Go Teen Writers
Edit Your Novel

Go Teen Writers

Edit Your Novel

STEPHANIE MORRILL & JILL WILLIAMSON

luminous

Go Teen Writers: Edit Your Novel
Copyright © 2013, 2018 by Stephanie Morrill and Jill Williamson.
Originally published as *Go Teen Writers: How To Turn Your First Draft Into A Published Book*

All rights reserved.

No part of this book may be used or reproduced in any manner whatsoever without written permission except in the case of brief quotations embodied in critical articles and reviews.

Cover Designer: Roseanna M. White
Interior Design: Jill Williamson and Stephanie Morrill
Editor: Roseanna M. White and Chris Kolmorgen

International Standard Book Number: 978-1-7328808-0-1

Printed in the United States of America

To the writers who hang out
with us at Go Teen Writers.
Thanks for your creativity,
questions, and support.

Table of Contents

A Letter from Stephanie and Jill 1

Step 1: Make Your Good Book GREAT

  The Macro Edit—Taking Care of Big Issues 5
    Chapter 1—Thicker Plots 7
      The Story Problem 7
      Story Structure 9
      Writing the Cream of Your Story 14
      Creating Plot Twists 18
      Filling in the Gaps 20
      Try-Fail Cycles... 22
    Chapter 2—Deeper Characters 25
      Main Characters—Someone Worth Following 25
      Writing a Strong Antagonist 28
      The Rest of the Cast 29
    Chapter 3—Richer Settings 33
      Picking the Right Contemporary Setting 33
      Creating a Mythical Storyworld 36
      Writing Historical Fiction 41
    Chapter 4—Weaving in Your Theme 45
      Digging Out Your Themes 45
      But . . . What If Readers Don't Like My Theme? ... 49
    Chapter 5—Do Your Research 51
    Chapter 6—Why Bother? 57
      Book Surgery 59

  The Micro Edit—Cleaning Up the Writing 63
    Chapter 7—Tracking the Details 65
      How to Create a Story Workbook............................ 65
    Chapter 8—Scene Structure 75
      Making Sure Each Scene Matters 75
    Chapter 9—Point of View 85
      Point of View Basics 85
      Tightening Point of View 91
      Giving Your Narrative a Boost 94
    Chapter 10—Your Character's Past................................. 97

    Flashbacks 97
  Chapter 11—Dialogue That Speaks 101
  Chapter 12—Cut Out the Telling 113
  Chapter 13—Weaving in Description 117
    Describing Through a Point of View Character..... 120
    Description Through Word Choice 123
    The Five Senses 125
  Chapter 14—Fresh Writing 127
  Chapter 15—Tightening Your Prose 135
    Passive vs. Active Writing 143
  Chapter 16—Formatting It Right 147
    Technicalities 147
    "Correctly" Using Italics 150
    Punctuation 152
  Chapter 17—How to Know When You're Done 165

Editing Issues That Don't Happen On the Page .. 169
  Chapter 18—Self-Doubt & Others' Expectations 171
  Chapter 19—Wrestling with Procrastination 175

Step 2: Learning the Ropes of the Publishing Industry

  Chapter 20—Behave Like a Pro Before You Are 183
  Chapter 21—Critique Groups 187
    How to Critique a Manuscript................................ 190
    A Different View on Critique Groups.................... 193
  Chapter 22—Traditional Publishing 195
    What the Process Can Look Like 196
    How Advances Work 203
    Independent Publishers 205
  Chapter 23—Self-Publishing 207

Step 3: Putting Yourself Out There

How We Got Started 219
  Chapter 24—Pitching Your Novel 225
    Defining Your Genre 226
    Your Target Audience 228
    Your Hook Sentences 229

Your Back-Cover Copy 231
Your Author Bio 234
Your Synopsis 236
The New Recruit Sample Synopsis 242
Compiling it All into a Book Proposal.....................243

Step 4: Finding a Good Literary Agent

Chapter 25—Literary Agents 251
 How to Find Literary Agents.................................. 251
 How to Query 254
Chapter 26—Dealing with Rejection 261

Step 5: Building a Career

Be a Writer Who Grows 267
Remember Why You Write 272
In Closing 277

Extras: Lists and Resources

The Go Teen Writers Self-Editing Checklist 281
Self-Editing Dialogue Checklist 289
Stephanie & Jill's Weasel Words & Phrases 291
Story Brainstorming Questions 293
Story Plotting Charts 295
Copyediting Symbols...297
Character Archetypes 298
Hobbies and Skills Brainstorming List 301
Character Traits Brainstorming List 306
Character Phobias Brainstorming List 309
Historical Periods 311
Glossary of Terms 313
Recommended Resources 317

Hey, Teen Writers!

The original version of this book was published in 2013. Which is approximately five million years ago in the publishing industry.

Many things have evolved, like self-publishing and social media. But many things have stayed the same, the biggest of which is this:

Even though we've both been pursuing writing for about fifteen years now, we still struggle with self-doubt. With insecurity. With creative droughts. We still have a lot to learn, and we still share vulnerably and honestly at GoTeenWriters.com, though we've been fortunate enough to add young adult author Shannon Dittemore to our team.

Something else that hasn't changed is that young writers are still asking, "How do I get published? What should I do next?"

With self-publishing being cheaper than ever, and the paths to traditional publishing seeming murkier every day, this is a big, complicated topic. Too big and complicated for mere blog posts as we decided in 2013, and the same holds true for this revised edition.

Every writer's journey is different, which we want to recognize and respect. Yet as we've reflected on our own journeys, and examined the journeys of the writers around us, we've landed on a handful of steps that you can take to turn yourself into a card-carrying novelist. (Just kidding, there are no cards issued. But there is a secret handshake . . .)

Here's what we did to get where we are now

1. We wrote a good book and made it great.

Without this, you'll get nowhere.

We regularly hear from writers who are itching to get published but haven't yet completed this step. There's nothing wrong with looking toward the future and being excited about seeing your book on a store shelf someday, but that won't happen without a well-edited book.

2. We studied the industry.

Publishing is an industry with its own etiquette. Investing the time to learn it can save you a lot of embarrassment.

3. We learned how to pitch our novels and put ourselves out there.

4. We found good literary agents.

5. We built a career by learning to network with other authors and make connections with editors.

The steps look simple and straightforward enough when you list them in such a way, but we all know publishing a novel is anything but simple. Step one can take years, the industry is ever-changing, and finding and signing with a literary agent sometimes takes longer than getting a book contract.

There are lots of great books out there about writing a first draft, which is a skill of its own, but we felt there was a need for a book that detailed everything that comes after. How do you edit a book? How do you know when you're done? Should you join a writing group? Should you go to a writing conference?

So. Many. Questions.

It's easy to lose heart and look for shortcuts. We encourage you to respect your dream enough to have the patience and endurance to stick with writing. We can't make the process easy for you, but our hope is that this book will serve as a tool you can turn to time and time again when you're thinking, "Okay . . . what next?"

Stephanie and Jill

Step 1
Make Your Good Book GREAT

Make Your Good Book GREAT
The Macro Edit-Taking Care of Big Issues

If you've written your first draft, it's possible you've already built in many macro edit elements—like a strong cast of characters or a perfect setting. We included them here because sometimes when you edit your book, macro changes are necessary. It would have been helpful to us as new writers if we'd known early on how to edit these pillars in our stories.

A note from Stephanie

Both Jill and I have found it's best to take care of the big issues first—the plot, the characters, the setting, the theme—before you focus too much on scene tension and sentence structure. Author Sally Bradley refers to this process in housing terms. You would make sure a house had a strong foundation before you started painting it.

Something else Jill and I have in common is our bare bones first drafts. We both write first drafts without stopping and save our editing for after we type "the end." Ideally, I give myself six weeks off from a story before I start edits. This not only provides me time to do laundry and say hello to my family, it gives me enough space from the manuscript to see the story more clearly when I come back.

The first thing I'll do is read through my book in one or two sittings. I keep a notebook next to me and jot down the big things I notice—the plot line I foreshadowed in chapter two but never carried through. The line in chapter twelve that has a special kind of weight to it, that I want to consider expanding into a theme. Those type of things. After I do that, I have a good idea of what needs work.

I've always found the rewriting process to be one of the most exciting components of producing a great book. I originally ended this spiel with one of my favorite quotes about rewriting, only to discover Jill began hers with the same one. So I'll just let her talk.

A note from Jill

One of my favorite quotes is from author Michael Crichton. "Books aren't written—they're rewritten. Including your own. It is one of the hardest things to accept, especially after the seventh rewrite hasn't quite done it."

That's so true.

But I can't rewrite a book that doesn't exist—at least in a very rough draft form. So I write my first drafts as quickly as possible. That way, I have something to go back and fix. I also leave comments in the manuscript when I encounter problems that will have to be fixed later.

I'm a visual learner, so the first thing I do after finishing draft one is to write out each chapter and its scenes on index cards. I lay these on the floor, storyboard style, which allows me to see the entire book at once. I'll rearrange and add or take away until I feel like I have fixed plot holes and created a stronger plot.

I move on to characters, and I might spend a few days thinking and asking them questions to learn more about their lives.

Then I make a list of things to fix in my macro edit. I scroll through my manuscript and jot down the notes I left myself in the comments while writing the first draft, then I add my storyboarding and character notes and anything else I can think of.

That done, I start at the beginning and take it one chapter at a time. I add description—since I skip it in my first drafts. I often stop to research to get my details right. And I look for places I can insert plot points and references to my theme. My goal is to get all the important stuff into the second draft. I'll have time to edit for prettiness later.

> There are no rules in writing. There are only guidelines.
> –Nancy Kress

1. Thicker Plots

The Story Problem
by Jill

I don't want you to think that what Stephanie and I share in this book are rules that *must be* followed. Every writer is different, and every story is different. That's what makes novels so great. The information in this book is meant to help you better your writing craft and increase your chances of getting published—or of self-publishing a great book.

That said, there are consistent problems Stephanie and I see in the work of beginning novelists. If your goal is publication, this book is meant to raise some questions that will get you thinking about what problems might exist in your story and how you can fix them.

One of the most important question to ask yourself is: What is my story problem?

I've read books where I was in the third chapter before I had a clue what was happening. And I'm not talking about a suspense novel. I'm talking about a character bumbling along through their life without any sign of a goal or conflict. Stories need both. Conflict is what happens when something gets in the way of the main character's goal of solving the story problem. Conflict is what keeps readers turning pages.

A story can't have conflict if the character has no problem and no goal. The reader must know the story problem so he knows why he should care and why he should keep reading.

So what *is* a story problem, anyway? This is the situation your character is going to spend the entire book trying to solve. It's character + problem + stakes.

But it shouldn't be any character or any old problem. You need to give your reader a compelling character. The problem needs to be big, noble, and/or important. And the stakes—the bad stuff that will happen if your hero fails—must be high.

The great thing about identifying your story problem is that you can use it as a quick pitch for your story. Here are some examples of story problems that sound like pitches:

A girl must fight to the death on national television. Twenty-four enter, one survives. (*The Hunger Games*) **Problem?** Fight to the death. **Why should the reader care?** Wants the main character to survive.

An orphan girl comes to her new home only to learn that her new family wanted a boy. (*Anne of Green Gables*) **Problem?** The family wanted a boy. They're going to send her back! **Why should the reader care?** Wants the sweet orphan girl to find a family.

A hobbit inherits an evil magic ring, and the enemy is coming to take it back. (*The Lord of the Rings*) **Problem?** Bad guys are coming to take the ring, which could destroy everything good in the world. **Why should the reader care?** Wants good to prevail.

If you want to hook your reader into your story, you must let them know the story problem as soon as possible. Because if your main character doesn't have a problem to solve, you don't have a story.

Make it Yours:
1. Can you identify your story problem?
2. Why should the reader care?
3. When does the reader learn the problem?
4. Could it be introduced sooner?

Story Structure
by Jill

Every story has a structure. It's possible you worked out your story structure back when you were plotting your novel, but if you haven't, now is a good time to make sure your story works structurally. A good story needs a plot, which is a series of events your character experiences in an effort to solve the story problem. Most Hollywood plots follow a three-act structure that divides a screenplay into three parts.

Act one is the setup of the plot.

Act two is the confrontation, the struggle, the emotional story behind the plot.

And act three is the resolution, where the plot and emotional story come together. Where the hero faces his fears and wins.

This works in novels too. I've put together a diagram of the three-act structure. As I walk you through it, I'll bold each of the areas from my chart so that you can refer back to it. I'm going to use the book *The Hunger Games* for an example since it's widely read. Just to warn you, there will be spoilers as I break down the three-act structure of this book, so if you haven't read it, go read it first!

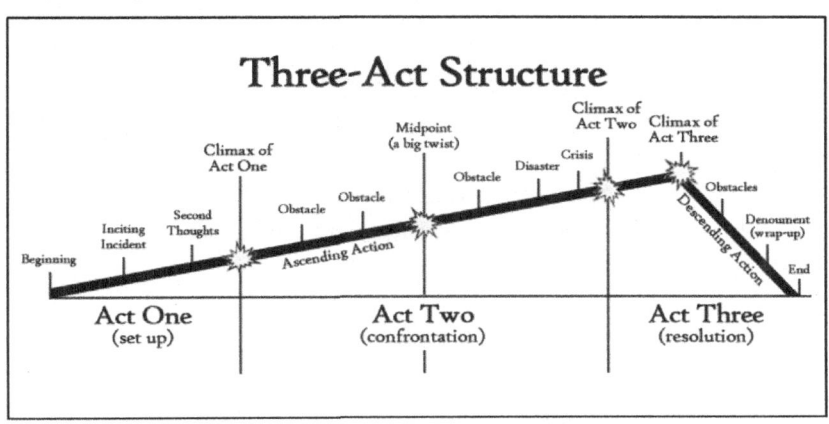

Act One: The Setup

Every story has a **Beginning** where the reader meets the main character, often in his everyday world before it changes. In *The Hunger Games*, we meet Katniss Everdeen on the day of the reaping, which is the day two names are drawn to participate in the Hunger Games. We meet her family and her friend Gale, and we see her hunting. We get a glimpse of her normal life before it changes forever.

Next comes the **Inciting Incident**, which is sometimes called the opening disturbance. This is an event that happens, usually by the end of the first chapter, to get the story moving. In the reaping, Prim's name is drawn, and Katniss volunteers to take Prim's place.

And now we have a story problem. Katniss is going to participate in the Hunger Games. Will she survive?

The rest of Act One shows Katniss saying farewell to her family and preparing for the games. She has a few moments of **Second Thoughts**, which leads us to the **Climax of Act One**, which is an exciting situation that puts the main character at a crossroads. She must choose a course of action that will change the direction of the story. She will make a plan and embark upon it.

In *The Hunger Games*, Peeta declares his love for Katniss on national television. This is a disaster for Katniss, who was already trying to fight her compassion for the boy who gave her bread back when she and her family were starving. How can she kill someone who loves her? And does he really? Or was this merely a trick to get the audience's sympathy?

This is a brilliant climax because it does so much in such a simple way. It raises the stakes for Katniss and Peeta, and it raises the expectations for the reader.

Act Two: Confrontation

Our heroine then sets out on her journey, meeting many obstacles along the way. She is going to look for every comfortable way to solve her problem. In *The Hunger Games*, the games have begun, and Katniss has gone off on her own to wait out the initial fighting. She's hiding in the trees. She's smart. But that won't help her for long. The first major **Obstacle** comes her way: Peeta has teamed up with the Careers and plans to work against her. Shortly thereafter, the gamers create a fire (another **Obstacle**) to draw Katniss out into the open. This puts her in the Careers' path (another **Obstacle**). She climbs a tree and the Careers camp out underneath, waiting. Katniss is stuck.

Now we're at the **Midpoint** of the book. The midpoint should be a bigger obstacle than the others and should end with some sort of **A Big Twist**. It should also give the hero a moment of introspection. The midpoint scene in *The Hunger Games* with Katniss in the tree ends with two twists. First, Peeta saves Katniss' life when she'd thought he had sided with the Careers. Second, Katniss makes an alliance with Rue, who reminds her of her sister Prim (introspection).

As we head into the second half of the book, the stakes are raised and we meet more obstacles along the way. Katniss and Rue make a plan to destroy the Careers' food supply. This is an **Obstacle** they set for themselves. Then Katniss can't find Rue, which leads to the **Disaster**: Rue's death.

The disaster is what screenwriter Blake Snyder calls in his craft book *Save the Cat* the "All is lost" moment, which feeds right into the **Crisis,** also known as the "Dark Night of the Soul." Snyder suggests that the "All is lost" moment should always include a whiff of death, be that the death of a character, a way of life, or a dream.

In *The Hunger Games*, Rue has become Katniss' ally. Her death is a disaster for Katniss as a contestant in the games, but it's also emotionally devastating because she reminded Katniss of Prim. This leads Katniss to a crisis point. Where the disaster is action, the crisis is reflection.

The crisis is all about how your main character is feeling in regard to the previous disaster. It's the "Poor me!" moment and rightly so. It's the scene right before the main character reaches deep down and brings forth that last heroic push toward victory. This is the point when Katniss decorates Rue's body in her attempt to honor her but also to silently rebel against the games.

Now we have reached the **Climax of Act Two**. In *The Hunger Games*, a rule change is announced: Two tributes can win if they are from the same district. This pulls Katniss away from her reflection on Rue's death. She is energized. She now knows what it's going to take to win. She must find Peeta. Together they can survive. They must win the Hunger Games for Rue, for their districts, for Prim, for vengeance. They now have a chance.

Act Three: Resolution

In the **Climax of Act Three**, the plot is at its highest escalation or tension and slowly begins to unravel toward the conclusion. Our hero sets off to accomplish her new goal, but more **Obstacles** stand in her way. Katniss goes looking for Peeta, finds him injured, and is determined to help him heal. And as the other tributes are killed, it's soon down to three: Katniss, Peeta, and Cato. They fight Cato, and once he is gone, Mutts attack, and once the Mutts are destroyed, the new rule that two tributes can win is revoked. Will Katniss die or kill Peeta to win the Hunger Games? She decides neither. She and Peeta, threaten to eat poisoned berries rather than be forced to destroy the one they love (which they had been faking for the viewers). Either they both win, or there will be no winner. They force the Capitol to choose.

The **Denouement** or wrap-up occurs after the climax. *Denouement* in the literal French means "the untying." This is the final outcome of the overall plot, where all the loose ends are tied up.

The Capitol declares Katniss and Peeta both winners of the Hunger Games. They are heroes, but as they travel home, they see they've stirred up trouble. The government didn't like losing, and Katniss' trick with the berries has put her loved ones in danger from the Capitol's wrath. Now she must continue to fake her love for Peeta or admit she was lying. It's a bittersweet **End** because it's the first book in the trilogy.

Every structure will vary some, but using the three-act structure will give your story a strong frame to build around. I've always found that planning a foundation doesn't squash my creativity; it forces me to tell a stronger story.

Step 1: Make Your Good Book GREAT

The Hunger Games Plot Chart

Beginning: Katniss and her family prepare for the reaping ceremony.

Inciting Incident: Prim's name is drawn. Katniss volunteers to take Prim's place.

Climax of Act 1: Peeta declares his love for Katniss on national television. How will she kill him now?

Obstacle: Peeta is working with the Careers.

Obstacle: A fire forces Katniss out into the open.

Midpoint Twist: Peeta saves Katniss's life, and Katniss forms an alliance with Rue.

Obstacle: Katniss and Rue set out to destroy the Careers' supplies.

Disaster: Rue is killed.

Crisis (Dark Night of the Soul): Katniss reflects on Rue's death.

Climax of Act 2: New rule: Two tributes can win if they are from the same district.

Climax of Act 3: Katniss offers the poisonous berries to Peeta. If they both can't win, no one will.

Denouement: Katniss and Peeta are heroes, but there was a price.

End: The Capitol is not pleased.

Make it Yours:

1. Using the breakdown of *The Hunger Games* as a guide, create a plot chart for your manuscript with the blank one in the Extras section of this book. You can also download a printable one at:
   www.jillwilliamson.com/helps/

2. How does your chart look? Could your story use some more obstacles or plot twists?

Writing the Cream of Your Story
by Stephanie

Shouldn't the middle of the story be the best?

This thought plagued me as I worked on a story several years ago. At the time, the book was a typical Stephanie story. The kind that's about a girl ... and it's summertime ... and she has this Big Problem ... oh, and there's this guy...

Also in typical Stephanie fashion, I wrote the first couple chapters without a hiccup. But as my main character made her choice during the inciting incident to go into the second act of the story, I ran out of steam.

For the first time (and this was the eleventh novel I'd completed) I had a disturbing thought going on in my head: The middle is where all the story stuff happens. It should be the best part of writing.

So, why was the middle something I dreaded? And not just me. Every writers conference I've gone to has offered a class called some variable of, "Fix your story's sagging middle!"

Then one day, weeks later, it finally clicked for me—middles are hard *because* that's where all the story stuff happens! And coming up with all those ups and downs, those twists and turns, takes work!

Say my story idea is a girl whose parents discourage her from going to college. That tells me two things about the timeline—my start and my finish. I'll need to start with my character at home, still at the age where she would be making college decisions. Those will be my first couple chapters. I don't have to follow through on anything quite yet, just show my main character's world, do some foreshadowing, and get her ready for her journey. And then the ending will be her going to college. Or not going to college.

The beginning and the ending must exist, of course, and they have their own unique challenges, but the middle is where your characters will spend most their time and energy. Jill's three-act structure chart is excellent, but I also like to imagine my plot as an Oreo cookie. A Double Stuf, preferably. That's how I roll.

The beginning and the end are those chocolate wafers, and if they're not perfect, you can tell the balance is off.

But what's an Oreo without cream, and what's a story without a middle? Not only is the cream delicious in its own right, it's what binds the chocolate wafers together. They all work together to make one amazing bite, same as your beginning, middle, and end must all work together to make a complete story.

The first element you need for a strong middle is a clear goal for your main character, typically related to the "story problem" Jill talked about at the beginning of the chapter. So if you haven't determined your character's goal yet, now's a good time to do so.

When your main character has a goal, it means he's invested in the journey and you have stuff you can take away. He wants to attend a fancy university? You can take away his financial resources, his straight As, and his college guidance counselor. He wants to stop Evil McVillain from taking over the world? You can trap him, take away his team, or strip away his defenses.

Another way you can ensure yourself a strong middle, or act two, is to give your character several people, places, activities, or objects to love. We usually think of that being a character-enriching exercise, but if your character has at least two things he cares about, it's easier to build conflict within him.

For example, when my middle son was about fifteen months old, he had two great loves in the world—me and his pacifier. (I learned the first time I referred to pacifiers on the blog that they go by many names including binkies or dummies. I'm talking about the plastic item we put in baby's mouths to soothe them.)

So we were on a family vacation and poor Connor was exhausted. I was on one end of the hotel room, and he wanted to be with me . . . but his pacifier was on the opposite side. Connor would start walking toward his pacifier, then remember I was the other way and start walking to me, then remember he wanted his pacifier, and turn to walk the other way. And the whole time he was bawling.

You want to create this kind of conflict in your plot, but you can only do that if you've given your main character multiple things to love and care about.

Of course the story can't be doom and gloom the whole time or you'll exhaust your reader. Yet too many good things happening to your character will drain away the conflict. So how do you balance it?

You use "the pendulum," where you swing from good news to bad news to good news and back again.

The pendulum is done very well in *The Hunger Games*, particularly when Katniss is in the arena. Jill talked about the scene in the midpoint of the book, the big crisis, so let's take a look at it.

- Katniss is found by the Careers and runs for her life—that's bad.
- She climbs a tree and it turns out they can't climb—that's good.
- They decide to wait her out at the bottom—that's bad.
- In the morning, Katniss discovers a hive of "tracker-jackers" hanging on a nearby branch—that's bad.
- She cuts it down and it explodes where the Careers are sleeping— that's good.
- In the process, she gets stung too—that's bad.

See what I mean? When the balance is done well, it makes those rays of sunshine brighter and those rain clouds darker.

The middle of the book is also a great time to add or subtract a character. Does your character have someone she can depend on? Someone who's always on her side? Try taking him away. If it's not the type of book where you can just "off" characters, take him away in a different sense. Maybe that person is absorbed with a new romantic relationship and no longer has as much attention for your poor main character.

For adding a character, can someone new move to town? Or get assigned to work with your character on a project? Or maybe you're not adding a completely new character, but just moving a character on stage.

In *Pride and Prejudice* we have examples of both. We have Mr. Wickham coming into town (brand new character) but later we also have Georgiana Darcy, whom we've heard about throughout the book, but whom we don't see until much later.

And there are few things I love more in the middle of a novel than a Big Reveal, which has a variety of forms:

- A misunderstanding coming into the light. ("All this time I thought Adam was the bad guy, but it turned out he was actually trying to

save the main character's life! Who knew?!")
- A secret past. ("Oh, wow, Jake has already been married once before?!")
- That secret the main character has been trying to keep finally exploding. ("What's gonna happen now that they all know the prime minister is her father?")

The middle of the book is probably always going to be trickiest for me to bring to life on the page. There's no formula for easy middles, but I've found these techniques to be helpful in revisions, and I hope you do too.

> **Make it Yours:**
> 1. In the first section, Jill asked you to think through your story problem. Does your story problem tie in with your main character's goal?
>
> Characters can have goals they know about–like in *Tangled* when Rapunzel longs to see the floating lanterns that mysteriously appear every year on her birthday. They also have goals they don't fully understand, like Rapunzel wanting to experience true love and acceptance. Have you given your character a goal he knows to chase and a goal he doesn't know he's chasing? How severe will the consequences be if he fails?
>
> 2. Are there multiple people or places your main character cares about? If he had to pick, which would it be? How can you make it to where keeping one means losing the other? What are some ways he could wind up with both and what are some ways he could wind up with neither?
>
> 3. Examine several key scenes from your manuscript. How's the balance of good events and bad events? Are you hammering your main character with an excess of bad news or making his life too easy?
>
> 4. You know that dull section about 40,000 words in? (That's where mine always is, anyway.) Can you add

someone? Can you take someone away? Brainstorm specific characters and write scenes with them just for fun. Keep what you like and toss what you don't. Or, better yet, save it in a different document in case you want to use it later, even for another project.

5. Time to dig into your characters' secrets. What kind of pasts do your other characters have? Is there a way their pasts can somehow ensnare your main character? (The show *Downton Abbey* is masterful at this!) What about your main character? Is he holding a secret, and when would be the worst possible time for it to come out?

Creating Plot Twists
by Stephanie

Hopefully while you wrote your first draft, you had one of those moments where an excellent plot twist appeared—*poof!*—as if by magic. I love that. And while I have that happen sometimes, more often I have to work for my plot twists in the second draft.

After I've done my read-through and found a few dull spots that need livening, I pull out a pen and paper. Brainstorming works better for me like that, somehow. I make a list of everything that *could* happen in this scene.

Let's say I'm reworking a scene where my main character, Madeline, is having an amiable discussion with her friend, Jack, about some troubles with their mutual friends. Here's the type of list I might make for how to punch up this scene:

- They could completely disagree instead of agreeing like they do now.
- They could discover their friends are listening to this conversation.
- Madeline could tell him she thinks her parents are getting divorced. (Are her parents getting divorced . . . ?)
- Madeline could tell Jack she thinks they're being followed. Maybe

they ARE being followed . . . who could be following them? What would they be after?

And so on. Sometimes I get a little goofy and write down stuff like *Jack falls and gets amnesia and now thinks his name is Fred*, but that's okay. It's brainstorming. A little goofy is okay and might lead to some kind of surprise breakthrough. But if you get way out there—*they're attacked by purple frogs*—you're not really helping yourself.

You'll notice toward the end of the list, I finally came up with a potential twist that I wanted to follow a bit more. It's possible I'll try it out and it won't fit for some reason, but it also might work.

Another thing I like to do—sometimes in the first draft stage but more often in the second draft—is try to come up with some unique, previously unknown connections between my characters. (This is an exercise I first read in *Writing the Breakout Novel* by Donald Maass, but I've adapted it a bit for my own needs.)

For this exercise, I pull out a pack of index cards. I pick five or so characters and write one name on each notecard, then stack them in a pile, writing-side down. Then I pick five or so big(ish) events in the book, like "Madeline's birthday party" or "the first day of school." I write one event on each notecard, then stack them in a separate pile. And then I'll pick out a few settings from the story—the vineyard, the dry creek bed—and write those down in the same fashion, then put them in their own pile.

Sometimes I spread the cards flat like I'm playing a game of Memory, and sometimes I keep them in piles and just draw the top card. Either way, you want to pick three cards. Maybe one from each category, or maybe it'll be more fun to pick from the same category. Your choice!

When combined, the cards typically make no sense. I might end up with Madeline's dad, the first day of school, and the vineyard. Those are three things that never intersect during the story, but then I sit there and try to come up with ways that I *could* make them intersect. And if not all three of them, maybe two. Is Madeline's dad at school for some reason on the first day? Why? Or is he at the vineyard? What could the first day of school and the vineyard have in common?

Once I've exhausted possibilities, I set the cards aside and draw a new set. I've found this is a great way to get me thinking creatively about my story, and I always walk away with something I love and never would've thought of otherwise.

This can also help you to fill in the "gaps" if you've spotted big holes in your story. Jill has another thought on how she does that.

Filling in the Gaps
by Jill

I'm constantly getting emails from teen writers who are frustrated with how to move forward with their stories. Some have finished books that are far too short, and they want to know how to make their books longer. And some are stuck because they have ideas they love, scenes they've written, but there are big holes in the story that keep it from moving forward.

When this happens to me, I spend some time brainstorming. But before I do that, I write out a list of the scenes I have written in a plot chart like the one I created for *The Hunger Games*. I leave lots of spaces in between the scenes so I can write in the new scenes I brainstorm. Then I sit down with a pencil and think up what could happen in between the scenes I've got. I think about each character's motivation and what might get them from one scene to the next. I also consider what the antagonist might do to get in the way of my hero accomplishing his goal.

When I'm done, I like to put each scene on an index card and lay them out on my living room floor in storyboard fashion, but the process works the same with a good list.

Here is an example of what a plot chart might look like. I've used my story *By Darkness Hid* for an example. The typed text indicates scenes I already had. The handwriting is what I filled in after brainstorming. Forgive the spoilers!

By Darkness Hid Plot Chart

Beginning: Achan gets into a fight while milking the goats. We meet Riga, Harnu, Poril, and Sir Gavin.

Inciting Incident: Sir Gavin offers to train Achan as his squire, even though it's against the law for slaves.

-Achan starts training as a squire, learning to use a waster.

-Achan discovers that Gren (the girl he loves) is to marry Riga.

-Sir Gavin suggests that the tonic Achan drinks is poison.

-Sir Gavin sends Achan to kill an animal and carry it back.

Climax of Act 1: Achan is declared a squire, but Prince Gidon is threatening to make Gren his mistress.

Obstacle: Poril demands that Achan help in the kitchens for Prince Gidon's coming-of-age celebration, but Sir Gavin tells Achan to compete in the sword fighting tournament

-Achan meets Lady Tara, Lady Jaira, and Bran Rennan in a game of Hoodman's Blind.

-Lord Nathak discovers Achan is Sir Gavin's new squire and sends him back to Poril in the kitchens.

-Sir Gavin introduces Achan to Prince Oren.

Obstacle: Sir Gavin has vanished and Achan must now serve as Prince Gidon's sparring partner.

-When Achan sees Lady Tara in the stands, he chooses to beat Prince Gidon in a sparring match and is whipped for it.

-Prince Gidon claims Gren as his mistress and demands that Achan bring Gren to him.

-Achan confronts the goddess Cetheria in her temple over his frustrations, but hears Arman's voice instead.

Midpoint Twist: Achan saves Gren from the prince by urging her marriage to Riga to happen right away.

-Prince Gidon discovers Gren's recent wedding and threatens to kill her if Achan ever leaves his service.

Obstacle: Prince Gidon leaves for Mahanaim and demands that Achan come along. He leaves his home forever.

-A person with a scratchy voice speaks to Achan's mind. Achan doesn't want to believe in bloodvoicing, but it seems clear that he has the telepathic gift.

-Silvo Hamartano and his friends beat up Achan.

> -Bran befriends Achan and offers to let him join the Mârad, a rebel group that is opposed to Prince Gidon. Achan refuses, fearing for Gren's safety.
> -Achan sees the memorial tree, the place where King Axel was killed.
> **Disaster:** Poroo attack Prince Gidon's procession and Achan is struck down.
> **Crisis (Dark Night of the Soul):** Accused of trying to kill Prince Gidon, Achan sits in the dungeon knowing he will never be free.
> -Achan befriends Vrell, a healer boy with the scratchy voice who had been bloodvoicing him on his journey.
> **Climax of Act 2:** Achan is rescued from the dungeon by Kingsguard knights.
> -Vrell is held hostage for Achan's return, so he and the knights stage a rescue.
> **Climax of Act 3:** Sir Gavin takes Achan before the Council of Seven and makes a shocking claim.
> -Prince Gidon tries to kill Achan. Bran and Sir Rigil rescue him.
> **Denouement:** Achan and the knights fight Prince Gidon's soldiers to get out of the castle.
> **End:** Achan and the knights flee into Darkness to avoid Prince Gidon's wrath.

Try-Fail Cycles
by Jill

Another way to help you keep moving when you're stuck is to use try-fail cycles. First, define what your character wants. Then ask whether or not he will succeed? The answer must be one of these two: "Yes, but . . ." or "No, and . . ." Here's how it works:

My character wakes up late. Will he make it to school in time?

- Yes, but he misses the bus and must walk, OR—
- No, and he locks himself out of the house, so now he's stuck outside.

You can continue this cycle by again asking what he wants, then answering the question of will he succeed with a "Yes, but . . ." or "No, and . . ." reply. Let's keep going.

Your character, locked outside his house, climbs a tree and tries to sneak in through an upstairs window. Will he succeed?

- Yes, but his neighbor thinks he's a burglar and calls the police.
- No, and he got his shirt snagged on a tree branch and can't get loose. Now he's stuck in the tree!

The point with try-fail cycles is always to be escalating the problems, making them worse and worse.

Our hero decides to call the girl he likes since she has a free period first hour. He asks her to come pick him up. Will she come?

- Yes, but when she arrives, so do the police! (So embarrassing.)
- No, and he accidentally called the wrong number: his mom.

It's simple, really, and can be a lot of fun.

Don't Get Discouraged

While figuring out what happens in your stories can be exciting, it can also be frustrating when you're stuck, when a scene is flat and you don't know how to make it better, or when things just aren't coming together like you hoped they would. In times like these, brainstorming with a friend, or exercises like the ones above, can help a lot. Sometimes the results are instantaneous. If not, don't be discouraged. Often the right solutions to story problems take time and energy and digging to get them where they need to be.

```
Make it Yours:
    1. Go back to your own plot chart and see if you can
brainstorm some new scenes to fit in between the scenes
you already have.
    2. Practice some try-fail cycles with your story.
```

> A character is no more a human being than the *Venus de Milo* is a real woman. A character is a work of art, a metaphor for human nature.
> –Robert McKee

2 Deeper Characters

Main Characters: Someone Worth Following
by Stephanie

Something we commonly get asked is, "Can you have more than one main character?"

While there are books that have two main characters (like my WWII era young adult novel, *Within These Lines*) and others with more of an ensemble cast, we generally advise sticking with one main character. Especially if this is early in your writing journey. Readers need a character to latch onto and cheer for. With an ensemble cast, it can be tough for the reader to bond because they aren't getting as much page time with characters.

I once had a meeting with a teen writer where she told me she had seven main characters, but later I figured out she meant that she actually had seven *point of view* (POV) characters. So let's clarify right off the bat that the reader can view the story from a variety of angles, a variety of points of view, but still there would be one main character. This is commonly done in the romance genre, where the hero and the heroine share the stage almost equally, but typically the heroine is still the main character, still the driving force of the story.

How do you know who the main character should be?

The answer is whoever has the biggest change to go through. Who has the most at stake in the story? Certainly you will have other characters that play huge roles, who are going through changes themselves, but which character's goal is driving the story forward?

This brings us back to the importance of giving your character a goal. The first time I heard that concept, it was a light bulb kind of moment.

A goal! Then my character will have something to *do*! Brilliant!

The goal should not only propel your character through the book, it should draw the reader into the journey. If you've done your job right, readers care about the character's goal and want to see him achieve it. They cheer when things are going well, and they weep when things are going poorly. Consider the Lord of the Rings trilogy and Frodo's goal of returning the ring to the fires of Mordor. It has everything a character goal should have:

- High stakes—Bad stuff will happen if he doesn't do it.
- It's noble—It's something he *should* want to do.
- Others come alongside him—Your character will need cheerleaders.
- There's opposition—It should be a strong enough goal that others *don't* want your character to reach it.
- It's achievable . . . but he can't do it alone—If the goal is too easy, the reader will lose interest.

Make it Yours:

1. Consider your main character's goal. Do the five things listed above apply to it? If not, how can you make them happen? Take a few minutes to brainstorm.

2. Asking "Why?" is the best tool you have for deepening characters. *Why* must he achieve this goal? *Why* does it matter to him? *Why* is he willing to risk everything to achieve this? When working on your character's goal, use "why?" to dig deeper.

Your main character not only needs a goal, she needs an inner desire.

For this I'm talking about your touchy-feely words. Love, respect, contentment, peace, acceptance. In her soul, your main character requires something, thirsts for something. Maybe she knows it. Maybe she knows she's materialistic, but what she's really searching for is contentment. Or maybe she doesn't know. Maybe she doesn't realize how deeply it scarred her that her mom was a workaholic. That's for you to decide.

Often the inner desire is tied directly to the character's goal. A character whose goal is to find her birth mother would likely have a corresponding inner desire for acceptance. But sometimes the inner desire and the outer goal can be seemingly at conflict with each other. What about a warrior whose goal is to win the battle, but whose inner desire is for peace?

What lie does he believe?

This is one of my favorite aspects of developing or enriching a character, discovering what lie they've bought into and why.

In my 1920s mystery, *The Lost Girl of Astor Street*, Piper believes she is the wrong kind of girl. That's what she's been told her whole life by adults, that she's not feminine or domestic enough.

In Sarah Dessen's *Once and For All*, Louna believes she has already had her chance at love and she's lost it. This is reinforced by the two primary adults in her life, who have never had anything more than a first love either.

In the movie *Tangled*, Rapunzel believes she isn't capable of taking care of herself in the real world and needs the safety of the tower. She believes this because Mother Gothel has told her this her entire life.

Make it Yours:

1. How does your character's lie drive their actions through the story? If you think of the lie like a disease, what are the symptoms?

2. What does your character need to learn that will help them defeat their lie? What will the medicine be that helps them cure themselves?

Writing a Strong Antagonist
by Jill

As we've touched upon, the most important thing you need to decide about any character in your book is: What does he want desperately? And how am I going to keep it from him?

This shouldn't change when dealing with your antagonist. The antagonist is the villain, by the way, but he needn't be evil incarnate. He might be a nice guy. If two best friends were going to try out for the track team, but there was only one position available, they'd instantly become each other's antagonists. An antagonist is merely the character who stands in the way of your hero achieving his goal.

Your antagonist can be likeable. The best villains are those the reader can relate to or sympathize with in some small way, like Loki from the *Avengers*. Yes, he's trying to stop the hero, but if the reader can understand his twisted logic, he'll be more realistic.

Make it Yours:

1. Take those questions you answered for your main character and answer them for your antagonist. Your antagonist needs ambition and goals too. He should be plotting and planning, not just taunting your main character. He thinks he *is* the main character!

2. If you were telling the story from the antagonist's point of view, what would be the beginning, middle, and end for him?

The Rest of the Cast
by Stephanie

One of the things I struggled most with as a new author was developing a robust cast of characters. I had given oodles of thought to my main character, somewhat less thought to my antagonist, and then my other primary characters were really there just to populate the story.

I think this mistake is common because we don't want anyone to outshine our main character. That's who we're all here to see, right? Everyone else is only there to support the main character and guide them (or oppose them) on their journey.

While the focus should be your main character, and all storylines should somehow relate to them, keep in mind that everybody thinks they are the main character. And your other characters will be much more alive on the page if you take that mindset with them.

Your main character's best friend doesn't think of herself as "the best friend." She thinks of herself as the main character, and that the main character is her best friend. Make sense? This means that the best friend has life goals same as the main character does. Not only does she have goals, but so do the other friends they hang out with. And the main character's parents. And the main character's wicked boss. The other characters in your novel should have goals they are taking steps toward achieving.

Now, maybe not everybody in your novel needs a goal. The receptionist at the office who says two things during the entire book might not need something to work toward but having a problem of her own can help jazz her up. It could be that her car wouldn't start this morning or that she dropped her cell phone in the toilet. Just something that keeps the dialogue from being boring ("Hi, how can I help you?") and from being all about the main character.

Everybody brings their own unique baggage into a conversation. That means the same words can land very differently depending on a person's past or their sensitivities. A character who feels he is overweight will respond differently—at least internally—to the question of, "Would you like a second helping of dinner?" than a person who feels happy with their weight.

When your characters are in conversations, think about where they've been and where they hope to go. Characters who grew up in stable, loving families will react to conflict differently than characters who grew up in unhealthy households. Someone who's been burned in relationships might be suspicious and untrusting. Someone who desires money and power might be charming if you have something they want, but cold and dismissive if you don't.

And these differences should come through in the way they speak. Making characters sound unique is tough. After all, they're all passing through the filter of your head. I have found this is something that's easier to correct during the second draft, after I've spent a lot of time with all these people.

When you're working on a character's voice and dialogue, make sure you're thinking through their education level, nationality, and home life. In *The Revised Life of Ellie Sweet*, my main character is seventeen and an aspiring novelist, so she uses bigger words and correct grammar. Another character in that book, Chase, is a guy with two older brothers in jail, and he's rather rough around the edges. Where Ellie might say, "My parents don't traditionally buy me presents for Valentine's Day," Chase would say, "My parents don't get me nothing."

Make it Yours:

Sometimes our characters all sound the same because we haven't taken the time to get to know them. Lots of authors use interview sheets, but those have never worked well for me. Partly because I find it boring to write out every character's favorite color.

In *The Art of War for Writers* by James Scott Bell, he talks about writing character journals. I completely fell in love with this exercise because it doesn't feel like meaningless paperwork, it feels like writing, like creating.

You can do them for your main character, of course, but it's *really* fun with secondary characters and the antagonist. Ask them "How do you feel about your name?"

or "What's your relationship with your mom like?" and then they just take over. Usually for pages. Because you're writing in first person, this works wonders for solidifying their voice and motives.

> Still round the corner there may wait, a new road or a secret gate.
> –J. R. R. Tolkien

3 Richer Settings

Picking the Right Contemporary Setting
by Stephanie

If you can pick up your story, move it somewhere else, and it wouldn't change a thing, you haven't found the right setting yet.

But how do you know what the right setting is for a book set in modern times?

Sometimes it's simply a gut thing. Maybe you have something you want to say about your hometown, so you set it there. That's fine. Stephen King, you'll notice, has a decent amount of books set in Maine.

But if you're struggling to find the right locale, even after your first draft, here are some questions you can ruminate over:

What would be more uncomfortable for my main character?

That sounds like a cruel question, doesn't it? But if your character is comfortable in her setting, your story is in danger of becoming boring. So how do you make her uncomfortable?

If your character has an embarrassing family, consider sticking him or her in a small town, where everybody knows everybody's business.

If your character is desperate to stand out, to be noticed, try putting her in a big city or at least a big school where there's lots of competition.

If your character is poor, figure out a way to put her in a ritzy setting. Or the reverse can work great too: a character with tons of money who finds herself in a place where money can't do anything for her.

Should I make up a place?

Possibly.

This works particularly well for small town contemporaries, like in Betsy St. Amant's *Addison Blakely: Confessions of a PK* where we get the small-town Kansas feel with the fictitious town of "Crooked Hollow" but you don't have the real-life residents complaining that Got Beans is actually on the west end of town, and how dare the author suggest otherwise . . .

With this, however, you still have to be mindful of the regional culture. Going back to the Kansas example, you wouldn't want to say anything about buying wine at the grocery store (because they don't sell it in the grocery stores) or reading the license plate on the front end of the car (because they only have license plates on the back of their cars). Messing up those kinds of details will snap all your lovely, wonderful Kansas readers right out of your storyworld.

Consider the Intangibles

There are tangible things about where we live—the flora and fauna, the seasons, the cost of a gallon of milk—and then there are the intangibles. Living in San Francisco, California is completely different than living in Dallas, Texas. Both are big cities, but the politics and the cultural priorities are different. When meeting someone for the first time, you would make different assumptions about them if you learned they were raised in Dallas than if they were raised in San

Francisco.

Wherever you choose to set your story, you must identify your character's emotions about where he lives. We all have a relationship with where we live; we have feelings about it. And sometimes our feelings conflict with each other—one day we might love that we know so many people in our town, that we can hardly go to the grocery store without bumping into someone we know. Another day, we might loathe that same thing.

If you build that into your characters, not only will your reader connect with your unique setting, you'll breathe life and movement into your story.

> **Make it Yours:**
>
> 1. Consider your current story setting—what's the opposite? How would your story change if you moved it there? Take a few minutes to brainstorm. Maybe even write a scene where your main character is in this opposite setting. How does it feel? Did you learn anything interesting about your character or your original setting?
>
> 2. Make a list of three things your character likes about where he lives and three things he doesn't like. First consider the things he likes—what are situations in which he'd cease to like those? Now consider the things he doesn't like and do the same. How could he come to like those? (An excellent example of this is in *Twilight*. Bella originally loathes the constant rain of Forks, Washington, but because the rainy days are the ones when Edward comes to school, she comes to look forward to them.)

Creating a Mythical Storyworld
by Jill

When creating a mythical storyworld, your imagination is the limit. That might seem a little overwhelming at first, so here are some ideas to get you started.

1. Pick a time period to model. Feudal Japan, ancient Egypt, a futuristic space station, renaissance France, regency England, the old west, modern-day Manhattan, a futuristic Australian Outback.

2. Pick a genre. Fantasy, science fiction, dystopian, time travel, steampunk, supernatural, paranormal, apocalyptic, etc.

3. Will this time period and genre create the right storyworld for your plot to work?

4. Consider the rotation of the planet. How long is a day? How long is a year?

5. Is there a country in the world or throughout history that you could use as a model for the style of government you'd like to portray in your story?

6. Is there a country you could use as a model for the terrain, climate, vegetation, and wildlife in your story? You don't have to use everything, but keep in mind what would be realistic and logical to readers. Having a moose show up in a desert might jar the reader out of your story. An oddity here and there *can* work in fantasy, but if you have too many inconsistencies, you risk losing the realism of your world.

7. Are humans the only type of people in your story, or will you have other beings who speak?

Using Maps and Floor Plans

You may not be an artist but sketching out a map of your storyworld can be really helpful. I've also found it useful to grab some graph paper and sketch out floor plans for character's homes or facilities or castles used in my stories. If you're looking for inspiration, here's a link to maps and floor plans I've made for my stories: www.jillwilliamson.com/maps. As you can see when you scroll down through them, not all of my maps are nice and tidy. Some were created only to help me visualize so I could describe better.

> **Maps Can Help You Plot**
>
> When you spend time drawing a map and adding in details, you'll come up with plot ideas. Where you place things on a map can influence your plot.
>
> For example, if there are two cities close to the only road that leads out of a mountain pass, that might create discord between the two cities as they fight for access to the road.

When I started to brainstorm my *Blood of Kings* trilogy, all I knew about the land was that half of it was covered in constant darkness and there was a half living/half dead tree in the middle of the land. I wanted a map, so I took a blank sheet of typing paper and drew a craggy shape. It was a little too big and looked a lot like Africa, so I erased a bit to get a more unique outline. Then I added a bunch of dots to indicate cities. I added about forty dots.

That seemed like way too many cities to have to name. So I erased half of them.

Better.

I shaded my half-darkness over the land. I added roads, rivers, and mountains. I added my half living/half dead tree.

I still needed to name all the dots. But how do you come up with name for the cities in your storyworld?

There are lots of ways. Tolkien invented his own language. Some people use street names. Some use a phone book to find interesting names. You could use a map of earth, pick a foreign country, and choose names of cities, rivers, or mountains from that place. (You might want to look up the meaning of foreign words just in case you chose one that has a troublesome translation.)

J.K. Rowling used Latin for many of her character names and most of her magic spells in the Harry Potter books. I thought that was clever, so when I was working on my map for *By Darkness Hid*, I looked on my bookshelf and saw a French dictionary and a Hebrew/Greek concordance. I thought Hebrew/Greek sounded more fantasy-like than French—it sounded kind of Klingon. Plus, I liked the idea of using words from the Bible.

So I went with it. For example, "allown" is Hebrew for "oak" or "tree." Guess what I named the city where my half living/half dead tree is? Allowntown. And "er'rets" is Hebrew for "earth," the same word used in the Bible when it says: "In the Beginning, God created the heavens and the *earth*." So I named my fantasy world Er'Rets.

I like having hidden meanings.

But I didn't want to name everything Hebrew because 1) it's really hard to pronounce and 2) I wanted to avoid creating a monoculture. So I came up with some more tricks. I gave each town a theme for brainstorming names. Allowntown, for example, is a city of orchards. I wrote a list of types of apples: Gala, Pippin, Cortland, Concord, Crab, Ginger, Fuji, etc. And when I needed a new character from Allowntown, I picked a name from the list.

Carmine is a vineyard town, so I made a list of things having to do with wine: Rioja, Flint, Terra, Keuper, Pinot, Concord, Malbec, etc. For Berland I used Inupiat names. For Magos I used Gaelic names. For Cherem, I used names of stars. For Nesos, I used Hawaiian names.

I also created a chart for each city and looked up information on similar locations on earth. For example, the landscape and climate of Barth is similar to northern Africa, so I looked up some countries in northern Africa and jotted down climate, crops, animals, plants, industry, that sort of thing. Doing this helped me understand what it might be like to live in each of my places.

I did this for every town on my map. If you'd like to see the chart I used, download the Civilization Worksheet from my website: www.jillwilliamson.com/helps.

```
Make it Yours:
    1. Draw a map for your storyworld. Add cities and
other landmarks. Name them.
    2. What have you done to make your world unique?
    3. Did drawing the map help you think of new plot
ideas? If so how?
```

Write a History

If your world is going to feel real, it needs more than a map and cool names. Write out a history of your land. Go back as far as you want. For inspiration, Google the history of our world. Look at the different eras and see how we've advanced over the years.

I wrote a history for Er'Rets starting 500 years before my story began, when the first king came to the land via a ship. I created a timeline of who was king when and what major events took place: wars, births, deaths, etc. I also wrote family trees for the lords of each major city so that I knew who married who.

All this gave my land character. For example, I knew why the people from Cherem hated the people from Magos. They'd been fighting each other for years. If a Cheremite and a Magosian were to meet in my book, it might get ugly.

And ugly is good because ugly means conflict.

Create Rules and Magic for Your World

Laws of nature make things possible or impossible on our planet. The same should be true of your world. Think about the environment, beings you've created, and magic. For each of these things, there must be rules. Without rules, you lose realism.

In my *Blood of Kings* trilogy, I created a telepathic magic called bloodvoicing that runs in one's blood, genetically, like blond hair or blue eyes. Bloodvoicers can speak to other bloodvoicer's minds, but they can also listen in on non-gifted individuals. They can learn to fight with their gift as well, forcing a person's soul from their body.

It was this ability that forced me to create different laws of nature for my storyworld. I invented the Veil, a spiritual realm into which bloodvoicers can go if they leave their bodies. This is the place between life and the afterlife, so when someone enters the Veil, his soul is pulled in one of two directions: Shamayim or the Lowerworld.

There are many other magical rules I created for bloodvoicing, but I hope you get the idea. If you add magic to your story, consider the source of the power and how the characters are able to harness it. Rumpelstiltskin, from the ABC show *Once Upon a Time*, often says,

"Magic always comes with a price." If you create a price for magical ability, you'll increase the conflict and risk for your characters, which makes the magic more believable.

Maybe you don't have magic in your story, but you have a race of people with the ability to walk through fire. Maybe your planet rotates faster than earth and the days are shorter. It could be that the climate of your planet is hot and all natural water is near boiling. Maybe your spaceships don't require warp speed because they can teleport from one location to another.

Your imagination is the limit.

A Note on Language

Many editors are wary of fantasy novels thick with fictional languages. You can have different languages spoken in your story, but you don't have to actually invent these languages á la Tolkien or Marc Okrand (Klingon). Spend the majority of your time learning to write and rewrite a great novel about compelling characters. Then, if you really want to invent a new language, go for it. Just make sure it enhances the story and doesn't take over.

Don't get stuck on creating the storyworld

Taking the time to brainstorm your storyworld does two important things: it makes it easier for you to write, and it makes your storyworld feel more authentic to readers. Consider making a three-ring binder with dividers for different cities, languages, history, or creatures to keep everything organized and easy to refer back to. You could also create a story bible in Word or Excel to keep track of things. Stephanie shows you how she does this in Chapter 7.

If you're looking for more inspiration on building fantasy worlds, check out my book *Storyworld First: Creating a Unique Fantasy World for Your Novel*. Be careful, though. You could spend months or years brainstorming a fantasy world. Have fun, but make sure you don't get stuck there forever and forget to write the book!

Writing Historical Fiction
by Stephanie

In the 2013 edition of this book, I wrote 357 words in this section. Some of those words included that I had once attempted historical fiction, failed miserably, and had concluded that as much I loved reading historical fiction, I wasn't cut out for writing it.

Two years after the original publication, I signed a contract with Blink/HarperCollins for my 1920s mystery, *The Lost Girl of Astor Street*. Now I have so much to say about writing historical fiction, that I offer a free ebook, *The Newbie's Guide To Writing Historical Fiction*, to those who are signed up for my author emails. You can grab your copy here: http://www.stephaniemorrill.com/innercircle/

But since we're talking about editing currently, let's focus on that. Maybe you've already written your historical novel, and it just feels kinda . . . off. Or maybe you keep trying, and you can't seem to get it off the ground. Since I don't know you or your book, I can't be completely sure, but my guess is that one of your problems might be that you haven't gotten specific enough with your time and place. I know that was a problem for me when I first tested the waters with historicals.

When I had the idea for *The Lost Girl of Astor Street*—*Veronica Mars* meets *Downton Abbey*—I immediately turned to my best friend, Roseanna White, who happens to be a historical fiction writer. That's handy, right? So, I sent her an email that was a half-excited, half-panicked, rambling mess that boiled down to, "What do I do first?!"

She said, "Before you can do much of anything, you need to know where your story is happening and at what point in history. Like, as specific as you can get. Then you'll know what's worth researching."

This is brilliant, and it's become the place I always start when I have a new historical idea. If you're trying to edit a historical novel for which you haven't yet gotten super specific about the setting, that's job number one. With some stories, that's easy. With others... not so much. Let's explore what to do in either situation:

If your story idea comes with a time and location included

Some story ideas are kind enough to come as a package deal with a time and place.

Like my idea of, "What if a Caucasian girl was in love with a Japanese American boy, and he was taken away to the concentration camps during WWII?" This idea became *Within These Lines*. I knew it would be set on the west coast of the United States in 1942, because that's when and where the Japanese Americans lived when they were taken away.

Or maybe you want to write a story that involves a character witnessing Jesus dying on the cross (*A Stray Drop of Blood* by Roseanna M. White) or about the culture in Mississippi during the Civil Rights movement (*The Help*, Kathryn Stockett). Those are ideas that quite conveniently come with details like *when* and *where* already solved for you. Even if they're just broad strokes.

Your job then becomes to get super specific about time and location.

Within These Lines went from being set on the "west coast" to San Francisco. Once I had decided on San Francisco, I then had to narrow to a neighborhood. And then a street.

Same with timing. Did I want to start before the bombing of Pearl Harbor (December 7, 1941) or after? It's okay to keep this timeline flexible while you're in the brainstorming stage, but you certainly need to know before you can effectively edit.

If your story idea does NOT come with a time and place

But some historical ideas don't come with a fixed time or location. Like *The Lost Girl of Astor Street*. Since my concept was, "*Veronica Mars* meets *Downton Abbey*," that left me like, "Okay ... when and where should I set this story?"

I could have told a similar story in tons of time and place combinations: 1930s New Orleans, 1880s Rio de Janeiro, 1910 Reykjavic. How do you pick?

I think it's best to start with your own curiosity and interests. Is there a time or place you're interested in or would like to know more about?

You're looking for a place that won't just be a pretty backdrop, but that will offer its own push and pull of the story and characters. A time and place that has something going on, something of interest to look at.

The 1920s was the first choice I made for *The Lost Girl of Astor Street*. My reasons were vague at first. I didn't want to deal with wars, so the teens and forties were out. The depression sounded, well, depressing, so I skipped that one. And I liked the hats girls wore in the 1920s. Done!

For Americans, the 1920s are best known for prohibition (it was illegal to sell alcohol in America) and the lawlessness that came with it, especially in New York and Chicago. I'm a Midwestern girl, and I've always loved Chicago, so I said, "Okay, 1920s Chicago. That's where I'm setting this story."

To find my specific location, I asked a friend of mine who grew up in Chicago for her thoughts on what would be an affluent neighborhood. Sally Bradley (author of several contemporary Chicago fiction titles) suggested the Gold Coast, right off Michigan Avenue, which in the 1920s was called The Astor Street district. As soon as I "visited" via Google Streetview, I was hooked

I picked my specific year because of when cloche hats became popular (1924) and my month on when my character wouldn't be too clogged up with school (the summer).

Again, there's no right or wrong with this. I could have told the story I wanted in Sydney, Australia during the winter of 1875, but that's not what I was curious about. Follow your natural curiosities, because they will carry you through the hours of research ahead of you.

If your story idea is just borrowing a historical time and location

But maybe you're not writing a true historical. Maybe instead you're writing a fantasy or paranormal novel, and you're actually borrowing an era or historical setting for world building purposes.

This is true for *The Hobbit* and The Lord of the Rings series, which are medieval fantasy. Fantasy can be set in any era you like.

Shades of Milk and Honey by Mary Robinette Kowal is a regency fantasy, or *The Scorpio Races* by Maggie Stiefvater has an early 20th century British feel to it.

If you're a new writer and working on a historically-inspired novel, it's easy to think, "It's fantasy. It doesn't need to be historically accurate."

True. But if you want your readers to get immersed in the storyworld, the historic details do need to feel authentic. Like it would be weird if Frodo picked up the telephone to call the Shire and see how everyone back home is doing, right? That would pull you right out of the story because the characters are using lanterns and swords, so logically a phone has no place in their technology. The setting needs to feel authentic for the reader to get lost in it, and historical inaccuracies break the authentic feel.

Jill mentioned her book *Storyworld First* in the fantasy settings section, but I'll recommend it again because it's an amazing resource for worldbuilding. You need it in your personal library!

> People ask me when I start one of these projects, what is your theme? I haven't the faintest idea. That's why you're writing the book, it seems to me, to find out.
> –David McCullough

4 Weaving in Your Theme

Digging Out Your Themes
by Jill

Theme, simply put, is what your story says about life and the human condition. It can be obvious or subtle. It can leave readers with a question or some kind of feeling. It can reveal a universal truth or inspire readers to a higher level of humanity.

When I attend writers conferences, I often run into people who, when asked what their book is about, say things like, "It's a book about animal rights," "It's about a group of teens that learn how bad premarital sex is," "I'm writing about a girl who learns that teachers make huge sacrifices for their students," "I'm writing to teach the consequences of lying."

These could all be considered worthy themes for novels, but when a writer comes at a story with a plan to lecture or "teach," the book is preachy before any word has been written.

And a book doesn't have to be about religion to be preachy.

Does this mean you shouldn't have a theme in mind when you start a book? Nope. But I would advise that you be on your guard against skewing the story toward your point of view. All authors have a worldview—personal beliefs that unintentionally come through the story and characters they write. Good authors should strive to hide their own voice and opinions and be true to their characters' beliefs. But this can be difficult to do.

When starting out with a new story idea, I often list potential themes. This might be something I hope my main character will learn on his journey. It might be a question he is asking about life or the world. It might be an adage he believes, like "What goes around comes around." These are places to start because my character's views will change as a result of what happens to him in the book. A story takes a character on a personal journey where he faces fears and grows because of it. With a forced theme, however, the author will do all she can to make it fit, even if it doesn't match who the characters is or the journey he has gone through.

So how do you portray a theme in your novel? Here are some ideas that have worked in other books:

The plot brings it out.

Your theme can come out in the action of the story. In *The Hunger Games*, the game combined with the storyworld and the Capitol's way of choosing contestants work against Katniss. Killing and war are not her ideas. The plot forces her into those events. And as Katniss journeys through the plot, the readers learn how she feels about all this. The themes? Survival and understanding the horrors of war.

Your character believes in a lie.

In *Matched* by Ally Condie, Cassia trusts The Society to make the right choices and protect the people. She learns over the course of the book that The Society is lying, and she has to decide if she wants to continue to live a lie or if freedom is worth the fight. The theme of *Matched* is freedom. Freedom to make your own choices, freedom of speech, freedom to remember.

The lie in *Matched* is something everyone believes. But characters often believe lies that are personal, and these can turn into great themes. Your character might believe she's ugly, unloved, or a bad person because of something that happened years ago. She might think she is a burden to her parents, better than everyone else, the right girl for her best friend's boyfriend, entitled to steal things, or unworthy of an education. Helping your character grow past that lie is a great way of working in a theme.

The story requires something noble of your character.

Sometimes the plot of your novel asks something of your character. In my *Blood of Kings* trilogy, Achan learns that a good king must sacrifice, that a king's hopes and dreams and wants are not as important when it comes to his people. Sacrifice is an overall theme of that series.

Whatever theme you wind up exploring in your manuscript, I advise you to portray the opposite point of view in an equal and fair manner. In *The Perfect Match* by Jodi Picoult, Nina is a trial lawyer who prosecutes child molesters. While she recognizes the bad parts of the system—criminals sometimes walk free—she also believes in the system. Until it's *her* son who gets molested. Does she put her faith in the system to give him justice when she's seen it reject justice for so many children? Or does she take matters into her own hands? It's a heart-wrenching read because both courses of action pull at Nina and, because of that, they pull at the reader.

Symbolism

You can use symbols to represent your theme. This can be done through word choice, animals, description (colors, light and darkness, temperature, size, etc), broken things, letters, characters, nature, or whatever you might fashion into a symbol. In *The Hunger Games*, the mockingjay is a symbol of independence, of something that has broken free from the control of the Capitol. When Katniss wears the mockingjay pin, she's saying without words that she's all about the things that bird symbolizes. She wears the pin, which the viewers turn into a symbol of opposition against the government.

The story asks a question.

A theme can simply pose a question to the reader, like: "Are angels real?" Then, through the story, that very question is explored. These types of stories work best when the author doesn't answer the question at the end but gets the reader thinking about what the answer might be, long after they close the book.

Allegory

An allegory is a story that can be interpreted to reveal a hidden meaning. Many themes can be found in allegories. *The Narnia* series by C. S. Lewis is one of the most well-known collection of allegories in fiction. It tells the biblical story of creation, Christ's crucifixion, and his resurrection all in the character of Aslan and how he interacts with the children in the series.

A bad habit

A bad habit might be a gateway to a theme. In *Fablehaven*, Seth is a rule breaker. One of the themes in *Fablehaven* is that obedience can protect you. Seth learns that the hard way when angry fairies turn him into a blobby beast after he breaks the rules.

Wait and see

I've often been surprised to finish a story and see that a theme has come out in the pages. A theme I didn't plan. No matter what themes I might hope to get the reader thinking about, when I write the actual story, they change, morph. Sometimes totally new themes emerge. So don't stress too much about nailing down one strong theme for your story. It will come.

Once you know your theme, you can tweak it as you rewrite so that it becomes more prominent. However, one of the biggest problems in storytelling is lack of subtlety, so don't forget that less is always more.

> **Make it Yours:**
> 1. Write down one or two themes from your story.
> 2. What lie does your character believe? In what ways does that lie reinforce the theme of the book, and in what ways does it oppose the theme?
> 3. Does your main character have a bad habit that could play into a theme?
> 4. Does your story pose a question?
> 5. Make a list of ideas that could show symbolism in your story.
> 6. Does the plot of your story ask something of your main character? (Like in *The Perfect Match* where Nina is asked to be patient and trust the system or in the *Blood of Kings* trilogy where Achan is asked to sacrifice.) If not, brainstorm some ideas of how it can.
> 7. Try writing a scene or two with what you brainstormed and see how it feels.

But . . . What If Readers Don't Like My Theme?
by Stephanie

I'm not the type of writer who plans a theme ahead of time. When I'm working on a book, the way it feels to me is that my story is wrapped around a core issue . . . but I don't know what it is yet. I have to keep drilling deeper into the characters and plot to uncover the truth inside.

Sometimes writers—especially writers who have a debut about to release—tell me they're worried about getting bad reviews, or they're worried readers won't like a particularly controversial element of their plot. It's something I get nervous about too. I'm a people pleaser, and I want people to like me. I hate reading reviews that rip apart how I handled an issue, and I won't lie and tell you I'm tough about it—I cry. And then I mope. And then, days later, I slowly ease my way back into writing.

But something I regularly remind myself is that my goal is not to please everyone—thankfully, since that's impossible—but to tell the truth. And sometimes the truth is hard to stomach, and sometimes it's going to make people mad because they don't want their worldview being messed with.

Not only is it okay if readers get mad about what you have to say, it might even be a good thing. Writing a book that touches someone's heart, that speaks to them, often means you're writing something that will repel another person. Art is so subjective, and every reader will react differently.

> When you take stuff from one writer, it's plagiarism; but when you take it from many writers, it's research.
> —Wilson Mizner

5 Do Your Research

by Jill

Research not only teaches you about necessary elements for your story, it can inspire you. Stories written without the help of research often fall flat. You can research things for your story before you write a word, while you're writing that first draft, and during the editing stage to add interesting details.

If you're writing historical fiction, accurate information is very important, so you'll likely need to read many nonfiction books about your chosen era. Research isn't necessary only for historical writers, though. Sometimes, to be able to write about certain subjects, you need to learn how those things work in our contemporary world, and researching the topic is the only way to figure it out.

But where to start?

Books

When I start a new project, one of the first things I do is collect a pile of books. If I'm working on a fantasy novel, I read other fantasy books. When I'm writing dystopian, I read other dystopian books. I do this for two reasons. First, it helps me to read books in the same genre to get my mind into that particular environment of storytelling and for a genre like Regency, it helps with voice and vocabulary. Secondly, it helps me know what's already been done so that I'll be aware of similarities in my story in time to change things.

I also read nonfiction books on related topics. When I wrote *By Darkness Hid*, I read a book called *Medieval Swordsmanship* by John Clements to help me learn sword fighting techniques. I wrote a proposal for a book about a girl in a sorority and read some nonfiction exposé books about Greek organizations. For a western steampunk idea, I read some books on Lewis and Clark's expedition and books on Native American tribes in the northwest, where my story was going to take place.

> ### A Note from Stephanie
> Some writers are adamant about not reading in the genre they're currently writing for fear of it stifling their own creativity or of unintentional "borrowing." I try to hold off on reading anything in my genre if I'm currently writing a first draft. It messes with my voice and fills me with doubts, so for me it's better to hold off until I'm in the editing stage.

Libraries

Unless you have an extravagant book allowance, research will put you on a first name basis with your librarian in no time.

Libraries are still excellent sources of information on all subjects. You can find books, magazine articles, and newspapers that sometimes go back hundreds of years. If the library is local to the area that you're writing about, there might also be a town history of some kind that you can look at. And keep in mind that most writers regularly use the interlibrary loan system, where you go through your library to borrow a book from a *different* library. I know I do.

Online

The internet is the most convenient tool for writers. You can find so much information in seconds. It's truly amazing. Be sure to verify any information you find online with at least one other source, especially if you're writing historical fiction.

Wikipedia- You can find almost anything on Wikipedia these days. It's not always true, so do be careful.

Etymonline.com- This is a great site to look up the history of a word and find out when it was first used and whether or not your characters might say it.

Google Maps- You can look up practically anywhere in the world by zooming in as far as possible and dragging the little orange man onto the road. You can actually "walk" this little man down roads one click at a time. I've done this for several books. I walked all over Phoenix, Arizona for my story *THIRST* and was able to describe landmarks without having to leave my Oregon home. I did the same for a drive Spencer went on in *The Profile Match* when he was driving to different mansions in the Hollywood Hills. Pretty sweet.

Google Translate- This is a great tool for helping you check the meanings of foreign words. It's not good for finding accurate language translations, though, so if it's important for your story to have accurate foreign language spoken, find a real translator. I used Google Translate often when researching Russia. When I stumbled onto foreign websites, I could copy and paste the Cyrillic text into Google Translate and was able to read it enough to understand. This worked for Japanese websites too.

YouTube- There are videos for almost any subject on YouTube. I watched so many videos for my dystopian series *The Safe Lands*. For *Captives*, I found videos of people exploring storm drains, police officers getting shot with Tasers, firefighters setting a controlled burn, and people smoking electric cigarettes. For *Rebels*, I watched videos of slaughterhouses, working cattle ranches, and immunizing cattle. For my *Blood of Kings* trilogy I watched videos on skinning birds and sword fighting. And for *The Mission League* series, I looked up videos for people visiting foreign countries like Moscow, Japan, and Cambodia. Invaluable.

Specialty Websites- There are millions of useful websites for the researching writer. Google "popular names from 1893" and you'll get several links. There are historical websites for all kinds of topics and countries. You can find sites on dog pedigrees, types of guns, vegetation and wildlife for different states, police procedures. Pretty much anything you could ever want. I've even found personal blogs with stories that match the topic I'm looking for, which can be really helpful when people are talking about having traveled to places you aren't able to go.

Interviews

Finding an expert on a certain topic is better than any website. I've interviewed firemen, hunters, doctors, and scientists for the books I've written. I also wrote a book about Venezuela that wouldn't have been possible without the first-hand accounts of the girl who traveled there. She was able to answer questions about smell, foods she ate, and concerns of the people who lived in the village. I couldn't have found that online. And when I was writing *Ambushed*, I talked to a recruiting coach for a college basketball team who explained how everything worked in the NCAA, which made Spencer's college visits realistic.

If you're going to interview someone, be sure and have a list of questions written up in advance. You want to be as quick and as thorough as possible without wasting too much of your interviewee's time. Always ask if you can call or email with any follow-up questions you may think of later.

Research Trip

If you're writing about a specific location, no amount of research can beat actually going to that place. If you get the opportunity to take a research trip, be sure to plan in advance. List the places you might want to visit, topics you want to investigate further, and have a list of questions you're looking to find answers for. Be friendly, introduce yourself as an author, and you'll be surprised how many people are willing to help.

Other Ideas

You can also get information from historical societies, by visiting museums, or by joining historical writers' groups. If you're a historical writer, you might consider joining some of these groups now. Making friends with other historical writers is a very good idea because you can help each other out later on.

Doing research and learning how to use it in your writing can make your book so much more realistic. Take the time to do it right.

Step 1: Make Your Good Book GREAT

> Inspiration usually comes during work, not before it.
> –Madeleine L'Engle

6 Why Bother?

by Stephanie

At this point in the editing process, you might be thinking, "Is it even worth it? This book has so many problems. Should I just cut my losses and move on to a new story?"

I have totally been in that place. And I'm guessing I'll be in that place again at some point.

One of the first things I ask myself in this situation is, "Does my idea have potential to be a great book?" (Ideally you ask yourself this *before* you ever start writing, but sometimes I get too excited about an idea and rush into it.)

Of course this begs another question: What makes a book great? Here are five elements that I think are critical:

A main character in a sympathetic situation

I'll use examples from *Harry Potter and the Sorcerer's Stone* and *The Help*, which are totally different genres but both great books. Harry is an orphan being raised by a horrid family, and Skeeter is a white girl in the south in the 1960s who wants to help black maids tell their stories. Both are sympathetic to the modern reader.

A main character who is a hero in some way and facing an impossible situation

As a baby, Harry somehow defeated the darkest, most powerful wizard, though he's not sure how, and Skeeter is risking her life to tell an important story and promote social justice.

A unique storyworld

Hogwarts School of Witchcraft and Wizardry, and Mississippi in the tumultuous 1960s.

A theme or takeaway message that will impact readers

After being treated wretchedly the first eleven years of his life, Harry finds himself capable of more than he ever imagined. It makes us feel like despite whatever obstacles are in *our* lives, we too are capable of overcoming.

In *The Help*, Skeeter breaks away from cultural norms to stand up for equality for people of all races. It makes us want to do the same for social injustices that we see in our society.

A great ending

Well, I don't want to spoil anything for anyone who hasn't yet enjoyed the Harry Potter series or *The Help*, but the endings pack a punch.

Can a book be successful without these elements? Definitely. *Gossip Girl* doesn't have a heroic main character or a noble theme, but it's still an engrossing read and addictive series. The unique storyworld (a peek at the life of unbelievably rich and spoiled teenagers from old money families in NYC) makes up for a lot.

If you're still wanting to trash your story, I'd recommend putting it away for a period of time. A month or so. Either work on another project you're feeling excited about or take a break from writing in general. After you've had some space, pull the manuscript back out and read through it. When I've done this, I've had times where I think,

"Yep. This is just as horrible as I thought." And I put it away again, often forever.

But other times I've thought, "You know . . . this isn't so bad. It's kinda good, actually. Maybe if I added this or that, it could work."

And when I do that, I'm often signing up for:

Book surgery

When I was working on the manuscript that evolved into my debut novel, *Me, Just Different*, I kept getting the same negative feedback from agents and contest judges—Skylar, my main character, was unlikeable. One agent wrote, "I don't like your main character. At all. I found her really annoying, actually."

For a few weeks, I indulged in inner protests that Skylar was *supposed* to be unlikable. That if the story was going to be about her reinventing herself, she had to start as someone who *needed reinvention*. But the evidence had piled up against me—she was a pain in the butt and no one wanted to spend time with her.

I shelved the manuscript, figuring I'd cut my losses and move on with other easier-to-like main characters.

But Skylar wouldn't let go of me.

Despite her pain in the butt qualities (or maybe *because* of them), I missed her. What I needed was a way to drum up some sympathy for her. Skylar needed a deeper reason for being aloof around boys . . . but also a reason to start dating her boyfriend, Eli. What I landed on was a near date rape, from which she was rescued by Eli.

I figured I'd open the story with the morning after the almost-date-rape, and then I could proceed with the story as planned. Just a 500-word scene addition, and I'd be good to go!

Um, not quite.

It seems incredibly obvious to me now that you can't casually toss in a character barely escaping date rape, but it wasn't obvious until I rewrote my opening scene, slapped it in the front of the manuscript . . . and admitted that book surgery was required.

Book surgery means you are doing something *major* to your manuscript. Not just beefing up a plot line or fleshing out sensory details, but stuff that affects the story as a whole. To seamlessly weave in the new stuff, you'll have to look at every scene and reconsider it. You'll have to ask yourself, "When I factor in the new plot thread or new character, would *this* still happen? Would the characters still feel and interact this way?"

I've found the easiest way for me to do this is to write out a sentence or two for each current scene in the book on the same color of index cards. Just enough to jog my memory of what's happening: *Skylar finds out that Abbie is pregnant; Connor overhears the discussion.*

I post all the index cards in chronological order on a bulletin board. Then I take a new color of index cards and write out scenes that I know will need to be added. Again, I just jot down as much information as I need to remember my idea for the scene: *Skylar tells Connor what happened the night of Jodi's party, and Connor now realizes why she dated Eli.*

Then I take those index cards and tack them up where I think they'll fit into the story. Sometimes in this process, I discover original scenes that will need to be cut, so I put an X through them. Or sometimes I'll see a scene that needs heavy revisions. Typically I write revision ideas on a Post-it and stick it to the card.

The index cards not only help me clarify the work ahead, they give me a tool to turn to when the book surgery feels overwhelming.

Sadly, scenes and plot lines that you love will have to die to make room for material that serves the new story.

When I had to do book surgery on *The Revised Life of Ellie Sweet*, the ending really gave me trouble. In the original manuscript, the book ended with Ellie moving to Kansas, but in the revised version, the book *also* ended with a triumph in her writing life.

I worked and worked to make everything fit, and one night it dawned on me that my endings were competing with each other. The story felt cluttered with both events happening at the end. Even though I loved the original ending, it had to die in order for the new story to work.

How do you know when book surgery is worth it or when you should scrap a project? With those completed manuscripts that I put away when I realized they needed serious surgery, I've never felt a longing to pull them back out. But Skylar had been in my "Retired Manuscripts" folder for about a month, and I was still thinking about her. I knew then that the extra work was worth it.

Since you're the one who has to do the hard work, only you can make that decision.

A Note from Jill

Not too long ago, my publisher asked me to cut 50,000 words from my manuscript, *King's War*. I about died.

When I got over the shock, I buckled down and did the best I could. I started out similar to how Stephanie does her book surgery. I created a sheet of paper with twelve blank boxes and I printed several. These had a similar use to Stephanie's index cards. Each box represented one chapter. In each, I listed all the scenes in that chapter and how many pages long the chapter was. Then I did some math and subtracted twenty percent from each chapter's page count. If a chapter had ten pages, I was going to try and make that chapter have only eight pages. I wrote my new target page counts at the bottom of each square and circled them.

Now, instead of a somewhat horrifying goal of cutting 50K from my story, I had close to one hundred tiny goals of cutting a few pages here and there. This was much easier to handle, as I was able to take it one chapter at a time. As I rewrote, I did cut some entire chapters and scenes, but I also had to add in some new scenes. That said, I didn't quite make my goal. I only managed to cut 33,000 words overall from the story, but I never would have been able to do that much if I hadn't split up the project into tiny pieces.

A Note from Stephanie

That's brilliant. I hope to never need this advice (50,000 words!!!) but that's fabulous thinking.

Make Your Good Book GREAT
The Micro Edit–Cleaning Up the Writing

A note from Stephanie on the sheer awesomeness of the micro edit

The micro edit can make you want to pull out your hair ... but it's also the time when your manuscript *really* starts to shine. By the end of this edit, you'll have a manuscript that's "clean as a sparkle" as my daughter used to say.

For a lot of new writers, these nitty-gritty things like POV or active writing can cause grumbling like, "Do readers *really* care?"

They do, they just don't always know how to explain it. My husband will sometimes say, "There's something wrong with this book; I just don't know what it is." (Though now that he's been faithfully reading the Go Teen Writers blog all these years, he can frequently identify issues by our writerly terminology!)

In my book club we read Kristen Heitzmann's wonderful *Edge of Recall*. Kristen is a master of deep POV, but none of the ladies in the group knew that. Yet one of them said, "The amazing thing in this book is I feel like I deeply understand every character." Even non-writer readers could tell how flawlessly POV had been done, they just didn't know to phrase it that way.

Many of the issues you address in a micro edit are like the mortar that holds together a brick wall. Your well-crafted characters and interesting settings and plot twists are the bricks, and the time you take in the micro edit to freshen up your writing and weave in your descriptions are what keep the bricks together.

Nobody but dorky writers will admire how few adverbs you used, just like nobody admires the mortar in a brick wall, but the reader will still be able to tell what a fine craftsman you are and how easy your books are to read.

A note from Jill

You might think I'm crazy, but the micro edit is my favorite part of writing (aside from brainstorming my initial story and world). The stress is gone. I have a rewritten draft of my book done. The story is all there. I just need to tweak and tighten and get rid of any errors.

I love it.

I start at the beginning and read, changing things as I go. I add description—since there's often little in my first drafts. I also often stop to research to get any last details right. I look for places I can insert plot points and references to my theme. And I fix spelling, grammar, typos, and sentence structure too.

Mostly I'm editing each point of view character's narrative voice, dialogue, and actions because I want to make sure they sound and behave like their unique selves. An example of how much I enjoy this can be found in my *Safe Lands* trilogy in the brothers Levi, Mason, and Omar. I loved writing these guys and trying to make them each sound unique. For example, when I was writing Omar's point of view, he noticed colors and beauty (since he's an artist). He once took home all the paper placemats on the table at a restaurant because he was poor and wanted something to draw on. His brothers would never have done something like that. They would have done other things, though. And that's the stuff I'm looking to fix or enhance as I do my micro edit.

When I'm done, I go through it again—as many times as I can before it's time to turn in the manuscript. The more the better.

> The difference between something good and something great is attention to detail
> -Charles R. Swindoll

7 Tracking The Details

How To Create a Story Workbook
by Stephanie

I have the best intentions when I start a new novel.

This time, I tell myself, I'm going to keep track of each character as I write. No more eye colors changing from chapter to chapter, and no more getting to the end of a story and realizing I have three characters named Jack. (Three!)

Maybe one of these days, I really will do a good job of keeping track of my story as I write it, but for now that remains a backseat item to be sorted out in edits. Specifically, the micro edits phase is when I turn to my story workbook and start getting all the details documented in one place.

What is a story workbook, and why do you need one?

A story workbook is a digital binder (though you could make it with a physical binder too) that helps you keep track of the minutiae of your story. The reason I prefer to make mine a digital binder is that when I'm working with an editor, I always send them pieces so they can double check my details.

With my story workbook, I track things like my characters and plot, but I also document how many hours I put into a story and what needs to be researched.

As I said before, I use most components of my story workbook during edits, but maybe for you it will be part of your brainstorming or first draft. That's the great thing about a tool like this—it's yours!

Getting Started

What's worked best for me is to use plain ol' Excel. If you're a Scrivener user, there's probably tools in there you can use (Scrivener and I don't get along great, so I can't help with this) but I like Excel for a couple reasons. One is that if you don't have Microsoft Excel, you can do many of the same things with Google Sheets. To do that, all you need is a Google account, which is free.

Another reason I really like using Excel for my workbook is how easy it is to share the finished product with my editor when the time comes. Using specialty software makes that tricky, but my editor already has Excel.

I'll walk you through how I format my story workbooks, and if you want a link to a formatted template, you can get that by going to GoTeenWriters.com and signing up for our free newsletter.

When you open a blank spreadsheet, it can feel overwhelming. The first thing I do is get my font and border preferences set up, because then the spreadsheet starts to feel like it's mine.

Start by selecting all (Ctrl+A) to format all your cells and your borders. I'm a Georgia font, size 12 kind of girl, and I like my headers bold and centered. I always choose "all borders" because I like how it looks when I print it, but you may find you prefer something else.

The next thing I do is get my "Tabs" added. At the bottom of your spreadsheet screen, you'll see where it says "Sheet1"and a plus sign for adding more sheets. I think of these sheets as my binder tabs, and here are the sections I include in mine:
- Work log
- Characters
- Timeline
- Backstory

- Research/To do
- Locations
- Acknowledgements

If you're a fantasy writer, you might also have tabs for your storyworld, or a timeline of the world's history.

Just remember that the workbook is a tool. Writing tools are only helpful to the extent that they serve the story. If it's not helping you get the story written or edited well, then it's not a tool you need.

Now let's look at what I put in each of my tabs:

Work Log

The work log is the first sheet in my spreadsheet because it's the one I use the most consistently.

Maybe you're not yet at a place where you want to track how much you're writing. I didn't really see a purpose in it until I had firm deadlines, and lots of things in my personal life pulling me away from writing time. (Primarily very cute, lovable things named McKenna, Connor, and Eli.)

I grew frustrated that I truly had no idea how long it took me to write my books. Yes, surprises happen along the way, but can you imagine operating another kind of creative business and being mostly clueless about how long it took you to do the creating? Florists are amazing artists, but they still need to have an idea of how much time it takes them to create a bouquet, right?

Here are the details I track:
- Date
- Time In
- Time Out
- Starting Word Count
- Ending Word Count
- Calculated Amount
- Location
- Notes

Why track location? I mostly write in my office, so I frequently don't specify anything in this column. But if you write in a variety of places, this can be helpful. You can look for patterns and see if you maybe work better on the patio than you do in your bedroom, or if having easy access to Wi-Fi makes a difference in your word count.

I use the "notes" column to track any details that may have impacted the data. Like if I have a kid who's home sick, or if I was able to repurpose 1,000 words from an old manuscript, making my word count abnormally high.

One last note about this section. At the end of a writing session, jotting down what I accomplished feels like a dorky-but-fun reward. Something that makes novel writing a particularly difficult art form is how long it takes and how many words there are to write and revise. When I keep track in this way, noting my progress feels similar to the satisfaction of crossing an item off a to-do list.

Characters

This is the piece of the workbook where it would be really helpful if I kept track of details as I worked on my first draft. Again, it tends to be a task I push off until edits, but you could even use it as you're brainstorming your story.

For characters, I find it helpful to track:
- Hair
- Eyes
- Skin
- General physical description
- Age/Birthday
- Personality descriptions

In addition to those, I almost always track:

- Primary Motivator
- Their role in the main character's story
- One-word descriptor
- What others say

Primary Motivator: What does this character want most and pursue during the story? For my main character in *The Lost Girl of*

Astor Street, she wants to find Lydia. That's what everything comes back to for Piper. But her friend, Walter, is focused on getting a starting spot on his minor league baseball team.

Tracking this detail for all my important characters does a couple things:

1. It forces me to think through their motivations, and that's a really important piece of delineating your characters from each other. If they are motivated by different things, it automatically prevents them from sounding the same.

2. It helps me identify opportunities for conflict that I might otherwise miss if they weren't all laid out side-by-side. Piper being focused on finding Lydia and Walter being focused on making the starting rotation may not directly pit them against each other, but it definitely grates on their relationship as the story goes on.

Their role in the main character's story: This is where I specify my purpose for having this character in the story. I tend to create overly large casts, so this is something that helps me make sure everyone has a clear purpose for advancing the plot. Like for Walter, one of my purposes for him is that he helps Piper see that growing up is going to happen whether she wants it to or not.

One-word descriptor and what other characters would say for their one-word: If your character described themselves in one word, what would it be? How do they see themselves? And then how do others see them, and what one word would they use? (For more details on picking a word for your character, go to GoTeenWriters.com and search "Your Character In One Word.")

Quirks: I especially try to note body language they use or expressions that are unique to them.

Personality descriptors: I mostly use this section to note the main character's observations. It helps me to make sure I'm being consistent and that any changes in her feelings toward that character are intentional rather than an oversight.

These are the things that I track because it's helpful to me as a writer. You only want to use the tool to the extent that it's helping you write the story.

Timeline

As I've transitioned into writing historical fiction and historical mysteries, this has become the most useful tool for me. I have a lot of information about specific dates and clues, and I need to keep it organized for the story to work. Especially by the time I'm on my fourth rewrite, and I can't really remember if my character already knows something ... or if that was the last draft where she found that out, or...

Obviously, you'll be tailoring this to your use, but here's what's worked for me. I usually track three-ish characters in their own columns, and then for other not-as-important characters, I throw their info into that last "Others" column. If you're telling a story from multiple points of view, you'll probably want a column for at least each POV character.

Chapter	Historical details	1924	Piper	Mariano	Villain	Others
3	Mafia territory battles	Tuesday, March 25th	Purchases replacement shirt for Walter	Investigate different case	Does villainous stuff	Walter sets up baseball game

The historical details are obviously only useful if you're writing a historical novel. I use this column to keep track of big world things that are taking place outside of the main plot of the story. If you're writing any kind of novel that involves a war going on, this can be a really helpful way to keep track of those important dates alongside the story details.

Where it says 1924, you would put whatever year your story is being told in. Or, if your story spans many years, you can put "Date." I put the specific year because I didn't want to bother with typing it out every time.

For this story, my main character is Piper. Her column is where I'll track most of the plot. Thus far, most my stories are told from just one point of view, so for me this ends up being where all the big action is. If you have multiple POV characters, that might not be the case.

I have found it super important to track what my villain is doing. After I sent the original draft of *The Lost Girl of Astor Street* to my agent, she was like, "What is your villain doing while your main character is doing her thing?" And I discovered I had huge chunks of time where my villain was just hanging around. So, it's really important to keep track of your antagonists, even if they're off stage!

The "Others" column is a great way to make sure that clues are getting planted early on, and that you don't have people doing something in town when they were supposedly gone for two weeks, or whatever.

A note about color coding: You'll also notice that a lot of that screen is grayed out. That's because I used this to show myself when something happened off stage. Another way I've used color coding is if I'm adding a plot thread. I'll pull up the timeline and start plugging in the actions, but I'll make the cells bright yellow or something. That way it's easy for me to make sure the new stuff is going to jive with the old.

Something else you might consider tracking is the weather. Even if this is a fantasy world with your own created weather patterns, it can still be helpful to make notes.

A Note from Jill

I create historical timelines for all of my fantasy worlds. How detailed they are depends on how much the history of my world comes into play during the story. I create a list of historical events that greatly impacted the countries in my world. I also mark down birthdates and marriages of characters if I need to remember if people were born before or after certain historical events or were children together.

If you need inspiration, look up a historical timeline of the War of the Roses or another historical era that might provide ideas for significant milestones in the history of a country.

I know I'm starting to sound like a looped playlist, but don't lose sight of the purpose of the timeline: To help you write your story. While it's a worthwhile investment of time to make your timeline readable and useful (if your editor asks you for anything of this nature, it'll be the timeline and your character details) it's easy to get obsessive about tracking and color coding every detail.

Backstory

I don't always need to include this tab, but I've written stories with very tangled backstories that involved different locations and character ages. I have yet to need this timeline to be as detailed as the actual story timeline, so I usually have just these columns:
- Date
- Event
- Location
- Other Details

A separate tab for the backstory can be super helpful for tracking details like a big family history, the development of a technology, or the history of your storyworld.

Research/To Do

This tab often gets added during the first read-through, but sometimes I keep a running list during the first draft or brainstorming process.

I create columns for details I need to research, story questions I'm pondering, and things I need to do.

The best part of making a to-do list is, of course, crossing items off. I use the strike-through feature rather than just deleting them because it gives me a greater sense of accomplishment.

> **A Note from Jill**
>
> An important part of my story bibles is to make a story calendar. For the *Mission League* series, I printed off four years-worth of blank calendars with the months and dates for the years Spencer is in high school. This helped me keep track of everything, and to know when weekends or holidays might need to be mentioned in my story. I write in where chapters begin and end, which helps my pacing. For my fantasy novels, I do the same thing, but I print calendars without months. You can look up printable blank calendars online and find a site that works for you.

Locations

Your story may not need this tab. When I wrote contemporary fiction, I didn't find it useful, but with historical fiction I do. Anytime I reference an address, or I have a person living in a specific house or neighborhood, I spend a lot of time on Google Maps finding the right place.

The sheet I use for tracking these locations is very basic with just two columns. One that says what it is ("Piper's house") and the other that lists the address. If I can, I also include a link to a picture.

Acknowledgements

Along the way, people help me with my stories. They give me information I need or encouragement, and I keep a running list so that I can thank them publicly in the back of the book. This is the simplest of all the spreadsheets, with one for the name, and the other for how they helped me.

The story workbook is a tool that helps me edit more effectively, and I hope you find it to be helpful to! If you want to get a template for free so you don't have to start from scratch, go to GoTeenWriters.com and sign up for our free newsletter.

> Every frame and every scene has to have an intention.
> -Mira Nair

8 Scene Structure

Making Sure Each Scene Matters
by Stephanie

When you write a novel, scenes are your building blocks. There is no one-size-fits-all for scenes. Some might be 500 words and others 2,500. You might have three scenes within a chapter. You might have one in a chapter.

Some start with dialogue, and others with description, almost like an establishing shot in a movie. You'll hear writing teachers say that all scenes need a beginning, middle, and ending, or that every scene needs a hook, or that you should write in scenes and sequels.

All these different styles and suggestions can make the question, "How do I write great scenes?" a bit confusing.

I often write my scenes by instinct rather than planning out the structure ahead of time, so the questions I talk about in this chapter are ones that I use as a checklist of sorts when I'm in the micro edit phase. If you're the charting, outliney sort of writer, you can use this list to brainstorm scenes before you write them.

Often the misguided question we ask as writers approaching our next scene is, "What is going to happen in this next scene?"

Writing or editing a story using this question will likely give you a book that feels more like a list of things that happen than an actual, cohesive story. Another symptom of asking this question is your characters' decisions might feel "off" or mismatched from their motivations.

The question that I think is better is, **"Because of what happened in the previous scene, what will my character choose to do now?"**

If we want our characters to come across as thinking, feeling, logically motivated people, then this is the much better question. The story's progression will feel more organic when you use the, "Because of this, now that," approach to your scenes.

The next question I think we should ask is, **"What is this character's plan or goal coming into this scene? What are they trying to make happen?"**

It's possible they have a goal completely unrelated to what happens in the actual scene. Maybe their goal is to take their dog for a quick walk around the block, but then on the walk they are robbed at gunpoint.

But most of your scenes will have your point of view character actively trying to obtain something they want, only to have something get in the way.

Let's look at an example from my World War II era historical, *Within These Lines*.

Early in the book, Evalina goes to the farmer's market to see her boyfriend, Taichi. That is her goal in this scene.

Your next question is, **"What obstacle stands in my character's way?"** Or another helpful way to think of it can be, **"How is my character's expectation foiled? What surprises them along the way?"**

Evalina arrives at the marketing expecting to see Taichi, but he's not there. That's her obstacle. Now I get to answer my favorite question: **"What decision does my character make as a result?"**

They can act, or they can choose to not act, but them making a decision is critical to your scene working.

Going back to my example from *Within These Lines*, Evalina

could have chosen to go home. She could have complained to a friend. She could have decided that she would ask Taichi about it the next time they saw each other.

But because Evalina is a bold sort, and because she is very afraid for Taichi, I felt she needed to make a big, showy decision. I decided that she would get on a ferry and go to his house. Not only does it fit her, which is important, but it feels interesting. I've learned that characters doing interesting things really helps with telling an interesting story. (Brilliant, right?)

While there are no official rules for what kind of decision your character should make, having them make an interesting decision will go a long way toward crafting an interesting scene. The decision should still be logical, and it should make sense for who the character is and the circumstances around them, but it needs to be interesting.

Next I like to ask, **"What is the outcome of my character's decision?"**

Sometimes we don't fully explore the outcome until the following scene, so it might be that you close your scene by hinting at the outcome or resulting disaster, but with just a sentence or two. With the scene from *Within These Lines*, I ended the scene with Evalina's decision. She talks to several others at the market, finds they don't know where Taichi's family is, and the scene closes this way:

> Mrs. Ling holds out a beautiful navel orange, round and bold. "Share this with your friend. May it bring you both good luck."
> The market doesn't officially open for a few more minutes, but San Franciscans already mill about the rows of tables, haggling over prices of the first spring vegetables. The men who stole the Hamasakis' spot chat with customers, and the sight makes my chest burn.
> I put the orange in my basket and pedal along the street. The fog has thinned, but my thoughts are hazy with anger.
> At the ferry ticket booth, I pull coins from my handbag and place them on the counter. "When does the boat leave for Alameda?"

I cut the scene off there, which makes for a very easy way for me to know what question to answer next. As stated above, when a character makes a decision, next we need to explore the outcome. So here the question becomes, "Because of Evalina impulsively deciding to take a ferry to Taichi's hometown, what will happen next?"

If you are looking for ways to surprise readers or add plot twists, try examining the way your characters' expectations are foiled and the resulting decisions that they make. If your character is making logical but surprising decisions, and they are having logical but surprising outcomes, then your reader will be surprised ... but not in a way that makes them doubt the plausibility.

But we don't want our stories to be action, action, action. Even if your genre is thriller or adventure, you still need to build in moments where your character has time to react to what is happening around them.

You may have heard this taught, as I have, as writing in "Scenes and Sequels," with scenes being the action part and sequels being the slow-down-and-react part. I've always found this teaching very confusing.

What *does* work for my brain is to think about how to provide opportunities for my character to process the decision they just made. Usually, the amount of processing time corresponds with how big the obstacle or decision was in the last scene. Meaning you'll never have a tiny obstacle result in chapters of reflection time.

So, after a decision, we want to ask, **"Does my character need time to process what has just happened? And should I show it?"**

Going back to my example from *Within These Lines*, Evalina made a gutsy decision by deciding to go uninvited to Taichi's hometown. Neither of their families know about the true nature of their relationship. Evalina has never been to his home, nor has she ever called him, for fear that they would be found out.

This is a very big decision that she made, and I chose for some of her processing to happen offstage. It's implied in the opening of her next scene that she spent the ferry ride over thinking through what to do now.

I could have chosen to show that, but one thing about these kinds of reaction/processing scenes is that a little goes a long way. Hanging out with Evalina while she's sitting on a ferry and contemplating the possible ripple effects her decision might have can get boring fast, so I chose to show none of it.

In Donald Maass's *Writing the Breakout Novel* he rails against "in the kitchen drinking tea" scenes, saying how much he loathes when he sees manuscripts where characters are sitting around, drinking tea, and thinking. Even if there's no tea around, these kinds of processing moments can too often turn into that. He says, "They are a pause, a marking of time, if not a waste of time. They do not do anything. They do not take us anywhere. They do not raise questions or make us tense or worried. No wonder they do not hold my attention."

There are many ways we can have our characters "sit around and drink tea" and it felt to me like having Evalina sitting on a ferry and feeling stressed would be one of them.

So instead, her stressing is implied, and I open her next scene on the phone with a friend:

> "Evalina, you have flipped your wig." But Gia sounds admiring, not admonishing. "I knew when you finally fell for a boy, you would fall hard, but you seriously took a ferry to Alameda?"
> "What else was I supposed to do? He wasn't at the market this morning, plus these articles in the paper ..." I swallow. "I thought maybe his family had been taken."
> "You are so dramatic sometimes. They're not going to be taken. It's all voluntary."
> "I don't think so, Gia." I twist the cord of the pay phone around my finger. "I think they'll all be made to go."
> "I still can't believe you took a ferry to Alameda. What are you going to tell your parents?"
> "Hopefully they'll never know. You'll cover for me if they call or stop by, right?"
> "Of course. I'm meeting Lorenzo for lunch, but I'll just say you were with us."
> Imaginary lunches with Gia's on-again off-again boyfriend are the only kind I can tolerate. "Thank you, Gia. I'll let you know when I'm home."

In this moment, readers are able to see what kind of thought Evalina has put into the outcome of her decision. Even though there's movement to the scene, it still feels like a beat of rest for the audience.

There is a great example of this in the movie *Tangled*. After Rapunzel has sung with the thugs that she has a dream, and the palace guards have come for Flynn, Rapunzel and Flynn escape into the tunnel underneath the Snuggly Duckling.

The writers could have just had them run right into the next action scene. Instead, while they are in a tunnel, the audience has about a minute in which the characters process what happened. This slowing down from the action gives us a moment to breathe, and it gives them a moment to bond. A lot of character growth and connection happens in these segments of the story.

Sometimes reaction scenes take up an entire scene, particularly in heist novels or movies. A heist will go awry, and then we have a scene where the whole crew is sitting in a room debating the various choices and consequences.

So, let's say you've given your character a moment—whether it's a paragraph or pages—to process what has happened, survey all their options and various consequences, and feel all the feels.

Now the next question is, **"Because of what happened, what will my character choose to do now?"** which you might notice is the *first* question we talked about.

> **Here's a compiled list of all the questions:**
> - Because of what happened in the previous scene, what will my character choose to do now?
> - What is this character's plan or goal coming into this scene?
> - What obstacle stands in my character's way? How is their expectation foiled?
> - What decision does my character make as a result?
> - What is the outcome of my character's decision?
> - Does my character need time to process and react to what has happened?
> - If so, what is the decision born out of his processing time?

What's really fun is that once you understand this natural pattern, then you are able to mix and match how you put together your scenes without losing impact.

Scene One could be your character setting out to achieve a goal, and it might end with their expectation being foiled. (Answering questions one, two, and three.)

Scene two could show the decision they make and the outcome of that decision. (Answering questions four and five.)

Scene three could be processing, making a decision, and pursuing a new scene goal. (Answering questions six, seven, and one.)

In a way, arranging your scenes is like arranging your individual sentences. If you use the exact same sentence structure every time, it becomes very boring. Beautiful writing comes from sentences being arranged in all different kinds of ways, and the same is true for building your scenes. If every scene begins with the character having a plan, the plan getting spoiled, making a decision, the outcome of the decision, and then repeat, the story will have a mechanical feel to it.

Other questions to ask when editing scenes:

How does this scene impact the plot? If I cut it, would it matter?

This is the best place to start when you're editing a scene. Otherwise you might spend a lot of time editing a scene and then decide you don't need it at all.

Can I make this scene work harder for me?

I like to ask this question next because sometimes in my first drafts a scene only accomplishes one thing when it could easily take care of two or three if I just use my brain a bit.

Let's look again at that scene from *Within These Lines* when Evalina is on the phone with her best friend Gia.

Their conversation is only 174 words long, but it accomplishes quite a few things:

1. Introduces Gia.
2. Shows a different perspective about the impending evacuation of Japanese Americans.
3. Shows that Gia is someone who Evalina has trusted when it comes to Taichi.
4. Introduces Lorenzo and Evalina's feelings about him.

That's some heavy lifting for 174 words! In my first draft, I was only doing items one through three on that list and decided that I could have my scene work harder for me by mentioning Lorenzo.

Am I telling it from the right point of view (POV)?

If you're writing from only one point of view, this is a moot point, but it's a very important question if you have multiple point of view characters. If you are confused about point of view, that's something Jill is going to address in the next chapter.

Did I arrive late?

Just like the age-old writing advice of, "Start your story in the middle of the action," your scenes should each start that way as well. Something should already be happening, like in my scene where Evalina is on the phone with Gia. We don't need to see her digging through her purse for a dime, putting the dime in, talking to the operator, etc.

I adore this quote from Donald Maass about the opening of books, which can be applied to individual scenes as well:

> Did you ever arrive early for a party? It's awkward, isn't it? The music isn't yet playing. Your host and hostess make hurried conversation with you while they set out the chips and dip . . . You feel dumb for getting there too soon. That's how I feel when I read the opening pages of many manuscripts. Pieces of the story are being assembled, but nothing is happening just yet, and often the guest of honor, the protagonist, hasn't arrived.

Wherever you start your scene, you want it to feel like something is already in motion.

Do I help provide context for my readers? (Who, what, when, where, and why)

Once you've found the right action for starting your scene, you need to give your reader context as quick as you can. That means answering the who, what, when, where, and why of your scene. Who is there? What is happening? When is this taking place? Where are we? And why are we here?

Let's take another look at the first 250 words of chapter three of *Within These Lines* and see how I did:

> "Evalina, you have flipped your wig." But Gia sounds admiring, not admonishing. "I knew when you finally fell for a boy, you would fall hard, but you seriously took a ferry to Alameda?"
>
> "What else was I supposed to do? He wasn't at the market this morning, plus these articles in the paper …" I swallow. "I thought maybe his family had been taken."
>
> "You are so dramatic sometimes. They're not going to be taken. It's all voluntary."
>
> "I don't think so, Gia." I twist the cord of the pay phone around my finger. "I think they'll all be made to go."
>
> "I still can't believe you took a ferry to Alameda. What are you going to tell your parents?"
>
> "Hopefully they'll never know. You'll cover for me if they call or stop by, right?"
>
> "Of course. I'm meeting Lorenzo for lunch, but I'll just say you were with us."
>
> Imaginary lunches with Gia's on-again off-again boyfriend are the only kind I can tolerate. "Thank you, Gia. I'll let you know when I'm home."
>
> I hang up and push my bicycle out to the curb. The day has grown warm, but the wind off the bay still bites, so I tighten my coat. Around me, families hurry into line to catch the ferry to San Francisco. The women are dressed in bright spring skirts and sweaters, and many of the men wear their uniforms. A group of three sailors stand nearby; one winks at me. He reminds me of Gia's boyfriend, so I angle away.

Who is there?: Gia and Evalina

What is happening?: They're on the phone; Evalina has called to ask Gia to cover for her.

When is this taking place?: We know from the previous scene, told from Taichi's perspective, that he's just left the house to pick Evalina up from the dock. From that, it's easy for readers to connect that Evalina is calling Gia while she waits.

Where are we?: After Evalina gets off the phone, we see that she is at the dock.

Why are we here?: Again, based on the clues from the previous scene, the reader understands that Evalina is waiting for Taichi to pick her up.

Do I leave early and give my reader a reason to come back?

As soon as I've accomplished my objective with a scene, I want to get out of there. Even if it's not the end of a chapter, but just the end of a scene, I always try to end with something snappy, reflective, poignant, or question-provoking. Here's the close of this scene from *Within These Lines*:

> "We'll find a way." Taichi pops a wedge of orange in his mouth. "We can't see it now, and maybe it doesn't exist yet, but we'll find some way through this. Some bridge across this canyon."
> "I don't want to wait for someone to build us a bridge," I snap. "I'll do it myself."
> Now Taichi's smile is full, as it often is when my temper flares. He leans forward and presses his mouth to mine, melting away the firm, angry line of my lips. His hand threads into my hair, and I try to lean into the moment. Try to not let its inherent joy be stolen by all my fears about what tomorrow or the next day will bring.
> "If you intend to build us a bridge, Evalina"—Taichi's forehead touches mine, and his whisper is warm and citrusy—"then I pity whoever gets in your way."

I liked ending here because it sets up the rest of the story very nicely. While Taichi will spend a lot of the book dealing with what is dished out at him, Evalina will spend her time fighting for a better life for them.

Make it Yours:

Using these questions, make sure your scenes are as strong as you can make them!
- How does this scene impact the plot? If I cut it, would it matter?
- Can I make this scene work harder for me?
- Am I telling it from the right point of view (POV)?
- Did I arrive late?
- Do I help provide context for my readers? (Who, what, when, where, and why)
- Do I leave early and give my reader a reason to come back?

> You never really understand a person until you consider things from his point of view.
> –Harper Lee

9 Point of View

Point of View Basics
by Jill

Point of view is a tricky thing to learn, but once you grasp it, your writing can make readers feel like they *are* your main character. That's one attribute of a great storyteller.

Point of view is the perspective of the story. There are four perspectives a story can be written in and each has a different level of narrative distance, which is the feeling of closeness between the point of view character(s) and the reader.

Once you choose a point of view perspective, you must decide if the story will be written in past tense or present tense. Past tense reads like it has already happened. Present tense reads like it's happening right now. Most stories are written in first person past tense or third person past tense. First person present tense is, at *present*, a popular choice as well.

When you write a story, pick one point of view, one tense, and stick with them. There are some novels that mix it up a bit (*The Help* by Katherine Stockett comes to mind) but that's tougher than it looks, so if this is your first novel or if you're early in your writing journey, go easy on yourself until you get the hang of this.

Let's cover the four perspectives:

Omniscient Point of View

In omniscient points of view, God or an all-seeing narrator tells the story. This is mostly told from a third person perspective, but the God-narrator knows all, sees all, and can communicate to the reader the thoughts of different characters in the book.

The degree of knowledge that the narrator has determines his level of omniscience. If he knows what every character is thinking, then he's fully omniscient. If the narrator only reveals what certain characters are thinking, he has limited omniscience.

Omniscient point of view stretches the narrative distance between the reader and the characters by bouncing from head to head. Full omniscient perspectives are not as popular in modern fiction.

The biggest problem with omniscient points of view is that if they aren't written well, they're confusing. Jumping from one person's head to another in the same paragraph makes it difficult for your reader to connect emotionally to the story. This is what makes the omniscient point of view the most difficult to master. I highly recommend learning how to write a single point of view before you attempt omniscience.

Here's an example of omniscient third person from the novel *Magyk* by Angie Sage. Notice how we start in Marcia's head, then move to Sarah's head, back to Marcia's, and end up in Silas's head.

> Marcia looked around her. It was true, it was not somewhere you would ever expect to find a princess. In fact, Marcia had never seen such a mess before in her entire life.
> In the middle of the chaos, by the newly lit fire, stood Sarah Heap. Sarah had been cooking porridge for the birthday breakfast when Marcia had pushed her way into her home, and into her life. Now she stood transfixed, holding the porridge pan in midair and staring at Marcia. Something in her gaze told Marcia that Sarah knew what was coming. This, thought Marcia, is not going to be easy. She decided to dump the tough act and start over again.
> "May I sit down, please, Silas . . . Sarah?" she asked.
> Sarah nodded. Silas scowled. Neither spoke.
> Silas glanced at Sarah. She was sitting down, white-faced and trembling and gathering the birthday girl up onto her lap, holding her closely. Silas wished more than anything that Marcia would go away and leave them all alone, but he knew they had to hear what she

had come to say. He sighed heavily and said, "Niko, give Marcia a chair."

Many classics are done in an omniscient style, but if you want to pull it off for the modern reader, I suggest you study some popular, modern books that have omniscient narrators.

Examples of popular books done in omniscient POV: the *Gossip Girl* series, the *Septimus Heap* books, the *Luxe* series, the *Redwall* series, the *Heist Society* series.

First Person Point of View

The first person perspective uses "I" for the point of view character. This is a great point of view to consider if you want to really get deep with your main character. Here's an example of first person past tense from *Out with the In Crowd* by Stephanie Morrill:

> All winter break, I'd planned for this moment, the one about to happen.
> "Hey," Eli said as we passed each other in the hall.
> I intended to say hello back, to smile like things between us hadn't changed, but something inside me bristled. I locked my jaw, turned away from his hypnotic smile, and picked up the pace.
> Then I mentally kicked my butt as I sped toward my locker. That was *not* how it should've gone.

And here's an example of first person present tense in Libba Bray's *A Great and Terrible Beauty*:

> "Lily Trimble is quite beautiful, isn't she?" I say by way of trying to make pleasant small talk with Tom, a seemingly impossible task.
> "An actress," Tom sneers. "What sort of way is that for a woman to live, without a solid home, husband, children? Running about like she's her own lord and master. She'll certainly never be accepted in society as a proper lady."
> And that's what comes of small talk.
> Part of me wants to give Tom a swift kick for his arrogance. I'm afraid to say that another part of me is dying to know what men look for in a woman. My brother might be pompous, but he knows certain things that could prove useful to me.

The frustration of writing in first person POV is that you're typically telling the story from *that* point of view the entire book. Not always. *The Help* is all in first person, but the narrators alternate. Same with *Poisonwood Bible* by Barbara Kingsolver, both of which are modern day literature triumphs.

For a book with one first person POV, you have the pleasure of getting to know the main character intimately, but you can have a tough time gaining perspective from other characters without it seeming forced, though Libba Bray had little trouble showing the reader what Tom was like based on his dialogue alone.

Examples of books written in first person: All Sarah Dessen novels, all Stephanie Morrill novels, *An Ember in the Ashes* by Sabaa Tahir, *Steelheart* by Brandon Sanderson, *We Were Liars* by E. Lockhart, *The Hate U Give* by Angie Thomas, *Storm Siren* by Mary Weber, *Children of Blood and Bone* by Tomi Adeyemi, Jill Williamson's *The New Recruit*, *Divergent* by Veronica Roth, *Matched* by Ally Condie, the *Percy Jackson* novels by Rick Riordan.

Second Person Point of View

This perspective uses "you" for the point of view character. This is a really rare style of storytelling, most often used in choose-your-own-adventure novels. Here's an example of second person past tense from *The Abominable Snowman* by R. A. Montgomery.

> You are a mountain climber. Three years ago you spent the summer at a climbing school in the mountains of Colorado. Your instructors said that you had natural skills as a climber. You made rapid progress, and by the end of the summer you were leading difficult rock and ice climbs.
>
> That summer, you became close friends with a boy named Carlos. The two of you made a good climbing team. Last year you and he were chosen to join an international team. The expedition made it to the top of two unclimbed peaks in South America.
>
> One night on that expedition, the group was seated around the cook tent at the base camp. The expedition leader, Franz, told stories of climbing in the Himalayas, the highest mountains in the world.
>
> "The Yeti is said to be a huge beast," Franz tells you, "perhaps a cross between a gorilla and a human. People cannot agree what it is."
>
> "Is the Yeti dangerous?" Carlos asked.
>
> Franz shrugged. "Some say it is. Other people say the Yeti is

very gentle."

"Have you ever seen one?" you inquire.

The pitfalls of this POV are obvious. It's tricky to sustain over an entire story, and it can be pretty distracting for the reader.

The book *Stolen* by Lucy Christopher is an interesting example of how you could use second person in a powerful way. Gemma writes from her point of view, but she is penning a letter to Ty, the man who kidnapped her. She calls him *you*. Much of the novel reads like second person as Gemma speaks to Ty. Other parts of the book read like first person when Gemma is not speaking directly to her kidnapper.

> From a distance, when I'd seen you at the check-in line, your body had looked thin and small, like the eighteen-year-olds at my school, but up close, really looking, I could see that your arms were hard and tanned, and the skin on your face was weathered. You were as brown as a stretch of dirt.
>
> "I'm Ty," you said.
>
> Your eyes darted away then back again before you reached out your hand toward me. Your fingers were warm and rough on the palm of my hand as you took it and held on to it, but didn't really shake it. You raised an eyebrow, and I realized what you wanted.
>
> "Gemma," I said, before I meant to.
>
> You nodded as though you already knew. But, of course, I suppose you already did.

Powerful, right?

There aren't many examples of books written in second person. Besides *Stolen*, you could check out *Ivory and Bone* by Julie Eshbaugh and *Hart's Hope* by Orson Scott Card, which has sections written in second person.

Third Person Point of View

This perspective uses the character's name or "he" or "she" for the point of view character. Here's an example of third person past tense from my children's chapter book *Tinker*:

> "Name of sponsor?" the man asked.
>
> Oh no. Tinker tried to look confused. "Sponsor?"
>
> "You have to have an adult sponsor to enter the race. Someone who will be responsible for your vehicle in the event of a crash. Plus

there's a ten rula entry fee."

Just like that Tinker's dreams turned to scrap metal. Uncle Noctis would never sponsor him. Not with Grezzer competing.

He sighed deeply. There was nothing to be done now. He supposed he could still watch the race. Was there a price to sit in the stands?

"Come on, kid," the registration man said. "I need to keep the line moving. Who's your sponsor?"

"I don't have—"

"Isaias Monn."

Tinker spun around, eyes wide.

Mr. Monn set one hand on Tinker's shoulder and slapped a ten rula bill onto the table with his other. "Don't be surprised to find out that you are looking at the winner of this race," he told the man. "Tinker is very talented."

"*Tinker?*" the registration man asked.

"That's my nickname," Tinker said, then beamed at his neighbor. "Thank you, Mr. Monn."

The old man wiped his handkerchief over his forehead. "You're welcome, Tinker."

Once you've chosen your narrative style, you also must decide whether to use a single point of view or multiple points of view. A single POV means that you will stick with one character's POV for the whole story, like I did with *Tinker*. The reader never sees the story from another perspective. In books with multiple points of view, the story could be told from many perspectives, one at a time.

The Sisterhood of the Traveling Pants is a good example of multiple points of view. There are four POV characters, and each character has her own chapters. Also, in each of the four books, a different girl gets her turn being the main character.

Examples of books written in third person: There are tons! I mentioned two in this section—my book *Tinker* and *The Sisterhood of the Travelling Pants* books by Ann Brashares. Some more third person books are, *Uglies* by Scott Westerfield, *Caraval* by Stephanie Garber, *Mistborn* by Brandon Sanderson, *Captives* by Jill Williamson, *Three Dark Crowns* by Kendare Blake, and any Melanie Dickerson book.

> **Mixing Things Up**
>
> Not all novels are written strictly in the same point of view for the entire book. Jill's *Mission League* books are mostly first person from Spencer's snarky point of view, but in each book there is a handful of third person chapters from another character that Spencer will meet later in the book.
>
> Shannon Dittemore's *Angel Eyes* trilogy takes this even further. In these books, the main character Brielle's chapters are all told in first person, while any other point of view characters (Jake, Marco) are written in third person. James Patterson did something similar in his *Maximum Ride* series. In all of these examples, the authors stayed in the same point of view style for an entire chapter. That is a smart way of trying something different but still keeping things as clear as possible so not to confuse the reader.

Tightening Point of View

If you're trying to write a deep point of view, work hard to get your writing as close as possible to your point of view characters. This means to use only one point of view at a time. Some things to watch for as you edit are:

1. Don't tell us anything the character doesn't know.

Say you write, "Little did Shelley know, the monster was right behind her."

In deep point of view, if Shelley doesn't know that the monster is right behind her, then the reader can't know either. Not only does this sentence break deep point of view, but it's a nasty bit of telling. You spoiled the story by telling the reader about the monster! Try instead, "Shelley's gut tightened at the rank smell of rotten fish that came in a humid gust at the back of her neck. The hairs on her arms danced. Something was behind her!"

That's Shelley's point of view. She senses that something is behind her but doesn't know for certain until she turns around. And this way the readers experience what she's feeling, hearing, seeing, tasting, smelling, and sensing. They experience her fear.

2. Don't jump into someone else's thoughts.

It doesn't work in real life, and it doesn't work in fiction, unless you're writing in omniscient point of view or about a telepathic character. Consider the passage below.

> Kate glared at Edward. What a pain little brothers were! Why did he get away with taking her stuff all the time? Maybe she could ship him off to Australia media mail. That would teach him.
> If Kate wouldn't always boss him, he'd behave more. Edward really only wanted his sister to play with him. The other kids in third grade didn't have a big sister as cool as her, but she always yelled at him. He almost cried the last time, which was totally wimpy, but at least she was paying some attention to him, even if it was yelling.
> Mr. Jones always took his son's side. How could he not? Kate was careening through some bizarre teenage girl phase beyond his understanding. She constantly tortured the family, especially Edward. As a good father should, he stepped in, but Kate always took it as a personal attack.

The switches in POV from Kate to Edward to Mr. Jones are confusing. Most readers want to follow one character at a time. They don't want a new one every two sentences. When that happens, it's hard for a reader to know which character to invest in, which brings us to:

3. One at a time, please.

If you want to write multiple points of view, you can. Just do one at a time. That is, one per scene or one per chapter. I would rewrite the example above to come from Kate's point of view. If I wanted the reader to know how Edward and Mr. Jones felt, I could use dialogue. They could all have a big fight, or Mr. Jones could come up to his daughter's room and try to talk some sense into her.

Step 1: Make Your Good Book GREAT

> ### A Note from Stephanie
>
> Because I write in first person (so far it's just how all my stories have wanted to come out) I always skipped over lessons on POV and head hopping. After all, I wrote in first person so it was therefore impossible for me to head hop, right? Nope. Here's what head hopping looks like in first person:
>
> > I glared at my little brother. "I take it back. I no longer want you helping me with this."
> > My statement shocked Edward. "Well, if that's how you want to be, then fine. Be that way," he said, feigning coolness.
>
> To keep the point of view with Kate, everything must pass through Kate's filter. So instead you'd write:
>
> > I glared at my little brother. "I take it back. I no longer want you helping me with this."
> > Edward seemed unaffected by my harsh words. An act? "Well, if that's how you want to be, then fine. Be that way."
>
> It's tempting to want our readers to understand everything that all the characters are feeling at all times, but it really is better that they don't. It creates a breeding ground for conflict and misunderstanding—bad in real life, but great in stories!

Make it Yours:

1. Pick a scene from your book that involves more than one character. Try writing the scene from a different character's point of view. How does it feel? What did the new character describe that the original character didn't? Were there things the new character didn't even notice? What does the new character hear the original POV character say? Is it what your original POV character intended?

2. Now take a look at the scene as you originally wrote it—are there any changes you want to make?

Giving Your Narrative a Boost

All stories need an even mix of narrative, action, and dialogue, but I've read a lot of manuscripts that don't have enough narrative from the point of view character.

Narrative is the stream of consciousness that passes through your character's mind to depict his feelings and thoughts. It's his inner monologue. Not the italicized thoughts. Those are treated more like dialogue. (We'll get to italicized thoughts in Chapter 16.)

Here's an example of narrative thoughts from *The Amulet of Samarkand* by Jonathan Stroud. The point of view character here is Bartimaeus, a snarky demon.

> At last it looked as if the urchin was plucking up the courage to speak. I guessed this by a stammering about his lips that didn't seem to be induced by pure fear alone. I let the blue fire die away, to be replaced by a foul smell.
> The kid spoke. Very squeakily.
> "I charge you . . . to . . . to . . ." Get on with it! "T-t-tell me your n-name."
> That's usually how they start, the young ones. Meaningless waffle. He knew, and I knew that he knew, my name already; otherwise how could he have summoned me in the first place? You need the right words, the right actions, and most of all the right name. I mean, it's not like hailing a cab—you don't get just anybody when you call.
> I chose a rich, deep, dark chocolaty sort of voice, the kind that resounds from everywhere and nowhere and makes the hairs stand up on the back on inexperienced necks.
> "Bartimaeus."

Narrative thought can also be used in between dialogue. Here's an example from my book *The New Recruit*. Spencer is a sarcastic fifteen-year-old.

> Outside, dawn had lit the campus in pale light but not enough to raise the temperature. I poured on the speed, hoping to ditch Arianna.
> Unfortunately, she jogged to keep up. "How long did you use the broom before you realized it was a prank?" she asked.
> "Not long."
> "Isn't this neat? I hoped I'd get called. I speak three languages

already, but that doesn't guarantee—"

"How come you wear those weird skirts?" I asked, hoping rudeness might shut her up.

"You like them?" Arianna said, glancing down at her skirt. "I think our uniforms skirts are immodest, so I—"

"They go to the knee," I said. As did our cheerleaders' skirts, unfortunately.

"Exactly," Arianna said. "So I petitioned to get rid of them. Mr. McKaffey turned me down but said I could wear a longer skirt if I wanted to, as long as it was navy blue. So I sewed up a dozen different styles. This one is my favorite."

"Wow." And I meant it.

"Every year I ask God to give me a word, and this year he gave me the word *service*. And now this opportunity has come! It's such a God thing."

Arianna dove into an oration on being a servant of God, as if that would somehow make me want to be one too. Weird strategy. I ignored her babbling while zigzagging through the mob. I turned down the freshman hallway, which was filled with rowdy students and clanging lockers.

Arianna stopped off at her locker. "See you in homeroom."

That settled that. I'd skip homeroom for the rest of the year if only to avoid any more heart-to-hearts with Mission-Ari Sloan.

As you can see from both of those examples, narrative thoughts help the reader get to know the point of view character. Because the reader is privy to his inmost thoughts, the reader feels as though he is Bartimaeus or Spencer.

And that's the goal of writing a great point of view.

> I try to leave out the parts that people skip.
> —Elmore Leonard

10 Your Character's Past

Flashbacks
by Stephanie

One of the toughest things for me to overcome as a writer was my desire to explain everything to the reader. Because I had invested so much time thinking up these characters and their histories, I wanted the reader to "get" them right away. And because of that I loaded down my stories with flashbacks and backstory.

Flashbacks are scenes where the writer cuts away from the current action to transport the reader to something that happened in the past. It's like when Harry Potter fell into Dumbledore's pensieve—that kind of feeling.

Backstory is the explanations that get littered throughout your story. They feel more like a whispered aside to the reader. *Hey, Jenna is acting this way because Dylan dumped her last week.*

Backstory isn't bad writing, but it gets a bad rep because it often gets used clumsily. I certainly fumbled with it in my early writing days. This is a snippet from a high school manuscript of mine. I've bolded the part that's backstory:

> This day was different, however. Today she stood in the doorway a stranger to them all.
> **At the end of freshman year, Paige had tearfully moved away from Brawder, California to some unknown town in Missouri, and no one had heard a word from her.** Now here she was, a year later, on the first day of junior year.

This paragraph happens on the first page of the story. While eventually, yes, the readers need to know what happened to Paige, they don't need to know right away. The beginning of a story is a time for planting questions, which is what I did with "today she stood in the doorway a stranger to them all." Since the readers have just learned that the other students know Paige already, they're (ideally) intrigued by why today is different, why she's a stranger.

Planting questions is great. Answering them in the next sentence is not.

If the readers don't need the information in order to understand what's happening, then it's not the right time to hand it over.

But of course your story would be confusing and your characters flat if you didn't weave in backstory. I think the key to making those sentences interesting is they should come through the filter of the POV (point of view) character.

Here's an example. Again, I've bolded the backstory:

> "I think you guys should just be friends," Meghan says to me.
> Of course. **Ever since Joel stomped on her heart last spring, Meghan has been all about being "just friends" with boys.**
> I dry the counter with a towel. "You know, you don't always have a choice in the matter."

Much better, right? In that story of mine from high school, the backstory sentence felt more like Stephanie-the-author was explaining to you what was unusual about Paige being at school. But in this one, it feels like the POV character is telling you why Meghan is behaving the way she is.

It tells us everything we need to know at that moment. Which is that Meghan's advice is tainted by her experiences, and that our POV character is aware of it. We don't need an additional paragraph explaining what exactly happened between Meghan and Joel and whose fault it was. Maybe we'll need that later, but not yet.

But sometimes a sentence or two, or even a paragraph of explanation, doesn't capture the emotion of the character's past. And that's when you might consider a flashback instead.

Because flashbacks cut away from the forward progress of your plot, they should be chosen wisely.

When to use a flashback

- This is a moment in time that has forever altered your character.
- You've spent time in the story building up tension about what happened on "that night" or "that afternoon" and your flashback reveals what went down.

When not to use a flashback

- You wrote the scene, but then your timeline changed, but you really want to put it somewhere . . .
- It's a cute scene and you love it and you think readers will find it a fun bunny trail. (I was totally guilty of this as a new writer. Flashbacks are not about fun, but about revealing something deeper.)

Sometimes flashbacks are used in prologues, which I'm not a fan of. Typically, the reader doesn't have enough information about the characters for the flashback to have the emotional punch it might have later in the story. With that being said, *The Apothecary's Daughter* is one of my favorite books, and Julie Klassen opens with a flashback prologue. So it can be effective in the hands of a skilled writer.

As a general guideline, I would suggest only one or maybe two flashbacks per story.

In the Skylar Hoyt books, before the first book opens, she's nearly date raped at a party. This is, obviously, a very important turning point in Skylar's life. It's also not really something she likes to think about, and because she's pushing the pain away, there's no need to flashback to the scene in book one, *Me, Just Different*. Or in the second book, *Out with the In Crowd*. It isn't until halfway through book three, *So*

Over It, that we find out what happened that night, and then the scene is given almost an entire chapter.

But by now, the reader has gone through two and a half books of not knowing exactly what happened that night (Skylar's also a little fuzzy on the details, as it turns out). By the time the readers reach the flashback, they understand the significance of it. Whereas if I'd put the scene in the first book, or if I'd opened Skylar's story with it, the way I'd considered, the reader wouldn't have understood as deeply.

You don't need to strip all the backstory and flashback scenes from your novel, but hunt them down and assess the pacing and their contribution.

> Some people have a way with words, and other people ... oh, uh, not have way.
> —Steve Martin

11 Dialogue That Speaks

by Stephanie

Is there anything better than well-crafted dialogue? It's my favorite part of reading and writing, and if it's off, the whole story can feel flat or forced to me. While I can't always picture my characters the way some writers can, by the end of the first draft, I can *always* hear them—the tenor of the voice, their stutters, their unique way of stringing sentences together.

You have two nuts and bolts type tools when you're writing dialogue—word choice and punctuation.

Punctuation

We can all agree that these three sentences have the same words but mean completely different things:

"Grandma always made pumpkin pie."

"Grandma always made pumpkin pie!"

"Grandma always made pumpkin pie?"

Or maybe your character trails off or makes an aside comment:

"Grandma always made pumpkin pie . . ." (Or you can make a trailing off question, "Grandma always made pumpkin pie . . . ?")

Or maybe your character doesn't even get all his words out. For a character who's interrupted, you want to use the em-dash:

"Grandma always made pump—"

Be purposeful with your punctuation. What I see overused the most is the exclamation point. Those you'll want to really examine. If you're unsure at all, I would try going without. Some publishing professionals even say they only like to see one exclamation point per *book*.

You can use punctuation to show your pauses as well. Here's one with an ellipses:

"Grandma always made pumpkin pie."
"So maybe we should make one too . . . to honor her."

I'm also rather fond of em-dashes for pauses. *The Chicago Manual of Style* instructs it be formatted this way:

"Grandma always made pumpkin pie. And so today"—I take Joel's hand in my own—"that's what we're gonna do."

But I've seen variations of this format in published novels. Until a publisher tells you to do otherwise, sticking with *The Chicago Manual of Style* is a safe call.

I like how the em-dashes give the reader a glimpse of corresponding action. And I like that about using an action beat or character's thoughts to indicate a pause or hesitation:

"Grandma always made pumpkin pie."
Joel blinked a couple times. "She did?"

"Grandma always made pumpkin pie." **How could I say this to him? He was gonna be crushed.** "But today we're having pecan."

Maybe grammar isn't your thing—it's not mine either—but punctuation helps you communicate your words clearly. It's like if you were giving a speech, and your words were beautiful and your message great, but your microphone kept cutting out or making your voice sound weird. Your listeners would be distracted even if the speech was brilliant. The same is true with your dialogue. Like a microphone, punctuation will help pass your message along clearly, and it shouldn't call much attention to itself.

The Word Choice

Let's turn our attention from punctuation to the actual words being used in your sentences.

In an early manuscript of mine, one of my teenage boy characters kept using the word "fabulous." Everything was fabulous—weather, clothes, classes. But it's a rare male who says fabulous that often. I don't think my husband has *ever* used that word.

While a character's backstory isn't a "nut and bolt tool" for your dialogue, it's a support beam for your word choice. Where's the character from? How educated is he? How educated were his *parents*? Applying a character's backstory to the way he speaks is the key to creating character voices that differentiate from each other.

I used this example earlier too, but in *The Revised Life of Ellie Sweet,* my main character Ellie is sixteen, but because she's an aspiring novelist, I have her using bigger words and *who* and *whom* correctly. But her friend Chase was raised by parents who speak broken English, and he's pretty rough around the edges. Where Ellie might say, "My parents don't traditionally buy me presents for Valentine's Day," Chase would say, "My parents don't get me nothing."

Make it Yours:

List ten or so of your characters on the left side of your paper. Across the top of your paper, write several items or phrases that people say differently. I've selected a soft drink, purse, bathroom, and what they say when they say in a moment of surprise or disbelief. Then make a list of what each might say.

Here's an example:

	Soft Drink	Purse	Bathroom	Surprise/ Disbelief
John	Pop	Bag	Toilet	Really?
Sally	Soda	Handbag	Restroom	No way.
Lucy	Coke	Purse	The necessary	You're kidding me.

What's your problem?

Another way to keep your characters' voices from running together is to give them their own problem instead of letting their world revolve around the main character. (I also talk about this in the cast of characters section.) In my early drafts, conversations all hinged on my main character—her problems, her needs, her issues.

When your main character is interacting with other characters, be sure those other characters have their own thoughts and lives going on. If your main character wants to talk all nostalgic-like about Grandma's pumpkin pie, then have the other person wanting pecan pie. Or have him bring up the Thanksgiving where everyone fought, and he finished the day scraping pumpkin pie off the ceiling. Or he can bring up how Grandma never made pumpkin pie when *he* came to visit.

When you allow the other characters to have their own thoughts and problems, dialogue instantly becomes more interesting.

"Grandma always made pumpkin pie."
"Maybe for *you* she did."

Or:

"Grandma always made pumpkin pie."
"I know—but her pecan pie was so much better."

While you want your dialogue to have a real-life quality to it, you don't want it to read like a real-life conversation. Because that would be bo-ring. Alfred Hitchcock said that a good story was, "life, with the dull parts taken out." Apply this to dialogue too. At a real-life Thanksgiving dinner, you'll get cornered by Aunt Trudy and she'll talk to you for twenty minutes about Grandma's pumpkin pie and how she actually grated fresh nutmeg and always picked her pumpkins from so-and-so's pumpkin patch.

Don't make your readers sit through long monologues or pleasantries. ("Hi, how are you?" "Good, how are you?") Occasionally it might work for the story, like an awkward moment when two people who broke up last week are seeing each other for the first time, but in general "Hi, how are you?" discussions can all be nixed.

> **Make it Yours:**
> Pick a conversation in your manuscript at random. What was the non-POV character thinking about before the POV character started talking to him? Is that coming through in the dialogue? How would the dialogue change if the non-POV character had been thinking about something completely different?

The Strategy

A problem I often see in dialogue is characters that employ no strategy in how they deliver information.

My husband and I have been together since we were freshman in high school, yet still when I come to him with news, there's strategy involved. I'm not talking about me trying to manipulate him into doing something; I mean *any* news I share. News that will make him happy I share in a different way than news that will upset him. How will this affect him? When would be the best time to share it?

And this is a man who I'm confident isn't going to leave me, no matter what I say to him. Real life conversation involves strategy, and story world conversation should too.

Of course it can be a lot of fun to toss in a character who tends to say whatever pops into his brain, but how often do you say everything you're thinking?

When you're put on hold for ten minutes and someone finally comes back on the line and says, "I'm so sorry for the wait," what's your answer? I always say, "Don't worry about it," even though I've spent the last nine-and-a-half minutes grumbling snarky comments like, "Don't worry—my time isn't important. I'm not spending precious kid-free minutes trying to sort out this stupid billing error that's *your* fault. Take your sweet time."

> **Make it Yours:**
> Find a conversation in your manuscript in which one character is delivering information to another character. Does he have a strategy? If so, what is it? Why is he sharing this particular information right now? What if he had another motive? Fear, anger, jealousy, hope, love. How would that change the flavor of the conversation?

T.M.I.

Sometimes writers try to work information into dialogue that should *not* be in there. One of my writing pet peeves is an exchange that looks like this:

"Sally, how long have we known each other?"

"For ten years."

"That's why I'm giving you this ten-carat diamond."

I've seen variations of this on TV, in books, and in movies. Makes me crazy! Because that's not the kind of thing we say to each other. I never turn to my husband with moony eyes and say, "Honey, how long have we been married?" Not only is it information we both know, it's information we both *know* that we both know.

Now, I might say, "I can't believe we've been married for fourteen years," or, "I can't believe you've put up with me for fourteen years," but I've yet to say to him, "How long have we been married?"

I often see this kind of info dumping with dates and timeframes. Like, "Since today is Wednesday, do you have that report for me?" Or like this little gem from one of my early manuscripts:

"My father . . . is being transferred at the end of June."
"The end of June?! We're a week into June already!"

How forced is *that*? Sheesh. It's much more natural, I think, if the response is, "That's, like, three weeks away!"

Dialogue has to be natural. Read it out loud and ask yourself honestly if people would talk about things in such a way. If they wouldn't, find another way to get the info into the story.

Group Conversations

Of course, not all your conversations are going to be between two people. Often times you have a big group of characters engaging with each other. While necessary, it can really drag down the pacing.

A strategy for handling those is using sub-conversations. Say you're at a dinner party, seated at a long table. Rarely does everyone at the table engage in the same conversation. Typically you talk to whoever is across from you or next to you. You might catch snippets of other conversations, but mostly you interact with those closest.

That means as a writer, you want to be strategic with where characters are positioned in the conversation, because those are the characters your point of view character will be interacting with. You want to optimize the tension.

There are six characters in this conversation from my WWII era novel, *Within These Lines*. My main character, Evalina, is at her family's restaurant with her two best friends and their parents for a recurrent Friday night dinner.

Notice how when the whole group is talking, the topic is something that engages most or all members, and then we go back to a sub-conversation:

> Beneath the table, Gia kicks my foot. I startle and find the adults at the table—my parents, Mr. and Mrs. LaRocca, and Mr. and Mrs. Esposito—blinking at me with polite smiles.
> Mama swoops in. "You'll have to forgive Evalina. She didn't sleep well last night, I'm afraid." She smiles at me. "Mrs. Esposito asked how you think the yearbook will look."
> "Oh. I think it will look fine." I offer an apologetic smile to Mrs. Esposito. "We expect it back from the printer any day now."
> "I'm sorry you didn't sleep well, honey. Is it end-of-the-year stress?" Mrs. Esposito looks at Tony, who sits on the other side of me. "Tony has been working so hard to prepare for the end of the year. It's a shame that such a momentous time as high school graduation has to be shrouded with stressful exams."
> I wish my stress was as simple as concerns for my final exams.
> "I'm not stressed about school," Gia says as she scoops herself another helping of eggplant parmesan.
> "I think a little more stress would be good for you, Gia." Mrs. LaRocca shakes her head at Mama and Mrs. Esposito. "I cannot get her to care about her finals. Zola, you are so lucky to have a daughter who has worked hard enough to earn a scholarship. You would never know from Gia's grades that she's so smart."
> "A girl as pretty as Gia doesn't need good grades," Mrs. Esposito says as she reaches for a bowl of olives.
> Mrs. LaRocca is unsuccessful at hiding her pleasure over this comment. "Still. I never would have dreamed of doing less than my very best in school."
> The mothers fall into conversation about their school days, leaving Tony, Gia, and me alone to talk as we please.

If someone isn't contributing to useful conversation, you need to get them out of there. They need to go to the bathroom or see a friend walking by. Or they need to break into a side conversation with someone else.

Several lines after the above dialogue, I have this:

> Gia checks her watch. "I need to go. I'm meeting Lorenzo." She pauses and then cuts a look across the table at me. "He did call me by the way. After school today. Not that you've asked."

"Gia ..."

But she's already carrying her plate back to the kitchen without a glance over her shoulder.

"She'll be fine," Tony says in his rich, soothing voice. "Easy to injure but quick to heal."

"I know." I eat my last meatball even though there's no room in my stomach for it. "I'm more worried that she'll actually marry Lorenzo. He's not good enough for her."

Now, I have just Evalina and Tony in a conversation. Much more manageable!

Group conversations are necessary to breathe realism into the story, but too many of them will slow down your plot. You want to cut away from them and focus on your main character as soon as you can.

Action Beats and Dialogue Tags

Action beats are a tool you can use to support your dialogue. They're like framework, really. They help you keep the pacing and the context of both your group and one-on-one conversations. You can do it with dialogue tags too, but I prefer the effect of action or thought beats.

A dialogue tag is: he said, she shouted, he yelled, she questioned. It tells the reader who's talking, and it sometimes tells the reader how the speaker is saying his dialogue, but that's all it does—*tells* us. It doesn't show us what the speaker is doing. Consider the differences:

With dialogue tags:

"Grandma always made pumpkin pie," I said tearfully.
"Sure she did," Joel retorted.

With action beats:

I wiped the tear from my cheek with my flour-dusted hands. "Grandma always made pumpkin pie."
Joel snorted. "Sure she did."

Look at the difference that makes—we now have context and

emotion. Our main character is crying, and her hands are covered in flour.

Let's view it with a thought beat thrown in now:

> I wiped the tear from my cheek with my flour-dusted hands. "Grandma always made pumpkin pie." Would I ever make one without thinking of her?

Now we don't just have context and the physical manifestation of her emotion (tears), but we have her exact thought.

When you're using action or thought beats, you want to be sure to put them in the same paragraph. Otherwise this happens:

> "Grandma always made pumpkin pie."
> I wash my hands.
> "Sure she did."
> Joel walks out of the room.

What's wrong here? You can't really tell who is saying what. It could be the narrator speaking or Joel or someone else. The reader can't know for sure and needs some clues to help him know who is saying what.

> I wash my hands. "Grandma always made pumpkin pie."
> "Sure she did." Joel walks out of the room.

Putting the narrator's action with the "Grandma always made pumpkin pie" dialogue shows the reader that "I" said those words. Putting Joel's action with the "Sure she did," shows his response.

The action tags in that example, however, are a bit generic. In first drafts, my manuscript is always filled with generic action tags. Things like: He nodded. She shrugged. She rolled her eyes. He grinned. He walked. She smiled. While your characters might shrug or gasp or shudder or smile, these things don't build tension or emotion and tend to get overused.

Keep an eye out for generic action tags and replace them with meaningful action or narrative thoughts. Try to make each tag unique and show something important about the character or the setting.

> Kim clicked her long, red fingernails on the steel countertop. "I don't eat red meat."

Here we learn Kim has long, red fingernails, that the countertop is steel, that she doesn't eat red meat. Her actions and dialogue work together to show something to the reader.

When I first learned about action beats, I was amazed to see how they instantly tightened my writing, and I think you'll find the same for yours as well.

> **Make it Yours:**
>
> 1. Do a search in your manuscript for the word "said." Do you need it? Or could you strengthen the dialogue by either showing the action or sharing the character's thought?
>
> 2. Do the same with replied, retorted, shouted, or any of your other favorite dialogue tags. Instead of telling the reader that your character shouted something in anger, could you show the anger in his words by having him throw something instead?

Step 1: Make Your Good Book GREAT

> Don't tell me the moon is shining; show me the glint of light on broken glass.
> –Anton Chekhov

12 Cut Out the Telling

by Jill

Someone reads your work and says, "There's too much telling here. You need to show."

Huh?

The whole "show, don't tell" issue is a great mystery for beginning writers and even for some writers who've been at it a while.

What does "telling" mean, anyway? And how do you "show?"

I'm a visual learner, so when I was trying to figure all this out, it wasn't until I saw examples that I started to understand. That's why, in this chapter, I've listed several ways I see authors tell rather than show, and I've given examples of each in hopes of "showing" you exactly what I mean.

Telling the Senses

Using the five senses in your writing is great, but be careful not to "tell" the five senses. If you're using the actual words—felt, saw, heard, smelled, tasted, sensed—or other versions of these words—noticed, found, spotted, experienced, looked, watched, wondered, listened, tried, thought, etc.—you're probably telling.

> Telling example: Bill felt tired.
> Showing example: Bill yawned. His body ached. He hadn't slept in three days.
>
> Telling example: Shannon spotted a bird.
> Showing example: A blue jay flew across the gray sky.
>
> Telling example: Jessie heard the tinkling of a bell.
> Showing example: A bell above the entrance door tinkled.
>
> Telling example: Angie smelled fresh bread.
> Showing Example: The scent of fresh bread wafted on the breeze.
>
> Telling example: He tasted blood.
> Showing example: A metallic tang flooded his mouth.
>
> Telling example: She sensed foreboding.
> Showing example: Her skin prickled as if something was wrong.

You can't avoid every word from my list above, nor should you. And I'm not saying those words are bad news. They are perfectly fine words, and sometimes exactly the one you'll need. But use them carefully. Show action whenever you can rather than telling the facts. Showing gives you the opportunity to describe setting, characters, senses, and action. It helps you be specific. Every word matters. Choose wisely.

Adverbs

Adverbs that end in "ly" tend to be overused by new authors. And "ly" adverbs are *always* telling. Every once in a while it's okay to use one—I've even had editors add them to my writing!—but for the most part, cut them out. Instead, use strong descriptive verbs to convey emotion and action rather than relying on lazy adverbs.

Telling example: "Come here," Meg said loudly.
Showing example: "Come here!" Meg yelled.

Backstory in Dialogue

Flashbacks and backstory can be considered telling, and Stephanie went over that in Chapter 10, but telling backstory can also happen in dialogue. Can you see the backstory in the example below?

"How are you, Mike? I know you broke your leg last week. How is it feeling?"

"It's better, but I couldn't play in the basketball game last night like you did."

"I'm sorry. I know how much that means to you."

Or . . .

"I don't want to go to the party tonight. I'm tired of trying to meet boys," Megan said.

"But Meg, you're so pretty," Jessica said. "Your blonde curls make me jealous. And you have great posture and a nice figure. You're shorter than me, too, and I know boys like that."

My, what a "telling" way to sneak in some character description! Ha ha.

Assumptions and Interpreting Minds

Unless you're writing an omniscient point of view, you should always be inside the head of one character at a time. When you're working on your edit, watch for places where your point of view character knows something he shouldn't.

Be careful of using "seem," "I could tell," or "I knew." These words

and phrases often tell the emotion of characters your POV character sees, but your point of view character can't really know how another person is feeling by interpreting the look on her face.

Meg looked at John. He seemed to think she was lying.

Meg can't know that. She can't read John's mind. She could guess, but it's stronger to do a little more work on your rewrite. What about John's words or behavior gives Meg the impression that he thought she was lying? Did he huff and walk away? Fold his arms and scowl? Did he say, "Meg, you're full of it"? Make sure your main character isn't simply interpreting minds.

With a

Another signal that you might be telling is using the phrase "with a." Consider the difference between these two sentences.

Telling example: "Give up already," Dave said with a wink.
Showing example: Dave winked at Grace. "Give up already."

In the second example "winked" is a verb rather than a descriptor. It's stronger that way.

```
Make it Yours:
    Do a search in your manuscript for some of the
words mentioned above. You can also search for -ly
words, and even for phrases like "with a." Examine the
sentences you find. Are you telling? Is there a way you
could be showing instead?
```

> Description begins in the writer's imagination, but should finish in the reader's.
> –Stephen King

13 Weaving in Description

by Jill

Editors vary on their insistence that setting and characters be described fully. Some say leave it out and let the reader imagine everything. Others say you need to paint that scene for the readers so they can see it. I think somewhere in the middle is best.

If you describe nothing, you have what's commonly referred to as talking heads, which is a string of dialogue coming from people the reader can't see.

And if you describe too much, you keep the reader from experiencing the action of the story.

When I go back in to edit, I often find that I've described very little. If you write books on the shorter side, this is good. Going back and adding words will beef up your word count. This is always trouble for me, however, because I write such long books, and adding description to an already long novel is tricky.

There are two things I want you to know about description in fiction writing. 1) Description is necessary, and 2) Description is not always "telling." Description *can* be a form of telling, but that doesn't mean you can get away with describing nothing. If you don't describe the scene and characters, how will readers know where your character is or what anything looks like?

Props on the Stage

Ever see a play? A few years ago, my son acted the part of Linus in *A Charlie Brown Christmas*. When we entered and took our seats, the first thing we saw was the stage, decked out for Christmas. A piano and desk with a sign that said, "Psychiatric Help 5¢," sat on one side of the stage. On the other side, Snoopy's dog house had been taped to the wall, decorated with twinkle lights, and a red plastic dog dish sat on the floor in front of the blacked-out dog door. A tin can was sitting on a shelf in the background, and later, my son got to knock it down with his Linus blanket.

Everything the actors needed for the entire play was on stage from the start, waiting to be used.

You don't have to go *that* far. But near the beginning of every scene, you should give your readers some sort of description. Prepare that stage. It doesn't have to be much. It simply needs to share with the reader the following information: the location, what characters are present, and any objects that might be integral to the forthcoming scene, like the tin can for Linus to knock down or Linus's blanket.

If you plan to have a character pick up a chair and throw it later in the scene, you'd be wise to plant at least one chair in your initial description. Having a chair appear suddenly when the character needs to throw it might be confusing to the reader if you never mentioned there were chairs in the room.

Let's look at a few examples of description at the start of a new scene. The first example comes from *Code Orange* by Caroline B. Cooney.

> On Friday, Mr. Lynch walked around the classroom making sure everybody had written down the due date in their assignment books. Luckily, he started at the far side, giving Mitty Blake time to whisper to his best friend, "Due date for what?"

You might not see much description in that example, but we know we're in a classroom filled with people, we know the teacher is on the other side of the room, and we know our POV character, Mitty, is sitting beside his best friend.

How about this example from *Holes* by Louis Sachar.

> There were six large gray tents, and each one had a black letter on it: A, B, C, D, E, or F. The first five tents were for the campers. The counselors slept in F.
> Stanley was assigned to D tent. Mr. Pendanski was his counselor.
> "My name is easy to remember," said Mr. Pendanski as he shook hands with Stanley just outside the tent. "Three easy words: pen, dance, key."

The author's description allows us to see the layout of the camp, and we get Stanley and Mr. Pendanski's location before they start a dialogue with each other.

Let's look at one more. Shannon Dittemore does a good job in this description from her novel *Angel Eyes*.

> Damien leans against the warehouse. With human eyes he stares—at the burned-out church across the street, at the dark stretch of road before him, at the abandoned half-built skyscraper covering the site in shadow.

Can you picture it? Creepy. And this description leads right into Damien's goal for the scene. Whenever you are able to combine description with action and motivation, it's a very good thing.

If we tear these examples apart, you can see that all of the scenes let the reader know where the point of view character is and who is with him: Mitty is sitting at a desk in a full classroom beside his friend. Stanley is standing outside a tent with Mr. Pendanski. Damien is leaning against a warehouse, alone.

> **Make it Yours:**
> Check the beginning of each scene. Have you given a description that mentions the location, what characters are present, and any important objects? If not, do so now!

Describing Through a Point of View Character

The way things are described in your story depends on which point of view character is describing them. Some descriptions will be generic. Other times, if you're writing a girl, she might point out clothing details or compare her looks to the person she's describing, while a male POV might just think: She was a chick in a dress. On the other hand, some males might observe a specific model of a car and know what kind of an engine it has, whereas most females might only notice that the car was old and an ugly shade of green.

Those are general stereotypes, of course. There are plenty of fashion-conscious guys out there and girls who know cars. My point is, not every character will notice the same things or choose to think about them. Always try and bring out your point of view character's personality when you describe. Here are some examples of different ways to use description. Notice which examples characterize the POV character as well as describes something.

Narratives

> As always, [Nick's] face, clothes, pose, and perfectly gelled hair looked like something from the cover of GQ magazine. He was tall and thin, but I had four inches on him.
> —*The New Recruit* by Jill Williamson

> Medium height, stocky build, ashy blond hair that falls in waves over his forehead. The shock of the moment is registering on his face, you can see his struggle to remain emotionless, but his blue eyes show the alarm I've seen so often in prey.
> —*Hunger Games* by Suzanne Collins

Dialogue and Action Tags

> "Speaking of faces, love the nose."
> Tally giggled, pulling it off. "Yeah, no point in being uglier than usual."
> Shay's face clouded. She wiped off an eyebrow, then looked up sharply. "You're not ugly."

"Oh, come on, Shay."

"No, I mean it." She reached out and touched Tally's real nose. "Your profile is great."

"Don't be weird, Shay. I'm an ugly, you're an ugly. We will be for two more weeks. It's no big deal or anything." She laughed. "You, for example, have one giant eyebrow and one tiny one."

Shay looked away, stripping off the rest of her disguise in silence.

—*Uglies* by Scott Westerfeld

"I have to go." I start up the hill again, nearly sprinting now, but again he comes after me.

"Hey. Not so fast." At the top of the hill he reaches out and puts a hand on my wrist to stop me. His touch burns, and I jerk away quickly. "Lena. Hold on a second."

Even though I know I shouldn't, I stop. It's the way he says my name: like music.

—*Delirium* by Lauren Oliver

Action

I'm saved by a Centro bus. It coughs and rumbles and spits out two old women in front of the grocery store. I climb on. Destination: The Mall.

—*Speak* by Laurie Halse Anderson

At that moment Alex struck. It was another classic Karate blow, this time twisting his body around and driving his elbow into the side of the man's head, just below the ear. The guard didn't even cry out. His eyes rolled and he went limp.

—*Stormbreaker* by Anthony Horowitz

. . . Harry was still looking out of the window, feeling increasingly nervous. Ernie didn't seem to have mastered the use of a steering wheel. The Knight Bus kept mounting the pavement, but it didn't hit anything; lines of lampposts, mailboxes, and trash cans jumped out of its way as it approached and back into position once it had passed.

—*Harry Potter and the Prisoner of Azkaban* by J. K. Rowling

Voice

There are two types of voice: author voice and character voice. An author's voice is the way he or she puts words on a page. A character's voice is how an author puts different characters' voices on the page.

I like to write character-driven stories, so I strive to hide my author voice and make every word sound like that of the point of view character.

As I mentioned previously, I had a lot of fun doing this in my book *Captives*. Since this book has four point of view characters, I sometimes had to describe the same thing through the eyes of different viewpoint characters. For example, three of my viewpoint characters met General Otley. And each described him differently because they're different people and don't think alike.

Mason

> One man stood out from the rest, towering over the others like some monstrous bat. His eye shade had been pushed to the top of his helmet, though a pair of sunglasses and a thick beard covered most of his face. The skin that did show was pale and flaky. He had the thin plague.
>
> Mason had only ever seen body piercings in Old movies, but this man had overdone it, in his opinion. Gold rings looped through each eyebrow and the center of his bottom lip, and a gold spike curled out of each nostril like a section of the barbed wire that topped The Safe Land walls. He had a white number eight tattooed to his cheek. His name patch said Otley.

Levi

> A third enforcer ducked through the doorway. He looked like an elk walking on its hind legs. He had dark, frizzy hair, parted down the middle, that tangled with his bushy mustache and beard. His eyes were a freakish yellow. Even weirder, two coils of gold metal shot out from each nostril like feelers on an insect. Medals and bars and fancy patches covered his uniform. The word *Otley* was embroidered on a front shirt pocket. The number eight glowed on his cheek.

Omar

> . . . and Otley himself, sitting behind his desk with his beefy arms folded across his massive chest. Omar would sketch Otley as a giant boar ramming its tusks into the side of a house.

All three brothers compared General Otley to an animal, but chose different animals. Mason, a doctor, noticed his flaking skin and piercings. Levi, the outdoorsy hunter and leader of the Outsiders, paid more attention to Otley's beard, eyes, and metals. And Omar, an artist, thought about how he'd sketch the man to poke fun.

Each character is unique, and each voice should sound unique to that character.

> **Make it Yours:**
> Pick out three side characters from your book. Ask each of them, "How would you describe the main character?" Try writing the answers in first person, almost like a journal entry.

Description Through Word Choice

C. S. Lewis said, "Don't use words too big for the subject. Don't say 'infinitely' when you mean 'very'; otherwise you'll have no word left when you want to talk about something really infinite."

The words you use are important in writing, but especially so in description. You want to be specific and clear to paint the best image in your reader's head.

Simple Words

In any description, always try to state where the character is in one simple and strong noun: forest, bedroom, office, coast, classroom, sea. Pair the noun with descriptive verbs: curved, stretched, crouched, stood, towered. And occasionally add adjectives: rocky, thick, bare, crowded, grassy, colossal, or specific colors. I try to avoid "ly" adverbs unless I *really* want one.

Emotion Words

You can sometimes glean a character's mood from the words chosen in the description. Not all authors do this, but it can be a great way to bring out a certain feeling in a scene or even to convey imagery or symbolism. Let's look at a couple examples again. I've bolded the use of words and phrases that help to evoke emotion.

> Damien leans against the warehouse. **With human eyes he stares**—at the **burned-out** church across the street, at the **dark** stretch of road before him, at the **abandoned half-built** skyscraper covering the site in **shadow**.
> —*Angel Eyes* by Shannon Dittemore

> "I have to go." I start up the hill again, **nearly sprinting** now, but again he **comes after** me.
> "Hey. Not so fast." At the top of the hill he **reaches out** and **puts a hand on my wrist** to stop me. **His touch burns**, and **I jerk away** quickly. "Lena. Hold on a second."
> Even though **I know I shouldn't**, I stop. It's the way he says my name: like music.
> —*Delirium* by Lauren Oliver

In the *Angel Eyes* example, word choice paints a creepy, dark feeling for the reader: fear. The example from *Delirium* also evokes fear, but it's a different kind of fear, and it all changes quickly at the end of that example.

Word Pictures

Metaphors and similes create word pictures, which can be powerful when they create an instant mental image for the reader. A great simile or metaphor can help a reader connect, but be careful. Get too creative with this and you can jerk the reader out of the story. Make sure the ones you use work well. You can check your manuscript for similes by doing a "find" search in Microsoft Word for the word "like." Only keep the ones that flow and don't distract from the scene.

> The cafeteria was at full volume when I walked in. Feeding time at the monkey house.
> —*Twisted* by Laurie Halse Anderson

> [Arianna] was wearing a long, ruffly brown skirt with beige lace peeking out the bottom. All she needed was a parasol, and we could put her in a time machine and send her back to the Gold Rush.
> —*The New Recruit* by Jill Williamson

The rain came down in long knitting needles.
—*National Velvet* by Enid Bagnold

The Five Senses

Always try and work the five senses into your descriptions: sight, sound, touch, taste, and smell. Everything but sight is often neglected in books. This is such an easy way to connect with the reader. You don't need to give all five senses every time, but do try and use different ones.

> The house smelled funky, like mold, bacon grease, and cigarettes. The floors were bare. Cheyenne could tell by the sound of their footsteps that they were made of wood, not tile or linoleum. She shuffled her feet so that she could hear the echo from the walls. The room sounded small.
> —*Girl Stolen* by April Henry

> I lie in bed and listen to nine people breathing.
> I have never slept in the same room as a boy before, but here I have no other option, unless I want to sleep in the hallway. Everyone else changes into the clothes the Dauntless provided for us, but I sleep in my Abnegation clothes, which still smell like soap and fresh air, like home.
> —*Divergent* by Veronica Roth

Make it Yours:

Pick a scene in your book, preferably one that you haven't spent much time finessing yet. Examine the words you use in your descriptions. Are they simple and descriptive? Do they convey emotion for the scene? Do they paint a word picture? How about the five senses? Have you included some? For practice, try and use at least one sense per page and see what happens. Remember, not every description needs to do all of these things, but try to work in some of these tricks where you can.

> All the words I use in my stories can be found in the dictionary—it's just a matter of arranging them into the right sentences.
> —W. Somerset Maugham

14 Fresh Writing

by Jill

Part of rewriting is looking at how you've put your words together and whether or not you've done that in the best way. You want to craft every sentence and paragraph so that they sweep your reader along, page after page.

Seek out all things awkward, bland, repetitive, tiresome, and cliché, and work hard to make everything just right.

Paragraph and Sentence Length

We live in a "get it now" generation. Everyone is in a hurry, and attention spans are short. Most readers like lots of white space. If you pick up a book and flip through it, notice the amount of text on each page compared to the amount of white space (where there is no text). You want a good balance in your manuscript. When readers flip through a book and see pages covered in text with long paragraphs and little dialogue, it looks like a lot of work to read, which isn't appealing. Keep that in mind as you edit.

Paragraphs

Watch for super long paragraphs. They're not wrong, but if you're writing fiction that you hope will appeal to a wide variety of readers, you'll want to avoid them because readers tend to skim over long paragraphs. I recommend trying to keep paragraphs no longer than six lines in your Word document, because they'll be even longer once the text is put into book form.

Also, vary the length of your paragraphs. If you have too many really long ones, see if you can break up a few. This makes your text look more interesting to the reader and lets him know that a break is coming. And don't underestimate the power of a really short, one-sentence paragraph every now and then.

They rock.

Sentences

The same applies to the length of sentences. Too many long sentences are work for your reader. Too many short ones feel choppy, intense, and child-like. And if you write every sentence in the same structure and length, your writing will seem bland. A blend of short, medium, and long sentences with different structures is best. Below are two examples from different stages of my book *The New Recruit*. The first is an older rewrite. The second is the final version. Notice how similar the sentence lengths are in each paragraph in the first example, and how I managed to vary things in the second.

Example 1

"Is that you, Spencer? This is Lil Daggett. How are you, dear?"

"Fantastic." Spencer groaned inside. Lying to Mrs. Daggett was the only way to make it through the conversation without strangling himself with the phone cord. Grandma's friends from her quilt club had no concept that a sixteen-year-old boy had no interest in quilting.

"I need some help, Spencer. Alice suggested I call you."

No! Spencer whimpered in his head, focusing to keep the dream of Duke's offer fresh in his mind.

Mrs. Daggett went on. "I was over this morning, you know, for the quilt club."

The quilt club happened so often Grandma should charge rent. And she wondered why he rarely left his room. What had she volunteered him for this time?

"I have some calico for Alice."

Spencer shifted his weight from one foot to the other. "A cat?"

A laugh that sounded like crumpling paper crackled through the receiver. "Calico fabric, dear, not a cat. Alice needs it for a project. It's very important. Can you come right away?"

Spencer hung his head in defeat. "Sure, be right over."

Example 2

"Spencer? This is Lillian Daggett."

The low, rasping voice of Grandma's closest friend made me relax. Not McKaffey. Good. "Grandma's not home."

"I'm looking for you, actually. I have your lawn mowing money," Mrs. Daggett said. "Could you stop by sometime this evening? If I keep it any longer I'm afraid I might spend it on more fabric." She chuckled, but it sounded more like someone gasping for breath.

I perked up at the mention of money. I'd been saving up for a decent USB headset so I could talk to Kip while playing *Planet of Peril*. "Yeah, sure. I'll be right over." I hung up, excited about the cash. Mrs. Daggett hadn't paid me in so long she owed me, like, fifty bucks. If all went well, I'd be talking live on *PoP* tonight.

It's also wise to vary sentence length based on your characters and the current action. If you have a point of view character who rambles, he probably uses more lengthy sentences than a point of view character who doesn't talk much.

And if you have a fight scene or a battle of some kind, short sentences give the sense of excitement and fast-paced action. Long sentences do the opposite.

> **Make it Yours:**
>
> 1. Take a look at your paragraph and sentence lengths. Can you combine short sentences or divide some long sentences to come up with a more varied flow?
>
> 2. Consider the pacing of the action in each scene and whether the scene might benefit from some shorter or longer sentences.

Making Cliché Phrases Your Own

A cliché phrase is an expression that's so common it has lost its originality. They could be dialogue like, "Mark my words," sayings like, "there's a method to my madness," idioms, which are impossible phrases like, "It's raining cats and dogs," or overused descriptions like "alabaster skin." Clichés have been used so much that they make the reader "roll her eyes."

Avoid clichés in your writing. It can be hard to find them because some are so common you often don't even realize how cliché they are. Do your best to keep an eye out for them as you rewrite. If you're curious, there are many websites with lists of clichés.

When you find a cliché in your story, you can delete it or you can tweak it a little or a lot to make it your own—whatever works best for your scene, character, and storyworld. Here are some examples on how you could rewrite clichés.

He smelled like a dirty diaper/rotten eggs.
vs.
He smelled like the outhouse after Uncle Dan used it.

We're all in the same boat.
vs.
We're all in the same wagon. (Great for a historical.)

It had coal black eyes.
vs.
It had eyes that looked like someone had blacked them out with a Sharpie.

The voice of your character matters a great deal too.

She was higher than a kite.
vs.
She was as high as a 747. (Dad's voice.)
She was as high as the balloon my sister lost today. (Teen's voice.)
She was as high as Mariah Carey's vocal range. (Woman's voice.)

Hackneyed Plots, Twists, and Stereotypical Characters

Once upon a time (cliché phrase!) every idea that is now cliché was new and original and so brilliant that it inspired people to copy it, but over the years, so many people have used those same brilliant ideas that they're no longer brilliant. Now they make readers (or viewers) groan or roll their eyes.

Let's try to avoid having our readers groan and roll their eyes.

Cliché plots or twists to watch out for

- The love triangle.
- The line, "Don't you die on me!"
- A story about a chosen one.
- A prophecy being fulfilled.
- Prologues with an abandoned baby.
- Portals to another world.
- The sequel where the couple has split up and must be reunited.
- The magical item of great importance.
- Prologue that happens many years before your story begins.
- The main character falls in love with his best friend.
- The fake death. We saw him die, but . . . he's alive! (Uhm . . . I did this one.)
- A character goes to a magic school of some kind.
- The minority best friend, sidekick, or comic relief sidekick. (How about a minority hero or a funny hero instead?)
- The evil other woman, ex-wife, parent, etc. (People aren't ever *that* evil.)
- A retired guy called back into service because he's the *only one* who can get the job done.
- The bad guy who is really the main character's parent.
- The minor character who is planning to retire in just a few days. You know he's going to die . . . and he does!
- The "we look alike, let's switch places" plot.

- Big guys are dumb and oafish.
- Just before the big battle someone says, "Are you ready?" And your hero says, "I was born ready."
- The evil, dark lord of whatever.
- The main character is tutored by an old man. (I did this too!)
- The rakish hero who falls for the virginal heroine. He's a heart-breaker, but now he's met the one woman who can tame his wild heart. Sure.
- The bad guy could have killed the good guy but he monologues instead, giving the hero time to get away. (*cough* James Bond)
- The couple that hates each other at the beginning but end up together by the end of the book.
- The plain girl who gets a makeover and all of a sudden she's gorgeous and all the guys love her. (It was the glasses and ponytail.)
- The dying man's line, "Tell my wife and kids I love them!"
- The orphan who turns out to be someone really important. (Yeeahh . . . I also did this one. Oopsy.)

If something in your story is cliché, don't worry. You can still write your story, even keep the scene, character, or storyline (though that might not be your best bet). My point? You need to be aware of what's cliché and understand that an editor, agent, or reader will likely recognize that. Then you'll want to fix the cliché to make it work better before you submit or publish your story.

You might brainstorm ways to change the cliché. Introduce a new character. Bring back a dead character. Maybe the cliché character isn't who we thought he was. Make that cliché plot twist one more time with a fresh angle so that the reader thinks he knows where you're going, but you surprise him.

Readers love surprises.

Here are some other ideas to consider, but keep in mind that every character is on a journey and every scene should move your plot forward.

- Do the opposite of what you planned or something unexpected.
- Create your own creatures, weapons, and phrases. Who needs dragons and elves and dwarves? Forget swords, bows, and guns. Create your own species. Create your own weapon. Have fun with it! I created chams (fire-breathing bears) and gowzals (rat-like birds) in my trilogy, and they worked pretty well.
- Vary your characters' ages. I mean, it's pretty coincidental that the same-aged males and females are always going on epic journeys together, isn't it? Consider not having everyone in your story be the same age.
- Skip the prologue. Write it for yourself if you want to work out the history of your characters or storyworld, but maybe leave it out of the book. Too many people have used them.
- Don't become paranoid over every little thing. No one is going to call your medieval fantasy novel cliché because your characters use swords.

These are merely ideas to get you thinking. When you go back in to rewrite, work hard to make those clichés work for you. See what brilliant treasures you can come up with that will be so amazing people will be copying *you*.

> So the writer who breeds
> more words than he needs,
> is making a chore for
> the reader who reads.
> –Dr. Seuss

15 Tightening Your Prose

by Jill

Once your book is complete, and you're combing through it in editing mode, make sure that every word counts and belongs on the page. Seek out bland words, fluff words, needless words, and poor sentence structures. Fixing these things will make your manuscript tight. It will make it sing.

Cut Needless Words

When you're writing, you may feel the urge to add lots of descriptive words to make sure the reader gets it. Adjectives are often overused and can be redundant. Fluff words, also known as modifiers, often do nothing but take up space in your manuscript. Keep in mind: less is more. Remember this magic formula: 1 + 1 = ½. That means, if you overuse descriptive words, you might be making the story worse, rather than better. Whenever possible, one word is better than two or more. Here are some examples of fluff and how it might be tamed a bit for tightness and clarity.

> Poor: Luke was excited and thrilled.
> Better: Luke was thrilled.

One emotional word at a time packs a bigger punch. Plus, "excited" and "thrilled" are redundant since they have such similar meanings. Whenever you catch two similar words together in your story, pick your favorite and delete the other.

> Poor: The sculpture was totally gigantic.
> Better: The sculpture was gigantic.

The word "gigantic" implies that the object is about as big as it can possibly be. The word "totally" in front of it adds nothing. Better to cut it. Unless your POV character uses the word "totally" a lot because you're writing a 1980s novel.

> Poor: Billy felt his insides freeze, and he just knew that at any moment, they would see him and beat him to a bloody pulp.
>
> Better: Billy froze. Any second they would see him and plant him like a rose bush.

"Knew" and "felt" are telling, so they can be cut. I also got rid of the cliché, "beat him into a bloody pulp." Also, making it two sentences increased the tension. Short sentences like, "Billy froze," almost make my spine shiver.

> Poor: She cared nothing of the rumbling noise in her stomach as she searched through the piles and piles of clothes, looking for her cheerleading skirt.
>
> Better: Her stomach rumbled, but she continued digging through the mountain of laundry. Where was that skirt?

"Cared nothing" is wordy and telling. I showed that she caring nothing for the rumbling noise in the second example by stating the facts: Her stomach rumbled and she continued digging.

Also, "digging" creates a more powerful word picture as to the size of the pile. "Mountain" is more specific than "piles and piles" and it is two fewer words, and "Where was that skirt?" is stronger than "looking for her cheerleading skirt" because it shows what she's looking for and it conveys her frustration.

The first sentences were twenty-five words long. My rewrite was seventeen.

Look in the Extras section for a list of weasel words, which are words you can seek out and try to cut from your manuscript.

Vague vs. Specific

As you edit, look for vague words. They weaken your writing, confuse the reader, and it often sounds like you, the author, aren't quite sure what you're trying to say. These types of words often facilitate telling.

Also, vague words of measurement can almost always be cut. Words like every, often, sometimes, a little, a bit, kind of, sort of, about, nearly. These words mean nothing. It's okay to use them in dialogue, but in narrative, be specific. It will help the reader see exactly what you mean.

As you go back through your manuscript, look for vague words that leave the reader wondering and get rid of them. Good writing is in the details.

In the following examples, I've bolded the vague words.

Sarah **was a little tired** from cheerleading practice.

John **climbed** the **tree** and **looked** at the **mountain**.

Kate ate **some** pizza and fell asleep **watching TV**.

Michael Manis is **so good looking**.

Rachel's hair **was pretty**.

What's wrong with these sentences? They're vague! They don't use words that evoke a clear picture in the reader's mind. Here are the same examples written with more specific words.

Sarah **was exhausted** from cheerleading practice.

John **shimmied** up the **swaying willow** and **gazed** at the **monstrous peak of Denali**.

> Kate ate **a whole** pizza and fell asleep **watching *Doctor Who*.**
>
> Michael Manis is **Clark Kent without the geek. He's got that Superman build, the dark hair with the curls, the piercing blue eyes, but no glasses, stuttering, or falling all over himself.**
>
> Rachel's hair **fell in black waves over her shoulders and down her back.**

These words are much stronger and offer a clear picture to the reader. "Sarah was exhausted from cheerleading practice" still bothers me, though, because it's telling. How about this?

> Sarah entered her bedroom and tossed her duffle bag and pompoms onto the floor. She trudged across her room and fell onto the bed, muscles aching. She awoke at the sound of her mother's voice.

Whew! That's better.

"But, wait," you say. "First you told us to cut words, and in these examples you're adding words."

So true. When you rewrite telling into showing, it almost always increases your word count. Editing is a tricky balance of adding and taking away. The goal is to make every word count. Sometimes you might decide to leave some telling simply because there is no more room, but other times you'll fight to make room for a few extra words. This is tedious and sometimes maddening, but it is great practice and helps you become a stronger writer.

Contractions

Depending on your genre, you may want to add or delete contractions from your story. If you're writing nonfiction or historical, you may not want any contractions, because the lack of contractions can make your prose sound more formal. If you're writing a contemporary or young adult genre, however, I suggest using as many contractions as you can.

Some writers prefer to only use contractions in dialogue, and that's okay too. Do keep in mind, though, that most people use contractions when speaking. There are always rare exceptions. In my book *By Darkness Hid,* Vrell is a noblewoman, so to set her dialogue apart, I tried not to allow her to use contractions. It made her sound a little prissy, which was what I wanted.

Tricky words

There are certain words that almost every author occasionally mistypes. It's not that the author doesn't know which word is which or can't spell, it's just that sometimes you get typing so fast, mistakes are made. Some mistakes are harder to find than others.

I like to use the Find function in Word to go back and search for some of those tricky words. It's tedious, but it makes me feel better every time I catch mistakes. And I always do. Two I mistype often are: though/through/thought and lose/loose.

> **A Note from Stephanie**
>
> My biggest are think/thing and image/imagine. Also, several times I've caught myself accidentally using the phrase, "I put my hand over my heart," as, "I put my heart over my hand."

Quirks and Habits

Every author forms habits that can become monotonous to the reader. I tend to add way too many metaphors and similes. I do a "Find" search for the word "like," but it's more difficult to find all my metaphors. Another habit of mine is to use triplet sentences like: He walked down the hall, got a drink from the fountain, and went outside. Triplet sentences are something I have to watch for, and my editor helps me, since he knows this is a sentence structure I overuse.

Work on making a list of your own quirks and habits, then keep an eye out for them as you edit.

Weasel Words

Weasel words are those pesky words that sneak into your sentences like "just" or "very." When I'm working on my final draft, I have a list of words that I do a Find search for. Again, it's tedious. But it really makes a difference in my manuscript. In the back of this book, you'll find a detailed list of our weasel words.

Action Out of Order

Fiction should be shown in order, action first, then reaction. If the reader is going to connect with your characters and plot, the reader needs to experience everything the character does in a logical way. When important actions are left out or seem to happen backwards, it disconnects the reader.

> Poor: Ryan ducked to let Mike's punch go over his head.
> Better: Mike swung a punch. Ryan ducked.

> Poor: The world was foggy as I opened my eyes.
> Better: I opened my eyes to a foggy sky.

Teleporting

A mistake often made by new writers is the character that seems to teleport from one location to another. Like when someone is on the couch, then he's suddenly in the kitchen without having walked from one room to the other.

> Rachel was reading her math book at her desk in Mr. Lawler's classroom when the bell rang. She opened her locker and put her book away.

But we've missed the action of her moving from the classroom to her locker, right? Fixed, it might look like this:

> Rachel was reading her math book at her desk in Mr. Lawler's classroom when the bell rang. She walked to her locker and put her book away.

Continuous Action Words

Trying to write things that happen simultaneously doesn't work. Watch out for the words as, when, while, after, and continued to. I know it's tempting to use these words—especially in a fight scene—but most of the time they can be omitted. If you do use them, be careful to put things in logical order: action first, then reaction.

> Poor: The car stopped as Katie ran into the street.
> Better: Katie ran into the street, and the car skidded to a stop.
>
> Poor: Maggie cried when she dropped her pacifier.
> Better: Maggie dropped her pacifier and cried.
>
> Poor: Ben wrote in his journal while eating a donut.
> Better: Ben wrote in his journal and munched on a donut.

Infinite Verb Phrases (Starting sentences with —ing words)

Avoid starting a sentence with a word that ends in "ing" because such words imply everything in the sentence is happening simultaneously, often creating physical impossibilities. These are called infinite verb phrases but are also known as a continuing action word.

> Poor: Grabbing a notebook, he stuffed it in his backpack, slammed his locker, and ran to class.
>
> Better: He grabbed a notebook, stuffed it in his backpack, slammed the locker, and ran to class.

Since he can't physically grab a notebook, stuff it into his backpack, slam the locker door, and run to class simultaneously, the first example is humanly impossible.

Progressive Tense

Progressive tense uses an active verb with an -ing ending and a helping verb. Most of the time, it's shorter and more accurate to use the simple past tense of the verb. If you want to convey that something is in the process of happening, use progressive tense. Otherwise, edit it out.

> Past Progressive tense: Jane was walking to practice.
> Past tense: Jane walked to practice.

Past Perfect Tense

Okay, this is going to get deep here . . . If you're writing in past tense, that means past tense is actually your present, so anything that you talk about in the past, needs to be written in past perfect tense.

You're like, "What?"

I know. Grammar. Boring, right? I also know it's a bit of a trend to ignore past perfect tense (Or maybe people just don't care anymore, or they think it doesn't matter. I don't really know). If you want to write correctly, be sure and keep an eye out for this one.

> Incorrect when writing in past tense: I picked up my report card and looked it over. Woah! **I was always smart**, but these grades made me look worthy of MIT.
>
> Correct past perfect tense: I picked up my report card and looked it over. Woah! **I always had been smart**, but these grades made me look worthy of MIT.

Or consider this next example. Pretend you just read a scene in which the character Joey almost got hit by a car because he wasn't paying attention.

> Incorrect when writing in past tense: Joey waved and bounded away. Strange. **The boy survived** another brush with death and didn't seem at all fazed.

Since past tense is our present tense, to say "the boy survived" would mean that just that moment he survived. You need the "had" to create the correct past perfect tense.

> Correct past perfect tense: Joey waved and bounded away. Strange. **The boy had survived** another brush with death and didn't seem at all fazed.

A Note from Stephanie

I've read this about ten times, and I *think* I understand. God bless my editors. If you struggle with grammar, try not to panic. I'm living proof that you can still make it as a professional writer.

Double Verbs

Watch out for sentences using "started to" and "began to." These double verbs imply that an interruption is going to happen. The character began or started an action, but something stopped him. Now if you are implying that something did interrupt the action, using these words is exactly what you want to do. If not, get rid of them.

> Kaylee began to tug on the handle of her purse. **(This means she began to tug on her purse handle but never quite managed to complete the tug.)**
>
> Kaylee tugged on the handle of her purse. **(Here she actually succeeds at tugging on the handle.)**
>
> Mike started to clean his room. **(This implies that he is not going to finish.)**
>
> Mike started to clean his room, but his cell phone rang. **(This is better because it gives the reader the interruption to match the use of "started to.")**
>
> Mike cleaned his room. **(This tells us that he succeeded.)**

Make it Yours:
Read the Self-Editing Checklists and the list of weasel words in the Extras section of this book, then go through your manuscript and see what you can cut out.

Passive vs. Active Writing
by Stephanie

Passive writing is an issue for a lot of new writers, and often they don't even realize it. I had no idea I struggled with it until a literary agent told me she liked my story, but that my sentence structure was way too passive. "If you can fix that, I'll take another look," she said.

"Sure!" I told her. "I'll revise and get it right back to you!"

And then I set about trying to figure out what in the heck she was talking about. *Passive writing?!?!*

I sat at my desk with *Garner's Modern American Usage*, *The Elements of Style*, and *The Chicago Manual of Style*. In each one, I looked up what they had to say about using an "active voice." And then I reread the article. And then I reread again. Then I studied my manuscript. Then I turned back to the books and read the articles out loud.

After doing all that, I thought I maybe-kinda-sorta knew what the style guides were talking about and thought I could possibly fix it.

The first thing I had to figure out was what it meant to write in a passive voice. The word "was" can be a good clue that you're speaking in a passive voice, or "is" if you're writing in present tense. These are some examples ripped straight out of an old manuscript of mine. I've bolded the passive phrases:

> **It was finally Kyle who** led her out of there.
> **Carter was there** before she could do or say anything.
> **It was Carter's** best friend Matt who asked the question.

These can easily be revised to an active voice. (And—bonus tip—the word "it" is often a bad way to start a sentence because it's very vague.) Here are those same sentences revised to an active voice:

> **Kyle led** her out of there.
> **Carter arrived** before she could do or say anything.
> **Matt, Carter's best friend**, asked the question.

To quote the wisdom of William Strunk Jr., author of *The Elements of Style*, "The active voice is usually more direct and vigorous than the passive." Which I think is displayed in the sentences above. The ones written in an active voice are just better sentences.

But was (or "is") is not an evil word. Here are some examples of when was is necessary:

> When I entered, Jane was stirring the soup.

> James was a handsome boy.

> The room was decorated in mauve and blue.

I was scrubbing the floors when the phone rang.

All fine uses. Because if you changed that first one to something like, "When I entered, Jane stirred the soup," it would take on a different meaning. It would sound like Jane saw you enter, and then she stirred the soup.

> **Make it Yours:**
> Search your manuscript for the word "was" (or "is" if you're writing in the present tense). Consider your usage. Is it necessary, or could you write your sentence in a more active way?

> It's not wise to violate rules until you know how to observe them.
> –T. S. Eliot

16 Formatting It Right

Technicalities
by Jill

Formatting your manuscript correctly for the first time can be seriously intimidating. Here are some quick bullet points to get you started:

- Your title page should be single spaced. The rest of the manuscript should be double spaced with no extra spacing before or after paragraphs.
- Use 12-point Times New Roman or Courier font. No exceptions. Don't use a fancy font. It will mark you as an amateur.
- Each chapter should begin on a new page. Don't hit "Enter, Enter, Enter" to get your cursor to a new page. You must insert a Page Break at the end of each chapter, then begin typing a new one.
- Start each chapter ¼ to ½ of the way down the page. I like to turn on the Paragraph Mark (¶) and count the lines to make sure I start every chapter in the same place.
- Use only one space between sentences, not two. Using two spaces after a sentence is mandatory for screenwriting, but it's no longer correct in writing books.

•Avoid all fancy formatting, like drop cap letters to the start of each chapter, flowery scene breaks, or any other decorative graphics.

•Don't put a copyright symbol on your manuscript (See the Q&A section for the reason why).

On the next few pages you'll find examples for what the first few pages of your manuscript should look like. I've created several video tutorials to walk you through how to format everything using Microsoft Word. To find them, visit: www.jillwilliamson.com/helps

```
Your Name                                          Genre
Street Address                                Word count
City, State, Zip Code
Phone number
email address




                          TITLE

                           by

                       Your Name
```

> 1" margins on all four sides

> Use 12-point, Times New Roman or Courier font on all manuscripts.

> Center chapter title 1/4 to 1/2 of the way down the page. Make sure that all other chapters start in the same place.

> Set indentations to .05 and double-space your text.

Chapter One

Martyr stared at the equation on the whiteboard and set his pencil down. He didn't feel like practicing math today. What did math matter when his expiration date was so near?

His wrist still throbbed from Fido's teeth. Martyr touched the strip of fabric he'd ripped from his bedsheet and tied around his wrist to stop the bleeding. He hoped the wound would heal before a doctor noticed it. A trip upstairs to mend it would be unpleasant, as the doctor would likely use the opportunity to perform tests. Martyr shuddered.

To distract himself, he glanced at the other boys. Every Jason in the classroom except Speedy and Hummer scribbled down the numbers from the whiteboard. Speedy sketched Dr. Max's profile, staring at the doctor with intense concentration. His hand

> 1" margins on all four sides
>
> *REPLICATION* / Williamson / 2
>
> darted over the paper, shading the dark face with a short, black beard.
>
> Hummer—as always—hummed and rocked back and forth, hugging himself.
>
> Martyr never understood why the doctors made Hummer take classes instead of putting
>
> him in with the brokens. Perhaps it had to do with Hummer's being so much older than

(Callout: Type your title / last name / page number in the header. The page number doesn't have to go in the header. You can center it on the bottom of each page or tab it over to the far right.)

"Correctly" Using Italics
by Stephanie

There are no hard rules about "Don't italicize your character's thoughts" but it's rather frowned upon. Kind of like overusing exclamation points or adverbs, too many italicized thoughts can give your manuscript an amateur aura, which of course you want to avoid.

You especially want to avoid italicized thoughts in a book written in first person since you're already so clearly in the character's head. Here's an example:

> I walked through the door into eerie silence. *Why is it so quiet in here?* "Mom?"

Revising it with no italics makes it so much smoother and deeper:

> I walked through the door into eerie silence. Why was it so quiet? "Mom?"

For those writing in third person, I better understand the writer's temptation to italicize:

> John walked through the door into eerie silence. *Why is it so quiet in here?* "Mom?"

Step 1: Make Your Good Book GREAT

The writer wants us to know what John is thinking, wants to dip into John's head so we can see the thought scrolling through his mind. We, the reader, want that too . . . but are the italics necessary? Consider this:

> John walked through the door into eerie silence. Why was it so quiet? "Mom?"

You still get that it's a thought, don't you? Again, it's because the writer has already established who we're following—John. Therefore we understand, without help from the font, that John is the one wondering why it's so quiet.

But what if you write your stories in an omniscient POV? I won't pretend to be an expert on using omniscient POV, but I still think you should avoid italicized thoughts. Because even with an omniscient narrator where we, the reader, might pop into several different minds in one scene, the writer still needs to have established which character we're talking about in that moment.

Like Cecily von Ziegesar does here in *You Know You Love Me* (a Gossip Girl book):

> Blair nodded impatiently. What did Ms. Glos think she was, a moron?

Even though that book is written with an omniscient narrator, the writer signals, "Hey, it's Blair's turn on the stage" by starting the sentence with her name.

So when *should* you italicize sentences?

Sometimes dream sequences work better in italics. Especially if it's a book that has several short ones throughout. (*Out with the In Crowd* does and my editor suggested putting the dreams in italics. It worked well for that situation.)

Prayers, especially "breath prayers" like *Thank you, Lord* or *Little help here, God?* are another good use of italics.

Also, you might run across the occasional thought that just plain works better in italics. I've had that in a few manuscripts and the only common thread I can pick out is that they're extremely vulnerable, involuntary character thoughts. I actually spotted one in *You Know*

You Love Me, again by Cecily Von Ziegesar.

> Dan nodded. *Do you have to go?* He was afraid to open his mouth . . .

That works and falls into that category I mentioned above. He desperately wants Serena to stay there with him, and that's his gut reaction when she says she's heading home.

So don't automatically unitalicize every thought in your manuscript, just determine why you chose to format it that way.

Punctuation
by Jill

Punctuation had never been my favorite thing. But I needed to learn the rules to be a professional author. And so do you.

Trust me.

One mistake here or there won't get you rejected, but if your manuscript is filled with punctuation errors and misspellings, an agent or editor won't keep reading. They will reject you.

We don't want to turn this book into an English punctuation textbook, so we've decided to include the top punctuation errors we see again and again in manuscripts.

I highly recommend picking up a punctuation book for your own reference. There are many style guides out there. In the publishing industry, the go-to style guide for fiction is *The Chicago Manual of Style*. It's a massive book that includes every rule there is. Add a used copy to your wish list. It's a great tool to have on your shelf. If you find that too overwhelming, grab Strunk and White's *The Elements of Style* or take a look at my book *Punctuation 101: A Fiction Writer's Guide to Getting it Right,* which I wrote after doing a series on the Go Teen Writers blog on the same topic. My book is different from others because it only covers information that fiction writers need to know.

Punctuating Dialogue

Stephanie talks about this in Chapter 11, but I'll briefly cover the rules here as well.

Said Tags

A said tag assigns the dialogue to a speaker by using the word "said" or a variation of that word (asked, yelled, whispered, etc). A said tag is connected to the dialogue with a comma, unless the dialogue is a question or requires an exclamation point. When using a said tag, the pronoun must be lowercase unless you are using a proper name. Pay attention to the underlined parts of the examples below for proper punctuation.

"I'm sorry," the girl said.

"I am the President of the United States," Abraham said.

"What do you want?" she asked.

"What do you want?" Kate asked.

"Leave me alone!" he screamed.

"Leave me alone!" Mike screamed.

"I can't believe I'm telling you this," Mindy said, "but I'm one of them." (Since the said tag interrupted the dialogue, a comma was used on both sides of the said tag. If you do this, make sure the interruption falls in a natural place for your character to pause. Read the dialogue out loud to see what sounds best.)

"I can't believe I'm telling you this," Mindy said. "I'm one of them." (Here the said tag came between two complete sentences.)

Mindy took a deep breath and said, "I can't believe I'm telling you this, but I'm one of them." (The "Mindy took a deep breath" part of the example is what's called an action tag. But if you combine action with a said tag, like I did in this example, you need to punctuate the sentence like you would for a said tag.)

> **A Note from Jill about Exclamation Points**
>
> Editors and agents like to say that an author is allowed only one exclamation point per manuscript. It's a joke, but there's a grain of truth to it. Their point? Use exclamation points rarely. They're distracting to readers and should only be used when your character is screaming. Let your dialogue show other forms of anger or attitude. And save the exclamation points for special occasions.

Action Tags

An action tag is a complete sentence that identifies the speaker by what he's doing. Because we see a character's action in the same paragraph as dialogue, we know he's the speaker. Since action tags are sentences, they're punctuated like sentences.

Krista rolled her eyes and sighed**. "W**hat do you want, Paul?"

"Get out**!" B**eth slammed the door in her mother's face.

"If you want to come, get in**." K**yle opened the car door**. "J**ust don't be mad at me if you get in trouble for missing curfew."

"If you want to come, get in**," K**yle opened the car door**, "b**ut don't be mad at me if you get in trouble for missing curfew." (This example used an action tag to interrupt the sentence.)

In special cases when an action interrupts dialogue in a quick way, you can use em dashes to set this off. Since the break belongs to the sentence, rather than the dialogue inside, the em dashes must appear outside the quotation marks.

"Before we start**"—t**he knight plunged one of the blades into the grassy soi**l—"**we need to go over the basics."

Commas with Coordinating Conjunctions

There are seven coordinating conjunctions: and, but, for, nor, or, so, and yet. Basically, these are words that connect two clauses in a sentence. If you have a sentence that has one of those seven words in the middle, how do you know when you need a comma before the conjunction or not?

Simple. If the words on both sides of the conjunction are complete sentences by themselves, you need the comma to avoid having a run-on sentence.

> "Almost everyone on earth likes chocolate, but I can't stand how sweet it tastes."

You need the comma before "but" because "Almost everyone on earth likes chocolate" is a complete sentence and so is "I can't stand how sweet it tastes."

If the sentence had one side that wasn't a complete sentence on its own, a comma would be incorrect. "Almost everyone on earth likes chocolate but not carrots." Since "not carrots" is not a complete sentence, a comma is not needed.

Note that for a very short sentence, you can omit the comma.

> The bus departed and we were on our way.

Commas After an Introductory Word Group

When you start a sentence with an introductory word group, you need to separate it from the rest of the sentence with a comma. A good rule of thumb is if the introductory word group is five words or more, use a comma. Less than five words, it's optional. This practice can also be omitted in a very short sentence.

> When Martin was ready to eat, the waiter brought him a salad to start with.

> In no time we were in a different state.

Commas Between Items in a Series

When three or more items are listed in a series, those items should be separated with commas. This applies to single words, phrases, or clauses. Note that a comma goes before the conjunction at the end of the sentence.

> My favorite candy is M&M's, Skittles, and Gummi Bears.

> You can choose from going on a hike up the mountain, playing paintball in the field, going on a canoe ride, or swimming in the pool.

Commas Between Coordinating Adjectives vs. No Commas Between Cumulative Adjectives

Adjectives are coordinate if they can be joined with "and" or if they can be scrambled and still make sense. Commas are required between coordinate adjectives.

> Michael is a strong, tall, talented basketball player.

To test this example we first see if we can join the adjectives with "and" and keep the same meaning.

> Michael is a strong and tall and talented basketball player.

Next we scramble the adjectives to see if this has an effect.

> Michael is a talented, strong, tall basketball player.

Same meaning? Yep!

Cumulative adjectives lean on one another, with each modifying a larger word group. They do not require commas in between. How do you know that they're cumulative, though?

> Four gleaming white doves flew toward me.

"Gleaming" modifies "white." "Four" modifies "gleaming white." And when we test this sample by joining the adjectives with "and" it doesn't work.

> Four and gleaming and white and doves flew toward me.

When we scramble them, it also changes the meaning.

Gleaming four white doves flew toward me.

This doesn't work nor does, "White gleaming four doves flew toward me." So we know we had it right the first time.

The Colon

A colon means *as follows*. It's used to introduce something (or a series of things).

1. Use a colon after a complete sentence to direct attention to a list.

> Marcia's daily workout was supposed to include at least the following: twenty sit-ups, ten push-ups, and fifteen minutes of cardio.
>
> Give us the following construction materials: wood, hammers, and nails.
>
> This summer our family plans to visit four western states: Arizona, Utah, Colorado, and New Mexico.

2. Use a colon after a complete sentence to direct attention to an appositive: A word or phrase that means the same thing.

> Shelby was shocked at what she saw: her reflection.
>
> We found the cat sleeping in her favorite spot: the tree in the backyard.
>
> There's one obstacle I must conquer before graduation: passing all my classes.

3. Use a colon after a complete sentence to direct attention to a quotation.

> Consider the words of Mother Theresa: "Even the rich are hungry for love, for being cared for, for being wanted, for having someone

to call their own."

Capitalization and the Colon

How do you know whether or not to capitalize the first word following a colon? Always have the word be lowercase except in the following circumstances:

1. If the first word is a proper noun.

The people who should be on the bus are the following: M̲ark, Christa, Drew, and Kelley.

2. If the colon precedes a definition or a direct quote.

When Christy got angry at Karen, Jill told her not to "Jake Out": A̲n act of turning into a werewolf, inspired by the book *Twilight*.

The poignant words of Douglas Adams state: "F̲lying is learning how to throw yourself at the ground and miss."

3. If the colon comes before two or more related sentences.

Robert had three options: H̲e could walk the six miles to the library. He could call someone and beg a ride. Or he could just take Grandma Nan's car.

4. If the colon introduces dialogue lines in a speech or drama.

Juliette: T̲hen, window, let day in, and let life out.
Romeo: F̲arewell, farewell! One kiss and I'll descend.

The Semicolon

1. A semicolon is used to separate closely related independent clauses not joined by a coordinating conjunction.
Say what?
Basically, use a semicolon if you want to glue two similar sentences together.

Martin Luther King Jr. said "Hate begets hate; violence begets violence; toughness begets a greater toughness."

Ten finalists performed to be the next American Idol; only two remain.

Mr. Sanchez is a great chef; however, he won't eat his own cooking.

Each of the independent clauses (sets of words between the semicolons) are complete sentences on their own. You can't use a semicolon if these are only phrases. You also can't use a semi colon if you have a coordinating conjunction (and, but, or) between the sentences.

If you were to put a comma where a semicolon is above, you would have created a comma splice, which is a very icky grammar error. Be sure to look carefully at all your clauses. If they are complete sentences, you need a semicolon. If they aren't, you don't need a semicolon.

2. A semicolon is also used between items in a series that contain internal punctuation.

> Some popular fantasy novels are *Harry Potter and the Sorcerer's Stone*, with the boy wizard with a lightning bolt scar; *Eragon*, about a young dragon rider; and the timeless *The Lion, the Witch, and the Wardrobe*, where four siblings enter a magical land through a wardrobe.

Dashes

There are two kinds of dashes that are used most often in fiction writing: the em dash—and the en dash–

Please note that there should be **no space** before or after either type of dash.

The Em Dash

To create the em dash, type a word, then type two hyphens, then type the next word, then type a space. Do not put any spaces until you are done with the sequence.

What you type will look like this: word--word(space)

When you hit that last space bar, the two dashes will convert to an em dash.

If you read Harry Potter, you'll see spaces with the dashes. That's because J. K. Rowling is a British author and the punctuation and grammar rules are different in that country. These are the rules for the United States.

1. Use an em dash to set off parenthetical material that you want to emphasize.

> Everything that went wrong—from her C- on our history project to Tom breaking up with her—Shelly blamed on me.
>
> Can you believe that Megan Walker—a band geek and a freshman—won homecoming queen?

2. Use an em dash to set off appositives that contain commas.

> When you apply the make-up—foundation, mascara, eye shadow, and lipstick—be sure to follow the guidelines.

3. Use an em dash to signify a break in thought.

> "I have so much to—did you just say she had the baby?"

4. Use an em dash to signify an interruption.

> "I don't know why it happened. Maybe it's because—"

The En Dash

To create the en dash, type a word, type a space, then type one hyphen, then type the next word, then type a space. What you type will look like this: word(space)-word(space)

When you hit that last space bar, the dash will convert to an en dash. Once the dash is converted, go back and take out the first space. There should be no spaces before or after a dash.

1. Use an en dash to connect inclusive numbers like page

numbers, dates, or Bible references. In this case the en dash means "up to and including" or "through."

Please read in your text pages 86—92.

I went to college from 1993—1997.

I read John 3:16—17 and it changed my life.

Ellipses

Ellipses are used to show thought trailing off. If your character is confused, insecure, uncertain, falling asleep, or passing out, an ellipsis is the tool to convey this. Put a space before and after an ellipsis, unless it comes beside another punctuation mark.

"Where could it . . . I had it right . . . the medallion, I . . . I must have dropped it!"

"I want to go there . . . first thing . . . in the morning."

". . . tell you who shot me. It was . . ." Kit's body went limp in John's arms.

Apostrophes

Use an apostrophe to replace omitted letters in a word. If your font uses curly quotes, make sure that the apostrophe curls in the right direction. Whether the missing letter is in the front, middle, or end of a word, an apostrophe should always curl to the left, like this: '

Take note that omitting letters can be distracting to the reader, so don't overdo it.

"There be no tellin' what he'll do now." (The apostrophe takes the place of the "g" in "telling.")

"All you kids do is sit around listening to that loud rock 'n' roll." (The apostrophe before the "n" takes the place of the "a" in "and." The apostrophe after the "n" takes the place of the "d" in "and.")

"Daddy, tell me the story 'bout the princess and the toad." (The apostrophe takes the place of the "a" in "about.")

Numbers

Numbers can be written two ways: spelled out in letters (two) or written in numerals (2). The rules are: Spell out numbers one through one hundred. Spell out rounded numbers (hundreds, millions). Spell out numbers in reference to age. Spell out all numbers that begin a sentence. Use numerals (1234) for all other numbers.

Michael crouched down. "There are millions of ants here!"

"I need fifty copies of the flyer," Megan said.

"I need 2,500 copies of the flyer," Megan said.

"She's ninety-six years old!"

"One, I can't understand why you hate me. And, two, I don't like you either."

Time

Always spell out the time of day unless you're referring to the exact time.

Drew went to bed at five o'clock exhausted from the tournament.

"Mom slept in, and I missed my nine-thirty dentist appointment."

"I get to church way early because the Sunday bus goes by my house at 7:10."

"Class starts directly at 8:35 tomorrow morning. Don't be late!"

Dates

Dates are written with numerals. Do not write August 1st. The correct methods are:

School starts August 1.

"The photograph is copyright April 1942."

"On January 1, 2000, there were no major fallouts due to the new millennium."

When a day is mentioned without the month or year, spell out the number.

"By the fifteenth, finals will be over and we can focus on the Christmas holidays!"

> Whatever it takes to finish things, finish. You will learn more from a glorious failure than you ever will from something you never finished.
> —Neil Gaiman

17 How to Know When You're Done

by Stephanie

"How do I know when I'm done editing my book?"

This is a question we get a lot, and it's so hard to know how to answer. Because when it's early in your writing journey and you're growing rapidly in your craft, it can feel impossible to discern when to stop fussing with your manuscript. So how do you know when it's time to take the plunge and share your book with your critique partner or start querying literary agents?

I'm going to start with a question that totally marks me as a mom: Have you done your best?

Your book isn't perfect, of course, but did you do your best with the knowledge and skills you have? Or were you lazy with character development? Is that plot twist at the end more of a cheap trick? Did you have an idea for how to improve it . . . but you weren't in the mood for yet another rewrite?

If you've written and rewritten and revised and edited and rewritten and revised again, and you feel this is the best story you can produce at this point in your journey, I say go for it. Send out the queries. See what happens. This can be a painful way to learn you're not ready, but sometimes that's the only way you'll really know.

I sent out my manuscripts for years not knowing if I was ready, and I honestly didn't know if my writing was "there" or not until an agent said, "I'm so excited about this project. Can you send me the rest right now?"

And I didn't dare say it out loud, but when she said that, my internal monologue was, "Really? I did it? It's good enough now?"

This is a rather uncomfortable way to determine the quality of your writing abilities, but it's about the truest mirror you'll find. Not to say that agents and editors don't make judgments in error or guess wrongly about what will sell and what the public wants. Most everyone has received at least a handful of rejections. But for my rejections, typically I knew in my gut if they were right or not.

Like on the first book I sent out. Hardly any editors bothered to read it (no surprise, since I printed out all 90 pages of it on purple paper and mailed it to anyone who accepted unsolicited manuscripts), but the one who did told me my ending lacked oomph. And you know, that resonated. As I considered it, I realized my book didn't have an ending at all.

By now, I have a definite procedure I follow before I declare myself done with a book.

Before I send anything to my agent or editor, I always:

1. Write a bare bones first draft
2. Let my draft sit for six weeks (unless we're on a major time crunch, but ideally I take a full six weeks).
3. Do the macro edit.
4. Do the micro edit.
5. Send the manuscript to my critique partner and wait for her thoughts.
6. Make her suggested changes and read through it again for typos.
7. Send it to my agent.

And to be honest, even as a published author, when weeks go by and I haven't heard back from my agent, I slide into a pit of thoughts like, "She hates it. She's wondering why she ever took me on as a client." Every time the phone rings, I'm thinking, "It's her. She's calling to say she hates it." Most my writer friends do something similar. We're a needy bunch.

While I've gained confidence in my ability to know if my story is a good idea or not, and while I'm mostly confident in my writing style and voice, I still tremble a bit before I send my stuff out, for whatever's that's worth to you. But at some point, you've got to go for it.

Make Your Good Book GREAT
Editing Issues That Don't Happen On the Page

A note from Jill

Writing is a solitary and emotional business. Working in isolation tends to create self-doubt, especially in an industry like publishing.

I started writing in 2004. It was August 2006 before I sold my first article. And, no, that one article didn't pay enough to support my family. I wrote some more articles, but since I wanted to be a fiction writer, I spent most my time writing books. My first book was published in 2009 with a small publisher that didn't pay advances. So it was another year before I saw any money for my efforts.

That's a long time to work without pay.

Now, I wasn't writing books to make money, in theory. I wanted to get published, sure, but it was fun and I wanted to create entertaining and inspiring stories for teen readers.

That's still my goal today. But I struggle with wondering if I'm making a difference, if anyone is reading my books, whether or not I have anything of value to say. I get hurt when reviewers are cruel or when a reviewer doesn't even try to see my heart in a story. I struggle with procrastination when I have deadlines. And I am always trying to find a balance between work and family.

It's a lonely business. I'm on my own at home, typing stories, trying to decide if they're interesting or not, always on the lookout for new test readers to give me honest feedback. There were people who never thought I'd succeed, people who thought I was crazy, people who still don't know I write books, and people who think I'm famous (I'm *so* not!) and who assume I'm making a ton of money (I'm *really* not!).

It's a strange job, writing. You have to really love it to put up with all this weird stuff.

Good thing I love it, huh?

> Don't let anyone look down on you because you are young.
> −1 Timothy 4:12

18 Self-Doubt & Others' Expectations

by Stephanie

Once upon a time, I knew my writing was hot stuff.

It was well-known among my friends that I wanted to be a writer. Anytime I wrote so much as a chapter, I immediately passed it out to a few friends and asked for their feedback . . . but what I really meant was, "Tell me how wonderful this is, please."

I craved their approval.

And when they thought it was amazing, my day was awesome.

When they suggested a character seemed flat or a plot line seemed implausible, I argued. Sometimes out loud, but mostly in my head. They didn't understand it, did they? They didn't get it! What do they know, anyhow?!

This is a horrible rollercoaster ride to be on, and I wasn't smart enough to take myself off.

Instead, I got bucked off the ride.

When my best friend told me my stories were boring and unimaginative, that I was wasting my time and she couldn't imagine me ever getting published, something inside me broke. On the outside I was snarky and vicious, but on the inside I was curled up in the fetal position, broken and—I thought—permanently scarred.

It took me years to come back from that, to recover both from the blow from my friend and also my dependence on the opinions of others. Here's what helped me to break free (somewhat) of my need for others' approval:

I write my first drafts behind closed doors.

This isn't for everybody, but this made a huge difference for me, and I encourage you to give it a try at least once. Nobody sees my first drafts. Ever. I don't even like sitting next to my loving, supportive husband on the couch when I'm working on a first draft.

Until I've done my macro and micro edits, I don't let anyone read the book. Otherwise I get too many voices going on in my head and I lose track of getting the story on the page. I start focusing on the wrong things—if it's good feedback, I get preoccupied with how amazing my story is. If it's bad feedback, I get preoccupied with how much it sucks.

There's certainly a time when feedback and collaboration is fruitful and necessary . . . but for me it's *not* during the first draft. That time is for me and my characters only.

One plus I hadn't expected when I first started closing my door was how it honed my voice as an author. I wasn't thinking things like, "Oh, Christine is going to gush when she reads this scene!" Or, "I should put in a steamy kiss because Lauren likes those." Instead my focus was on telling the story as it came to me, not on pleasing my friends.

Establishing Expectations and Trust

My first readers are people who I know love me, who have my best interests at heart, and who I know like my stories and writing. In short, I trust they will speak truth to me out of love, and I trust that they won't try to take over my story and make it theirs, but that they'll instead try to strengthen it in a way that fits with my voice and my genre.

Something that helped me open up to others again was clarifying my expectations. I would say something like, "I'm interested in how such-and-such plot thread feels to you, and if you have any ideas for making this character more unique." Not only does this help me get the feedback that I really want, it's helpful to me to release the notion that I think this is perfect. Somehow telling them, "I know this isn't perfect, I just don't know how to improve it," softens the blow for me when I get the critique back.

I also do this whenever I'm critiquing for someone. Does she want general guidance? A line edit? Are there story threads I should be paying careful attention to? This saves everyone time.

Baby steps, baby rejections

Eventually, if you want to get published, you have to start submitting your stuff to agents and editors. This can be incredibly scary. I found it best to query a few agents at a time so that if I received feedback I wanted to incorporate, I would have a stronger piece to show other agents.

Sometimes you get sharp, well-defined criticism—I don't like your main character, your plot feels cliché.

Sometimes it's too vague to know what to do with it—this doesn't work for me.

And sometimes it's just a form letter.

Every editor and agent has different preferences, and just because one of them thinks your plot is boring doesn't mean they all will. If it's something you *keep* hearing, you'll want to weigh it differently than if it's something you only hear once.

Dealing with others' lack of understanding

The process of getting published is mysterious to the average person, which means many people won't understand what you're doing. And, honestly, you just have to figure out a way to be okay with that.

People will think the process should be moving along faster—you should have been done with that book months ago, or if you were really good you would have an agent by now, and what's your backup plan for when this writing thing doesn't pan out?

You'll get bad advice from people who may truly want to help you but have no knowledge of the industry. Some of the advice I received along the way was:

1. Just go to Kinkos, get your book printed and bound, and sell it like that.
2. Print out that great bit of dialogue you wrote and send it to several agents saying, "This is what I'm capable of. Can you help me get published?"
3. Write wizard stuff. That seems to be selling.
4. Get an English degree so you can get a job at a publishing house. You can make connections and work your way "up" to writing a novel.

This is just part of the writing life, people not understanding the industry or your genre or how you make money. You can let it make you crazy, or you can smile, nod, say thank you for their interest in your career, and move on with your day.

And that's one of the reasons I urge you to find a community of writers to support and be supported by. I'm fortunate that my family is incredibly supportive of my writing, but nobody understands the sting of a rejection, the frustration of a lousy writing day, or the triumph of typing THE END quite like my writer friends.

> You may delay,
> but time will not.
> –Benjamin Franklin

19 Wrestling with Procrastination

by Jill

Before I was published, procrastination wasn't such a big deal. I really didn't have any deadlines. And even when I set my own deadlines, they were for me alone, to try and achieve certain word counts.

Those are good deadlines.

But once I was published, deadlines became a lot more solid and necessary. My editors set the deadlines, and I didn't dare miss one.

My first deadline wasn't much of a big deal. I had written and edited *By Darkness Hid* until I thought it was perfect before I sold it to Marcher Lord Press. Once I signed the contract, I turned in the manuscript and waited for my edits. I started tinkering around with book two, but I figured I had time.

Then came a content edit. My editor had made a list of problems he saw with the story and asked me to rewrite those things. I was pretty excited about his edits. They were things that made me say, "Duh, Jill. How could you have missed that?"

So I completed the edits and sent them back. A short while later I received the line edit. This was a much more severe edit, and my editor wanted it back ASAP! That surprised me. I really thought I had written a clean book. But I was about to find out that most editors have a lot of feedback to give.

Panic set in, and I worked hard to get the edits done. There were a few more stages this time around. Little things. But I had done it! I was a published author.

Then my editor asked me how soon I could have book two ready. Uh... book two?

That was the beginning of a very stressful year. Up until that point, I wrote whatever book I wanted to write. I had no rules or deadlines. I did what pleased me. But now I had a deadline for a book that I hadn't written a word of yet. And worse, I now had readers to please. I had been getting great reviews on *By Darkness Hid*, and I didn't want to disappoint my fans!

It was a rough time of forcing myself to write, even when I didn't want to. And when book three came along, it was no different. Once I finished the trilogy, I had the privilege of selling a book off a proposal. This means I got paid for an idea, for a book I hadn't written yet. One that I would write. I thought that was pretty cool, until I got my deadline.

Yikes! That wasn't very far away!

And here we go again.

That's the reality of being a career writer. Deadlines come. Publishers are looking for authors who can work fast and deliver. I'm still not sure how successful I am in that regard, but I'm learning. I work hard, and the deadlines keep coming.

Even though it may not always feel like it, it's truly a blessing to have deadlines.

How to deal with Procrastination

Procrastination comes in a lot of forms and usually stems from not being prepared, fear of failure, or simple boredom with the project. No matter the reason, it all gets the same result: nothing is done and you are frustrated. Here are some things I've learned to do to beat procrastination.

Set Goals

You may or may not already have a deadline. If not, set one for yourself. Then do some math to figure out how many words you need to write each day to reach your deadline. Doing this gives you a concrete goal to strive for each time you sit down to write.

Get Organized

This is why I like plotting my story out in advance. Because it gives me a To Do list of scenes to follow so that I have a basic idea of what I should be writing each day. I also keep my notes and any reference books I'm using beside the computer so that I have everything I'll need at hand.

Skip Ahead

When I'm really stuck, or I've come up on a difficult scene that needs some serious brainstorming time, I often skip ahead to a scene that will be easier to write. This way I don't waste my computer time, and I get my word count in. I can brainstorm later in the car or when I'm cleaning the house to figure my way out of that difficult scene.

Give Up Perfectionism

Your first draft doesn't have to be good. You can come in and fix it later. And if you're working on a deadline, sometimes you have to force yourself to get that story done. Some writers get dreamy about their jobs and wait too long for inspiration to strike, but when you're on a deadline, you can't afford to wait. Buckle down and do the hard work. There will be time to edit later on.

Get Rid of Distractions

It's far too easy to get distracted when you work from home. I have a rule that I try to check my email in fifteen minutes at the start of each workday. Then I close it. Facebook too. If I don't, I'll "reward myself" with little visits throughout the day, and those visits are BIG trouble.

When I write, I also tend to make excuses to get up from the computer that involve an endless sampling of snacks and beverages. So it's best for me to get a few snacks and fill my water bottle before I start writing. And if I don't have something, I can live until lunch.

Interruptions come too. If I worked at an office across town, people wouldn't stop by or call me at work. But since I work from home, people tend to think, "Jill's home," then call or stop by. And five to ten minutes here and there adds up when I'm on a deadline.

So, if I'm working toward my daily word count and the phone or doorbell rings, I usually don't answer. This might sound cruel, but if it's that important, the person will leave a message or call back. If it's later in the day and I'm working on something less important, I might answer. And I'll certainly answer if I'm expecting someone. Otherwise, I can't allow myself to get interrupted.

I know writers who like to go sit at Starbucks or the library to get away from the distractions of home. If this helps you, do it. Whatever it takes to get the job done.

Make it Yours:

1. Keep a log of how much time you spend doing certain activities. How much time do you spend on email? Facebook? Snacking? Talking on the phone or texting? Writing?

2. Evaluate and try to set a more productive schedule for yourself.

Step 2
Learning the Ropes of the Publishing Industry

A note from Stephanie

I believe at the core of my being that if I can get published, *anyone* can.

When I started on my journey of becoming a novelist, all I had was a love for writing stories.

I lived in Kansas City—a great town, but hardly a publishing mecca.

I didn't know anybody even remotely connected to the industry, not even a bookstore employee.

And I didn't have a clue about what I was doing. I didn't know what genre I wrote, that my characters should have goals, what literary agents did, or what a query letter was.

Everything I learned, I learned by doing it wrong first. In this chapter, we hope to equip you with some etiquette and procedural basics to make your path to publication smoother than mine.

A note from Jill

There's a lot of advice out there for writers. And you can't follow it all. Believe me, I tried. Whether you're seeking traditional publication or planning to self-publish, this is a wonderful industry, and there are so many great opportunities out there for you to connect.

When I first started writing, I sought information from all kinds of sources. I gave and gave, and sometimes no one gave back. I learned the hard way what worked or what didn't work. I got involved, I tried my best, and over time I made many friendships. (*An aside from Stephanie: This is so true. When I'm with Jill at a conference, there are constantly people stopping to say hi to her.*)

Always keep in mind, you can't please everyone. You can't become critique partners with every writer. You'll find reviewers who don't want to read your book. *Publisher's Weekly* might hate your book. So, do your best. Learn. Have fun. And always try to make wise choices based on what you've learned.

> There are no secrets to success.
> It is the result of preparation, hard
> work, and learning from failure.
> - Colin Powell

20 Behave Like a Pro Before You Are

by Stephanie

Shakespeare once said, "All the world's a stage." And that's never been truer than it is now with all the ways to put yourself out there with social media and blogs and review sites. So when you're dipping your toe into the industry pool, put into practice these five guidelines of professionalism:

Guideline #1
**Whatever you put out there,
assume agents, editors, and readers will see it.**

When an agent, editor, or reader comes across a writer they're interested in, one of the first things many of them do is run a Google search on the author. Which is why I assume that anything I say online could be seen by my publisher, agency, or readers.

In reality, they're all busy people and may not see very much of it. (Though I've had my agent say things to me like, "I assume you're still at the wedding," when I never told her, she just saw pictures of me at a wedding on Facebook.) But it's so much safer to run everything through the filter of, "My agent/future editor/readers will see this."

Unlike real life where we can't edit words after they've emerged from our mouths (a sad truth for those of us who aren't particularly articulate), we can edit our written words to our heart's content. We have total control over what's on our social media sites.

I urge you to be a good steward with that freedom. When you get a rejection, it's a bad idea to blast the agency or house on your blog. Or if you write humor, you don't want all your tweets to be depressing. If you write romance, refrain from spending all your time talking about how boys are stupid and marriage is nothing more than a piece of paper.

You don't have to be someone you're not—in fact, I'd recommend against it—just keep in mind that if you're working to build a platform, don't treat your social media accounts like a message board to your personal friends.

Guideline #2
Use your name

If you're beginning the process of querying agents or joining writers organizations, now is a good time to shed any email addresses or social media handles like, OneDirectionRawks@email.com or yurboyfrndwantsme@email.com.

Now is the time to get your own adult email address, which should involve your name or initials in some capacity. One that you're not squeamish about giving out, because you want people to be able to contact you. Mine is Stephanie@StephanieMorrillBooks.com. On Instagram and Facebook, I'm StephanieMorrill and on Twitter I'm StephMorrill. You're building you and your brand, and you don't want your brand to involve the TV show you love or the band you obsess over.

Guideline #3
Like it or not—grammar matters

Ever since the ink dried on my signed contract, I've had people asking me if I would take a look at their manuscript. I almost always say no, but sometimes it's easier than others. Especially when I get an email that says things like:

> Ms. Morrel,
> i have attatched the first chapter of my book for you to look at. can you do it this week????? you might not undertstand some fo the plot stuff but its a fasinating story. write me back as apap. i really want to get published!!!!!

If someone doesn't know where all the commas go, that's one thing. But if she hasn't taken the time to spellcheck, or if she didn't bother with something basic like capitalization, my assumption is she hasn't taken the time to do so in her manuscript either.

Agents, editors, and professional writers are super busy people. If you want one to invest time in you, put your best foot forward.

Guideline #4
Don't act entitled

This is a tough line to walk, because you certainly don't want to put yourself out there as The Next Big Thing . . . but you also don't want to be like, "I've attached my manuscript, which isn't perfect and probably still needs a lot of work."

Let your story stand on its own merits. Describe who you are and what your story is about without injecting your opinion of it. (Or your grandma's glowing endorsement.)

Also, be respectful and understanding that the professional you're contacting has a full calendar and to-do list. Professional writers have their own writing to attend to, agents have clients to service and deals to make, and editors have authors and deadlines and manuscripts to edit and all kinds of stuff. This is why you always send a query letter or email asking if it's okay to send your stuff. (We'll get to querying in Chapter 25) This is also why you should always:

Guideline #5
Say Thank You

Who doesn't like being thanked for stuff? You don't have to get ridiculous with it, but a simple, "Thank you for your time and consideration," at the end of your email can make a big difference.

I also recommend a thank you for when you receive rejections. Again, a quick "Thank you for your time and consideration" is all that's needed. Not only is it a rare kindness, but it's a great way of releasing the rejection's hold on you.

> Honest criticism is hard to take, particularly from a relative, a friend, an acquaintance, or a stranger.
> –Franklin P. Jones

21 Critique Groups

by Jill

If you want to become a better writer, if you've written something and want an opinion on it, or if you feel your piece is ready for publication, it's a good idea to get some feedback before you submit to a publisher or self-publish your book. Don't seek input from only your best friends and family, either. At some point, you need to find a serious critique group.

How to Find a Critique Group

Libraries often know of local writers' groups where you can meet people and form a critique group. Also, professional organizations like Romance Writers of America or the Society of Children's Book Writers and Illustrators have local chapters that make it easier to find other writers.

When I lived in a very small town, I had no access to in-person groups, so I used online critique groups. These are good because you can read and post from home at your convenience. You can easily find hundreds of critique groups by doing a Google search. Simply type in your genre and the words "critique group" and you'll get lots of options. Try "science fiction critique group" and see what comes up. You can also find online critique groups through professional organizations.

Not every critique group is a good fit. You might join some only to quit shortly after. That's okay. It's important that you find the right group for you.

> ### A Note from Jill
> ### About Professional Organizations
>
> A great way to meet other writers is to join a professional organization for writers. There are hundreds, and you don't have to join them all. I'm a member of three: two national and one state. Here's a short list of national organizations that I recommend, but be sure and look for ones in your state as well, since that will help you find other writers that live near you.
>
> Academy of American Poets: www.poets.org
> American Christian Fiction Writers: www.acfw.com
> Association of Christian Writers in the UK:
>   www.christianwriters.org.uk
> American Crime Writers League: www.acwl.org
> Australian Society of Authors: www.asauthors.org
> British Crime Writers' Association: www.thecwa.co.uk
> Canadian Authors Association: www.canadianauthors.org
> Canadian Society of Children's Authors, Illustrators, and
>   Performers: www.canscaip.org
> Crime Writers of Canada: www.crimewriterscanada.com
> Fellowship of Australian Writers: www.writers.asn.au
> Historical Novel Society: historicalnovelsociety.org
> Horror Writers Association: www.horror.org
> Military Writers Society of America: www.mwsadispatches.com
> Mystery Writers of America: www.mysterywriters.org
> Oregon Christian Writers: oregonchristianwriters.org
> Poets & Writers: www.pw.org
> Poetry Society of America: www.poetrysociety.org
> Realm Makers: www.realmmakers.com
> Romance Writers of America: www.rwa.org
> Science Fiction & Fantasy Writers of America: www.sfwa.org
> Sisters in Crime: www.sistersincrime.org
> Society of Children's Writers and Illustrators: www.scbwi.org
> Western Writers of America: westernwriters.org

What to Expect

Whether you're in an in-person group or an online one, expect to share one chapter of your work at a time. An in-person group might pass the chapter from person to person so everyone gets a chance to read it. In an online group, you might post your chapter so that people can download it to edit.

If you don't ask for specific help, critique partners tend to point out anything and everything that they feel is a mistake or could use improvement. So it's always a good idea to decide what kind of help you want before you share your manuscript. This will solve a lot of problems before they start.

Beware of the critique partner who is a new writer but thinks she knows everything and is always right. This type of person is rarely helpful. Look for critique partners who are humble. They will be the best fit. And stay humble yourself!

You don't have to take every bit of advice you get, but it's good to know what people are thinking. This is part of the learning process.

Here are a few things you can do before submitting your work for critique.

1. Decide what you'd like your critique group to look for. Do you want a full line edit? Or do you simply want to know if the story holds the reader's interest?

2. Check for grammar and spelling errors. The spellcheck is great, but it doesn't catch mistakes like: its/it's or their/there/they're. Train your eye to catch these things before you ask others to look over your manuscript. Always be as professional as possible.

3. Make sure that your manuscript is formatted correctly. One-inch margins all around. Double spaced. Times New Roman 12-point font.

4. Prepare yourself for criticism. Your critique group doesn't want to hurt your feelings. They're trying to help you improve what you've written and want the same help from you. Be ready for that. When you're waiting for your feedback, you might want to psych yourself up a bit because taking criticism can be hard. Try to keep in mind that all writers are criticized. Even bestselling authors get negative reviews. It's part of being a writer. A critique group is a great place to practice

getting used to it.

Also remember that a critique group should be a safe place to learn. Expect negative feedback, and try to embrace it as an opportunity to make the story better before you send it to a publisher. If your critique group is hurtful and disrespectful, however, you should probably look for a new one. Try not to be overly sensitive, though. By its very nature, a critique looks for the negatives in your writing—weaknesses and mistakes that we all make. No author is perfect. So it's logical that a critique group will spend most of its time talking about what's wrong with your piece rather than what's right.

When you get your work back, read the comments over rather quickly. If you're frustrated or angry, close the file or put the paper away and wait a day or two. Come back to it when you've had time to think and relax. Then, let it go. Sometimes you just have to agree to disagree, but if you find that three or more people have given you the same advice, you'd be wise to listen.

Things that Make Good Critique Groups

1. Have a leader, someone to organize and keep things moving so that no one person gets all the attention
2. Without some guidelines, you'll have no structure, so set up some rules for the members to follow. These could be: attendance, give a critique before receiving one, balance negative feedback with positive feedback, members must write new material, etc.
3. Meet regularly. Writers need to get used to writing consistently and meeting deadlines. A critique group is a great place to start this training.

How to Critique a Manuscript

One of the best ways to become a better writer is to learn how to critique the work of others. It can feel strange at first, especially when you can't seem to find anything negative to say.

Start out by asking the author what kind of critique he's looking for. He may want all the help he can get. He may simply want your overall impression. Try to give him exactly what he's asking for. This will save you time and keep you from unnecessarily frustrating him.

Even if he asks for the works, still try not to point out every single negative thing you can. That kind of critique is rarely helpful because if you do all the hard work in pointing out every error, he will never learn to spot those errors himself. Point out things once, and suggest that he make the change throughout the manuscript.

Here are ten tips for providing a good critique.

1. Read the chapter through without marking anything. This way you get the heart of the story. As you read, ask yourself these questions: Does the beginning hook you? Is this story realistic? Are you bored? Are you confused? Do you like the characters? Is there a problem the main character is facing? Do you feel drawn into the story? Would you read more?

Write down these thoughts at the end of the chapter. Try to keep your comments positive and encouraging. Be sure to point out positives first, then negatives. You can be honest without being cruel. Instead of saying, "This is so boring!" say, "The first few pages could use some more action. The pace seems slow." Also, it's best to avoid using "you" in your statements. Saying "you" always sounds like a personal attack.

2. Go back and read the chapter again, this time stopping to make notes when thoughts come to you. Try to make positive and negative comments. Even if the story is horrible, you can always find something positive to say. The purpose of a critique group is to improve your writing through constructive criticism, but people have quit writing because of harsh critique partners. Unless the writer asked you to rip it to shreds, don't point out every little mistake. We all learn a little at a time, so overwhelming someone with nothing but red marks isn't necessary. Baby steps, you know?

3. Consider not using a red pen. Pick a friendlier color like blue or green. If you're using Track Changes, you can choose a color, but it never seems to show up the same on someone else's computer.

4. Mark misspellings, grammar errors, and punctuation mistakes, but only if you're certain you know the correct rule.

5. Word usage. Does the writer use too many passive verbs (be, is, are, was, were)? Advise him to use active verbs instead. Does he

always use vague or bland words (walked)? Suggest he use more specific words here and there (inched, jogged, sprinted, loped, strode). Note where the writer's words stood out, good or bad. If a metaphor confused you or impressed you, say so. Point out when you didn't understand the description or when it hooked you into the story. Mention when you really liked a phrase. Say, "Good job here!"

6. Dialogue. Does it sound realistic? Do character conversations move the plot forward? Does the author use too many said tags or action tags? Not enough? Is the punctuation correct?

7. Viewpoints. Can you understand the point of view? Are the transitions from one point of view to another smooth and clear?

8. Did the author use the proper manuscript format? Get into the habit of writing in the industry standard format at all times.

9. When you finish, edit and proofread your critique to make sure it's clear, kind, and doesn't contain typos.

10. Remember whose story it is. The author doesn't have to accept your advice. Also, be careful not to critique personal preferences. We are all different. We don't want to critique to the point that we strip the personality from each other's writing. Our unique way of saying things is part of our budding voice. Don't squash that out of each other.

I always try to end my critiques with a statement like this: "These are just my opinions. Take what you like and throw out the rest."

When you give your critique back to the author, let it go, and don't be offended if he chooses to ignore some or all of your suggestions. The point of a critique is to give your honest opinions and advice. What the writer does with that information is up to him.

Sometimes the Group is Wrong for You

One of the first critiques I received on my manuscript wasn't helpful and it caused me a lot of confusion. I later realized that the person reading my story didn't understand young adult fiction or read it. Her remarks were negative and hurtful. She shamed me for writing a teenage character who got into a fist fight and told lies.

Thankfully I only doubted myself for a week before I realized what was really happening.

She wasn't one of my target readers.

Finding a good critique group or even a single critique partner isn't easy. Look for someone with similar goals and needs as yours.

When I first looked for a critique group, I couldn't find a local one. So I went online and found a group that had every genre and every level of writer. I got some good critiques there, but I also found a lot more people who didn't understand my genre. I met another writer in that online group who also wrote for young adults. She and I vented to each other about feeling misunderstood. I remember emailing her a comment: "Someone should start an online critique group just for writers writing the young adult genre."

The next time I checked my email, she had sent me an invite to an online YA critique group. She and I were in that group for many years. It was a fabulous group. We all learned a lot from each other, and many of our members are now published.

Once I got published, though, my needs changed. Suddenly I had deadlines and needed critique partners who could read my entire book quickly rather than one chapter a week. So I found new people to trade manuscripts with, rather than a large group.

Critique partners matter, so don't skip this step. Work hard at finding at least one person who will ask the right questions and point out plot holes and inconsistencies in your characters because good critique partners can make all the difference in getting your manuscript ready for publication.

A Different View On Critique Groups
by Stephanie

Confession: I never did the critique group thing. In high school, I totally would have, but none of my friends were writers, and the internet communities were not what they are now. (Geez, I'm old!)

I didn't make any writer friends until I was twenty-two, when I went to a writing conference in Florida. I was the youngest person there by about a decade, and several faculty members stopped to tell me how cute it was that I had come to a conference with grown-ups.

Several good things came out of that conference, but the best was that I hit it off with Erica Vetsch, who had an agent but hadn't yet sold anything. She told me about American Christian Fiction Writers, how she was planning to enter one of their contests and was saving her pennies for the national conference.

Even though she wrote historical romance and I wrote contemporary YA, we started exchanging full manuscripts. We were both so new that I don't know how much we were truly helping improve each other's writing, but just being able to encourage each other was so valuable!

Several years later, I tried a critique group that worked like Jill talked about (exchanging one chapter a week). We imploded after the first few exchanges due to all of us being stressed and overwhelmed by that format.

Writer friends and groups come in all shapes and sizes, and the work required to find the right one is totally worth it!

> Publishing is a business. Writing may be art, but publishing, when all is said and done, comes down to dollars.
> –Nicholas Sparks

22 Traditional Publishing

by Jill

Most writers dream of getting published, but few know what that really means or how to navigate the challenging process to get to such a point. If you want a publishing house to pay you for your book, you're actually looking to sell the rights to publish your story. You're shopping around for the perfect company to sell to.

What goes on over at those publishing houses, anyway? Why does it take so long to get an answer? Let's take a closer look at what has to happen to get your beloved novel in print.

First, you must have an incredible, flawless manuscript. This is no easy task and can take many years. Once you've reached that point, you're ready to submit.

To get published, you must get an **acquisitions editor** to like your book. An acquisitions editor is a person who works for a publishing house and is responsible for finding books for the company to publish. Getting your manuscript to an acquisitions editor can be achieved several ways.

1. Send it to the editor at the publishing house.
2. Query an editor.

3. Pitch it to an editor at a writers conference.
4. Enter a contest in which an editor is a judge.
5. Have your agent submit your novel to the editor.

Most traditional publishing houses will not accept an unsolicited manuscript, which is a manuscript the editor did not ask you to send. It's like showing up to a party uninvited. The host says, "Who invited you?" and you say, "I invited myself."

Get the picture?

Traditional publishers don't accept unsolicited manuscripts because they just can't look at that many manuscripts. It takes too much time, and they don't have the staff to do it. Many publishing houses will accept a query, however. This is a short email or one-page letter that pitches your story to the editor in hopes of snagging her interest. (We'll learn how to write them in Chapter 25.)

What The Process Can Look Like

But let's dream a bit. Let's pretend that you have an agent. Sweet, huh? You and your agent have worked hard to get your book perfected. Now she's ready to submit your story to an editor. She'll likely send a quick email to tell you, "Just submitted your story to Tom over at ABC Publishers. Now we'll wait and see what he says!"

What happens next depends on the publishing house. Some houses are really slow. Some move faster. So you might get an update from your agent in a few weeks, or you might not hear anything for many months.

Meanwhile, here's what Tom is up to over at ABC Publishers. As the young adult editor, he works from seven in the morning to about eight at night. He's on salary, so there's no overtime pay. He works on about twenty-five books in a year. Today he's working on a content edit for one title, slogging through some more pages of a line edit on another, he's got a meeting with a cover designer to give feedback on a reprint cover, he's got to talk to Rachel in marketing about a book trailer, he needs to call the publicist in New York to talk out some ideas one of his authors has for promoting her book, he has a meeting with his boss (the publisher) to touch base, and he has 356 emails in his inbox, including some projects to reject. He'd love to get his inbox to 300 before he goes home.

A few weeks later your agent calls to follow up. No, Tom hasn't had a chance to read your submission yet, but he promised to try and get to it today.

When Tom finally gets a chance to read it, he *loves* it! He still needs a good fantasy project in next year's spring line, and this could be the book! He's so excited he puts the project on the agenda for the next editorial board meeting. He doesn't have time to call your agent and let him know this, however. So you don't know either!

But Tom does bring your story to the next editorial board meeting. At ABC, this meeting is made up of four people: Tom, the YA editor; Sue, the children's editor; Kathy, the middle grade editor; and Mike, **the editorial director**, a guy in charge of all the editors. Even though each of these editors is responsible for different things, they work as a team when they develop the ABC children's line. In this meeting Tom will pitch your project to the other editors. If they hate it, they'll say so. If Tom can't get the editorial board excited about your book, he likely won't take it any further. Your book might be rejected here.

Below is a sample conversation from the editorial meeting after Tom presented your book to the team.

> **Kathy (middle grade):** I love it. But the premise sounds younger. Maybe you should send it to me.
>
> **Mike (editorial director):** Tom, you think this should maybe be a middle grade project?
>
> **Tom:** No. I want this one for YA. I think it has great appeal for an older reader.
>
> **Sue (children's):** My concern is that this is a new author. You're so busy right now. Do you have time to work with a new author? You know how they can be.
>
> **Tom:** I love this project so much it will be worth the extra effort. I'll work on it from home if I have to.
>
> **Mike (editorial director):** Wow, okay. Who's the agent?
>
> **Tom:** Melanie Smith.
>
> **Mike (editorial director):** Good! Melanie's great. She wouldn't

send us someone who couldn't follow through.

The editorial board likes the project, so Tom makes a note to include your book in the next pub board meeting and puts the whole thing out of his mind. He's got a lot to do, after all.

Since the pub board—publishing board—only meets once a month at ABC Publishers, the next time your agent follows up, she learns that Tom intends to present your project there. Tom tells your agent how much he loves the story and is hoping it will fill that last publishing slot in the spring line. Your agent emails you to relay this information.

Not Many Publishing Slots

The problem is that every house has a limited number of books that they publish each year. Some may only publish five books a year, some thirty. Of those, most of the slots are for the house's established authors. If you submit to a house that publishes Stephen King, he may have two of those thirty novel slots. The other slots are taken up with a host of other successful authors. The pub board will always fill the book slots with their well-known authors first. This only leaves a handful, maybe one or two slots, for new authors each year.

Your book is going to pub board! You're doing a happy dance. You want to tell everyone and their cat, but you hold back. There's still a long way to go.

Things are still crazy over at ABC, so crazy, in fact, that the next pub board meeting got pushed back two weeks to deal with a crisis from a bestselling author who demanded a six-month extension on a book that's already pre-sold 200,000 copies. It's "all hands on deck" at ABC to fix this thing. Thankfully, Tom is not the editor working with this bestselling prima donna, but he still gets pulled into the drama.

Eventually, the rescheduled pub board meeting rolls around. This meeting takes place in a long room at a big table with chairs all around it and a lot of snacks in the center. Since ABC Publishers is a smaller house, there are only ten people present. The **publisher** (boss), the editorial team (Tom, Sue, Kathy, and Mike), the **sales director**, his **top sales rep**, the **marketing director,** Rachel, her assistant, and **the finance director**.

Here Tom gets his (and your) big chance. He spent a few hours preparing a video presentation to illustrate your project to the pub board. Mike hands out paperwork on the project and tells everyone that Tom is going to present a young adult fantasy novel by a new author and that the editorial board thinks this could fill that last slot for spring.

> **Sales director:** I think this one is great. It's got a *Percy Jackson* meets *Hunger Games* vibe that I can totally sell.
> **Publisher:** I still don't understand what a crowl is.
> **Marketing director:** Offspring of the gods and an elf. Think Galadriel.
> **Publisher:** So it's Lord of the Rings meets Percy Jackson meets *Hunger Games*?
> **Sales:** I like adding Tolkien. That will tie in with the Hobbit movies.
> **Publisher:** But didn't *Percy Jackson* do the Greek god thing to death? Can we sell Greek gods anymore?
> **Marketing director:** This one isn't Greek gods. They're crowls, which are Greek-like gods set in a fantasy world.
> **Sales director:** I can sell anything I can relate to the Hobbit right now, you bet.
> **Publisher:** Okay, Tom, tell us about these crowls.

Everyone is silent as Tom shares your plot in pictures, almost how a book trailer might look, though Tom narrates the story himself. He also goes over a profit and loss statement (which lists how much money the project will cost and, hopefully, make), talks about sales figures for similar titles, shows them your popular YouTube channel where you post humorous video book reviews, and shares how he thinks you would be a really great author for ABC Publishers.

> **Publisher:** And you want this for spring of next year? You think a new author can turn around the edits that fast?
> **Tom:** Yes. And I'm willing to put in the extra time to make it work.
> **Mike:** The manuscript is done. And the writing is great.
> **Finance director:** But it's a lot to invest on an unproven novelist. Can you really sell twenty thousand copies on a new author?

Sales: With the Hobbit angle, I can sell fifty.
Finance director: *snorts* Sure you can.
Publisher: I still don't understand what a crowl is. It sounds like crone. What teen wants to read about old ladies?
Sales: A crowl is the new hobbit.
Marketing: A crowl is nothing like a hobbit.
Sales: It is if I say it is.
Marketing: Whatever.
Mike: Well? Do we make an offer on this one?
Finance: Cut that advance in half and I say yes.
Sales: I say yes. I've been looking for a Hobbit angle to sell.
Marketing director: I vote yes. It's clever and smart, but accessible.
Publisher: It's not my kind of book, but I didn't like vampires or the dystopian craze, either, so I trust your judgment, Mike. And if we can sell twenty-five at the lower advance, I'll go for it.

And so you get an email or phone call from your agent with an official offer from the publisher! The offer might look like this:

Rights:
1. World English language rights
2. All international language rights, worldwide
3. All electronic/digital and ebook rights to the text of the book
4. Non-dramatic audio rights, both on a hard medium (such as a CD) and digital audio download rights
5. DVD curriculum rights

Advance: $5,000 ($2,500 payable on the receipt of signed contract, $2,500 payable on acceptance of manuscript)
Royalty: 15 percent of net.
Format: Softcover, $9.99, approximately 300 pages

Here you might bring up your concerns with your agent over the advance or when the manuscript is due. Your agent will negotiate this with the editor, and, once she's done, she'll email you a copy of the book contract. You'll read this carefully, ask your agent any questions you have, and when you're satisfied, print three copies, sign each one, initial each page, and mail them off to the publisher, who will process them, keep a copy for themselves, mail one back to you and the other to your agent. Sometime later, you'll receive the first half of your advance payment in the mail, minus your agent's 15 percent.

But what happens now?

Even though your manuscript was complete when you submitted it, you now have a delivery date to officially turn it in. Tom asked for a few story changes in the contract, so you make those changes and go through the manuscript once more to make everything perfect. Once you officially turn it in, you have nothing to do but wait. You tell people you're having a book published. You start writing another book, but you've got to wait your turn for Tom to get to you again, because remember, he's a busy guy.

Eventually you get an email from the marketing director asking you to fill out a marketing information sheet. This asks for your author bio, how you'd describe your book, other possible titles, what you'd like on the cover, names of authors you'd like to get endorsements from, names and addresses of people you'd like to get a free copy of the book to review, names of your local newspapers and TV studios . . . things like that.

A few months later you get an email from Tom explaining that they've changed the title to *The Crowl*. You don't love this, so you email your agent for help. Your agent gets involved to express your concerns, but in the end, the publisher is too excited about a tie-in with *The Hobbit*, so you lose out.

A month later you get an email with your cover art attached. Other than the title, you love it. Whew! At least you don't have to complain again. You're really trying to be an easy-going author.

A few weeks later the marketing people email you a link to a book trailer they made for your book.

It's awesome!

Then, while you're on your summer vacation and hop online at a computer in the hotel lobby, there's an email from Tom with your edits. He wants them back in two weeks, and you won't be home for three more days! You shoot off a quick email to let him know where you are, then open the edits really quickly to see how they look. You see a lot of changes! This depresses you for the last three days of your vacation, but you get home and see that they're not so bad after all. You spend all day, every day, of the next eleven days getting your edits done and turned in on time. Then you wait some more.

The edits go back and forth between you and Tom a few more times before you're both happy with the manuscript. You don't hear anything for a while until you get a PDF galley of the final book to read for mistakes. This file looks like a book! Your name is at the top of every even page and the title is at the top of every odd page. You ask your critique partner and your best friend to read the PDF too. You make a list of any errors and email that back to Tom.

More waiting.

Then one day you receive a package with an advanced reader copy inside! It's your book! It's beautiful. You laugh and cry and dance and show everyone in town.

You start to get emails from the publicist, who forwards you reviews from *Publisher's Weekly, School Library Journal, Kirkus, VOYA*, and, if you're lucky, an endorsement from a well-known author. The reviews are mixed. Some love the book. A few hate it.

Sigh. Such is life.

Meanwhile, you've been trying to learn the ropes of self-promotion and have set up a release-day book signing at your local Barnes and Noble. You've invited all your friends and family. You get a box with your author copies of the final book and you have your friend video tape the moment and post it to YouTube. That night you sleep with a copy of your book under your pillow.

Bliss.

Your book is now showing up for pre-order on Amazon.com, BarnesandNoble.com, and other online retailers! You pre-order a copy from every store, just for fun.

Release day arrives! The book goes live online and you spend the morning watching the online rankings go up, hoping that everyone who promised to buy a copy will. That night you head over to your book release signing. Your friends and family are there to support you.

Your mom buys ten copies. Your family and friends all buy one, but you're most excited about the three people who were actual customers who walked by, asked what all the excitement was about, and bought a book. You're hoping they'll become fans and buy book two when it comes out!

So there you have it. Pretty cool, huh? All this takes about a year and a half from submission to the book being available in stores. And that's much faster than it used to be.

How Advances Work

Now that you're getting a big advance, you're finally going to make some money, right?

Not quite.

As per the scenario for *The Crowl* getting published, ABC gave you a $5,000 advance on the book. Think of this advance as a loan. It would be like your boss down at Subway giving you a year's salary in advance. You'd still need to work to pay it back, but you'd get the money ahead of time—in advance.

In publishing, an advance is not something you have to pay back, but it's an amount that you must reach if you are ever going to earn a penny more from your publisher on your book.

Your book advance is calculated on how many copies the publisher thinks they can sell. This is what was figured in that profit and loss statement. Once your book comes out, you must sell enough copies so that your royalties add up to $5,000 before you make any more money on your book. This is called "breaking even" or "earning out" your advance. Sadly, the majority of authors don't ever break even. In fact, many bestselling authors don't break even because they get such huge advances that their books never earn out. That doesn't mean the publisher didn't make money off those books. Just that each one didn't earn back what they paid out in an advance.

Once you break even, then you'll start to receive more money on your book. You'll receive your royalty rate from your contract on all future sales, which was 15 percent, minus your agent's 15 percent. Also, returns count against you. Every quarter you'll get a royalty statement. The first one might look something like this:

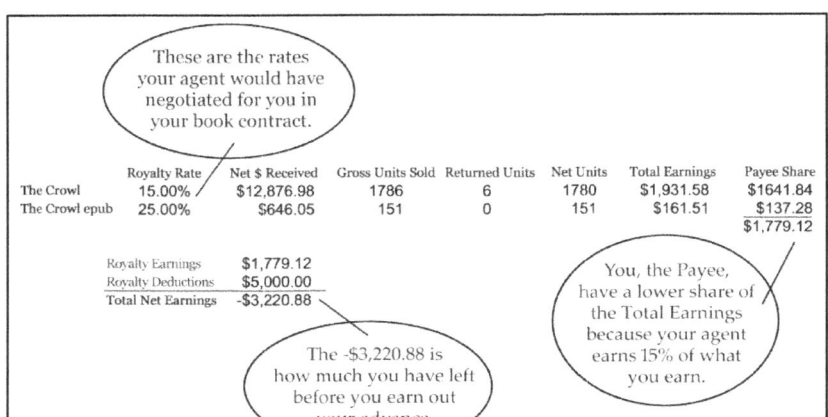

All this to say, the vast majority of authors need to have written multiple books that have earned out, are all still in print, and earning royalties before they can make a living. It adds up, but it takes time.

Something to Think About

If you have a favorite author, make a point of buying his or her books new, because authors don't make any royalties off used books or books you get free from their publisher. In fact, if you want to be an author, I suggest you make a point of buying at least one new book a month if you can. Because you know what it's like to be working hard to get published, and someday you're going to wish that someone would buy your book new.

If you can't afford to buy new books, request that your local library order them. Authors get paid for books purchased by libraries, and having your book in a library helps you find new readers.

Also, don't think that ebook piracy isn't a big deal. It is. Every ebook that someone emails to a friend without paying for it is another lost royalty for a hardworking, underpaid author.

Independent Publishers

Since it's so difficult to get published at a traditional house these days, many authors are starting out with small publishers. I did this, and it worked very well for me.

My first publisher did not pay an advance but offered a bigger royalty. He could do this because he used print-on-demand technology to produce the books. This means that a book is printed only when a customer orders one. This eliminates costs of large print runs where a traditional publisher might decide to print 5000 copies to start that will need to be warehoused until orders come in.

I worked very hard to market my book, and I did well. I got some nice reviews and won a few awards. I ended up writing a trilogy, which got me a small readership, an agent, and a publishing contract at a traditional house. Now I'm living the dream!

There are pros and cons to working with a small publisher.

Pros

- They need authors and your chances of getting published increase.
- You'll have a physical book that you can promote and sell.
- You might make a higher royalty rate.
- A smaller advance or no advance means that you can make royalties sooner.
- The indie publisher might not accept returns. If not, those won't count against your royalties.
- You might get a faster response on your submission because the staff is much smaller than at a traditional house.

Cons

- The editor helping to strengthen your story might not be as skilled as those who work in traditional publishing.
- The cover designers might not be as skilled as those who work in traditional publishing.
- Your book will likely be more expensive to produce, since the publisher can't get quantity printing discounts.
- If the publisher doesn't accept returns, bookstores might not carry your book, which can limit how fast people find out your book exists.
- It might be more difficult to enter certain contests or get

professional book reviews.

•The publisher may have no marketing budget to help promote your book.

Never rush into any publishing deal. Take your time, consider the offer, consult a mentor or agent, and make sure you feel comfortable. It's your book! If you're going to sell the publishing rights, you want to make the best possible choice over which publisher to sell to.

How to Tell if a Small Publisher is Legit

1. Are they going to charge you? If they are, they're a self-publishing company, not an independent press. You shouldn't have to pay a dime! That also means that they should not ask you to contribute to the marketing costs, purchase any amount of author copies, or pay for editing services or writing classes.
2. Are they listed in the Writer's Market?
3. Is their website professional?
4. Google "is name of publisher legit?" and read the articles you find.
5. What other books have they published? Research a few of the titles on Amazon.com. How are the sales rankings? Do they have reviews? Read a few reviews to see what people liked and disliked.
6. Ask if they have wholesale distribution or if they sell books online only.
7. Jot down the title of one of those books. Visit your local bookstore and ask about ordering one. If the bookstore can't find the book in the computer, that's not good.
8. Ask how many copies they expect to sell in the first year.
9. Ask to speak with the person who will edit your book. Is that person excited to be working with you? What changes does he have in mind?
10. Read the contract carefully. If possible, get an author, agent, or lawyer who knows publishing to look it over as well.

> The good news about self-publishing is you get to do everything yourself. The bad news about self-publishing is you get to do everything yourself
> – Lori Lesko

23 Self-Publishing

by Jill

Self-publishing (also called indie-publishing) is when you decide to keep the rights to your story and publish any ebooks, print books, or audiobooks yourself. In this scenario, you start your own business and you will pay for everything (editing, proofreading, cover design, typesetting, ebook creation, advertising, marketing, etc). You'll also have all the creative control and make all the money—if there is any after your expenses. Some authors don't want this pressure. They just want to write stories and let someone else run the business side. Other authors thrive on entrepreneurship.

As with the previous chapter on traditional publishing, this isn't meant to be a how-to manual on self-publishing but rather a snapshot of what the indie author lifestyle looks like. We have listed a few self-publishing resources in the Extras section of this book.

Two things I want to say about self-publishing:

1. You only get one chance to make a first impression.
2. Just because you can self-publish, doesn't mean you should.

Teens often throw out Christopher Paolini's name when this topic is broached. The fantasy novel *Eragon* was self-published in 2002 by Paolini International L.L.C., the company Christopher's parents had already published three nonfiction books under. Chris was nineteen in 2002, but he'd started writing at age fifteen, so he'd put in years of dedication into his craft by the time Paolini International L.L.C. published *Eragon*.

Financially backed by his parents, they went on a major tour to promote the book. Novelist Carl Hiaasen's son picked up a copy of *Eragon*, showed it to his dad, who eventually told Knopf about the book, which led to a major publishing deal.

The thing is, there are always one or two over-the-top success stories like this that motivate people. And that's good. But these kinds of success stories happen as often as someone wins the lottery.

They're extremely rare.

How many of you have parents who would quit their jobs, sell their house, and go on the road to promote your novel? Probably none. Nor should they! It's just too big of a financial risk.

Self-publishing used to be taboo. It was a sign of an author who'd cheated, skipped the hard work of learning to write, and paid to have his own book made. And while that's often still the case for many authors, self-publishing is not what it once was.

While no one is exactly certain when the first ebook was published, people began reading them on their computers in the late 1990s. It wasn't until Amazon released the Kindle in 2007 that reading ebooks became an entirely new type of experience. The Kindle wasn't the first ereader, but it made ebooks famous.

The publishing industry changed in a big way.

Today, many refer to self-publishing as indie-publishing, and while thousands of indie authors are making nothing on their books, many are doing okay, and some are doing well. The opportunity for success is greater than it's ever been.

Ebooks have changed the face of self-publishing. It's free to publish your own ebook, and it no longer costs much to self-publish print books, either.

This can be dangerous. Because while many authors (whether their stories were ready to be published or not) made a ton of money between the "golden years" of 2010 and 2015 when Kindle was new and readers were buying like crazy, there are now millions of self-published books out there. Readers are overwhelmed. Their Kindles are crammed with hundreds of free or .99 books that they will likely never read. And if they do try one, they will no longer tolerate a poorly written story. Because even .99 cents is too much to pay to read something filled with errors and no plot.

Today, if a self-published book is well-written, the author is faced with the same problem a traditional author has: discoverability. How do readers find you? When you're traditionally published, that's your publisher's problem. When you're self-published, it's your problem.

Don't get me wrong, a lot of indie authors still make good money, but it's not as easy as it used to be. Indie authors have to be constantly learning about what ads and newsletter lists to invest in and which marketing efforts will help them find new readers. The industry is always changing. All authors need to be paying attention to these changes, but if you're an indie, your success rests in part on how well you pay attention and the choices you make as a result. It can be pretty stressful.

Writing books is a business. It's also an art. Most people don't get good at anything without practice. So just because someone *can* self-publish an ebook—or a print book—it doesn't mean he *should*. And just because someone has a book on Amazon.com, it doesn't mean any readers will find it and buy it.

You only get one chance to have your first novel published. It's your name and reputation on the line. So make a good, smart, patient choice and wait until you're ready.

Now, there are many teens out there with self-published books. I've met dozens of them. Kind, smart, talented authors with fun stories. I'm not saying the fact that they self-published is a bad thing. I'm just saying it's TOUGH to sell those books.

Guess what? It's tough to sell any book.

I know because I've been traditionally published. And I've indie published too.

Both are hard.

In all honesty, self-publishing is best for people who have a speaking platform to sell their books. Say you survived a freak case of small pox and wrote your own harrowing tale. Medical groups across the country would be clamoring to have you speak at their summer retreats. So you self-publish your story and sell it on the back table. Because you have gigs—a place to sell your book—it makes sense to self-publish. The book will sell itself.

Or, if you happen to have 40,000 followers on Instagram—that will likely help you a great deal. When you're an indie author, your platform is important. You need people to sell to.

I've never wanted to be a representative for Pampered Chef, Creative Memories, Avon, Mary Kay, etc., because I don't like selling things to people. And I hate only getting invited to someone's house because she wants me to buy something.

So I am careful about how I promote my books to my "platform." I don't look at everyone I meet as a potential sale. It's not right. Your platform is about giving something to your readers—building a relationship with them. It's okay to sell to them, but that can't be all you do or your platform will shrink away and die.

All this to say, if you've been hard at work for years, getting kind rejections from agents and publishers—or maybe you have an agent and the market just hasn't been right—perhaps it's time to consider self-publishing.

So, let's dream a bit again. You've written several books. You've gone to conferences. You've met with agents and editors. You've gotten requests for full manuscripts. But you keep getting rejections. "The story isn't quite what we're looking for." Or "We already have a story similar to this one." You're frustrated. You decide to self-publish.

If you're going to self-publish, put up the money to get the help you need to do it right. Don't ask your mom to be your editor, even if she has a PhD in English. Find industry trained editors who know how to edit story content as much as grammar and punctuation. Research them. Ask for references. Buy a book they've edited and read it. See for yourself. I know it's tempting to create your own covers and get a friend to edit for you, but for your first time out, invest in your product just like a publisher would. This will give you the greatest chance of success.

There is a huge number of people out there who only read ebooks. This is good news for indie authors because the bulk of your sales will come from ebooks.

Ebook readers binge read. They love series, the longer the better. If you have a stand-alone, you likely won't do as well as you would if you had a six-book series. So if you can write series, it will help you. Indie readers also don't like to wait, so the faster you can publish those books the better. This can be dangerous it you're trying to write the best book you can. You don't want to rush things. If you're setting out to strategically launch a self-publishing career, you'd be wise to consider writing at least part of your series in advance, then releasing several at once or only a couple months apart.

So, let's say *The Crowl* got turned down by all the major publishers for the reasons we discussed above and you decide to self-publish. Before you go any further, you need to do some research on the area you live in and set up a small business since you'll be owning your own publishing house. Get a business license and pick a publishing name. You might even design a logo or pay someone to do that for you. You'll want something to put on the spine of your books to represent your company.

That done, create a simple budget. Below are some costs you'll need to consider for a single self-published book.

Editing... $500 (This is actually really low. Averages are between $1 to $5 a page.)

Proofreading... $100 (You can ask for proof readers among your friends and readers, but keep in mind that not everyone is good at it.)

Cover design... $200 (This is a low average. You can pay from $50 to $1000 for a cover.)

Typesetting... $500 (Most charge $3-$5 a page, but you can learn to do this. I typeset all my print books using Microsoft Word.)

Ebook design... $150 (You can learn to do this as well.)

Advertising... $200 (At least for the first month, but usually, the more you spend on advertising, the more you have the potential to make. Be ready to do some experimenting to see what works and what doesn't.)

Overall, you would be wise to budget between $700 and $1500 when self-publishing your first book.

For the sake of this example, let's pretend you've written this trilogy already. You schedule your release dates, then hire a professional editor who is trained in editing fiction and who has references from authors you admire. You send her book one. While you wait, you write your back-cover copy. You're going to need this back-cover copy for several things. It will go on the back of the print book. It will also go on your online book pages and likely also in the ebooks themselves.

The back-cover copy is so important in indie publishing. Since you won't have your book in a store, the description and the cover are the two places readers will look at when deciding whether or not to buy your book. Stephanie will talk about writing a back-cover copy in Chapter 24. There are some elements that are different for an indie author's back-cover copy than it would be with a traditional book. Google "how to write an indie back-cover copy" for help. Also, I wrote a GTW blog post on this subject too, so check that out as well: https://goteenwriters.com/2018/04/25/how-to-write-a-back-cover-copy-for-your-book/

Next you research keywords, write a logline, and finish your back-cover copy. You keep all this in one easy-to-find document. Once your book is published you'll add links to the different online stores and clips from online reviewers. This document will be a nice place to keep important information on the series.

Once this is done, you need to find a professional cover designer. Again you do your research and ask around to find someone whose work wows you. When you email the cover designer, you send them a Word document with examples of covers you like, pictures of inspiration for your story, like mountains, animals, trees, people who look like your characters . . . whatever you think will help the artist.

Keep in mind, self-published book covers need to look good in thumbnail size, since most of your sales will come from online bookstores. You'll want a simple image and the title text large and readable in thumbnail form.

This is also a good time to send your story to any professional authors you know who might be willing to read your story for an endorsement. Keep in mind, many will say no. There are just too many authors asking and it's impossible for authors to read everyone's book. But it never hurts to ask if you are polite, respectful, and especially if you're a big fan of that author and have supported them in the past. Be a giver in this industry before you start asking for favors.

Once the cover designer and editor are hard at work, you write a marketing plan. You're going to try and release all three books at the same time. (For advice on writing a marketing plan, go to GoTeenWriters.com and search "Creating a Realistic Marketing Plan For Your Book Release.")

Your edits come back, and you work through them. Once you're happy, you either send off your book for typesetting or start to create a typeset file on your own. As I mentioned before, I use Microsoft Word to typeset. Other people use resources like Draft 2 Digital or Vellum.

You also start your ebook file. I use Scrivener to create ebooks. Others use Draft 2 Digital and Vellum. You can find tutorials on YouTube for typesetting both print book and ebook files.

Once you're done, you create PDFs to send to proofreaders. You'll have two files, a PDF file of the print book and an ebook file, so make sure that both files get proofread.

Next you gather a list of people who will serve as a launch team to help you promote. These could be friends, family, and fellow writers who are excited about supporting you. You'll want to give these people PDF copies of your book so they can read it early and be ready to post book reviews as soon as they are able.

You decide not to invest in paying for "professional" review services, at least this first time. You're hoping your launch team will do the trick.

Once you have the typeset file, you calculate the spine width and pass that information along to your cover designer so he can create a full cover for paperback books.

You get the cover, but there is a typo in your bio. You email back and forth until that is fixed.

Once your cover and proofreading are done, you're ready to upload your book for publishing. You open your handy information document with your keywords and back-cover copy and start uploading both your print book and your ebook. You order a proof copy of the print book. It arrives and is gorgeous! You're proud of how the book turned out.

The release day for book one comes at last. The book is for sale online and is getting some sales and book reviews. You have a party to celebrate and give Facebook Live a try. You buy some Facebook ads in hopes the release video will bring in some new readers.

One month after your book release, you sit down and evaluate your marketing and release plan. You make notes of what worked and what didn't. Then you schedule out a few promotions over the next few months. As an indie author, you'll need to do promotions for your series at least every quarter if you want to stay on top of things.

So that's a peek at the self-publishing process.

Back in 2004 when I started writing, self-publishing wasn't what it is today. If it had been, I would have gone off and self-published my fantastical work of genius right then. I know I would have.

And that would have been a HUGE MISTAKE!

(Quick aside from Stephanie: ME TOO. I have actually prayed prayers of thanks that self-publishing wasn't really an option when I started out.)

Here's the deal . . . I know self-publishing is tempting. You just want to hold your book. Have it to look at. Get your start. Gather some readers. Show your friends and family you did it—that you're not crazy about this writing thing. I get that. I was there.

But if you want to have a career as a novelist—if you're serious about this thing—then wait. I'm not kidding. At least wait until you've spent a few years trying it the traditional way. Why? Because you need to put in the hard work of learning, suffering rejection, and persevering. If you don't, you cheat yourself of the struggle of becoming a great writer.

You cheat yourself of the journey.

Stephanie and I strongly encourage unpublished teen writers to keep writing. To be patient. To practice, practice, practice and learn, learn, learn. Read books on how to be a better writer. Read books in your genre. Get involved in a critique group or find a critique partner, and learn what other people say about your writing. Save up some money, and instead of spending that on self-publishing, invest it in a writers' conference where you can meet editors and agents face-to-face. I sold several of my traditional books at writers' conferences. Such events are the best place to show your writing to professionals who can give you feedback.

Our advice to all of you young, pre-published writers will always be: Wait. Have patience. Work hard. Learn the craft. Write many books. Go to conferences. Submit your story to agents and editors. And wait.

The better you get, the better book you'll write, the better chance you'll have of getting published by a traditional, royalty-paying publisher. And if you ultimately choose to self-publish, the better chance you'll have of becoming a successful indie author.

Both are really hard work, but both are SO worth the wait!

Step 3
Putting Yourself Out There

How we got started

Stephanie's story

I knew from first grade on that I wanted to write stories when I grew up.

And ten years later, when I finished my first novel, that was still basically all I knew—I wanted to write stories.

Which meant I needed a publisher . . . which meant they would need to see my story . . . ergo, I should just print off my manuscript and mail it to them. (I'm 100 percent serious—this really and truly was my thought process.)

But when I got online to find their addresses, I discovered a rather curious phrase on their websites—no unsolicited submissions. Oh . . . I couldn't just mail it to them?

So then I started looking for publishing houses—any houses—who accepted unsolicited manuscripts. I didn't pay attention to what kind of house they were, how their books were selling, or what genres they published. Honestly, I didn't even know what genre I wrote.

I found four. I printed off four copies of my 90-page manuscript, stuck it in an envelope with my SASE (self-addressed stamped envelope, another new term for me) and popped them in the mail.

Miraculously, two of them were kind enough to send me rejection letters.

Even more miraculously, one of them had actually *read* my manuscript. Like, the whole thing. The editor told me that for my age it was quite good, but that it lacked a strong ending. At the time, I was disappointed not to be getting published, but years later I see how amazing that response was. Not only was it a correct assessment, it's what made me dig into the industry a bit deeper.

I discovered genres, query letters, and literary agents. I quickly became so overwhelmed with how not-ready my manuscript was. This is when I became serious about writing a book that deserved to be published and about learning the ropes of the industry.

For me this meant going to writers conferences, reading craft books, entering contests, going to more writing conferences, stalking writing blogs, and more. We'll talk about querying in the next chapters, but for me the magic always happened at writing conferences. Some conferences were definitely more magical than others, and some left me curled up in the fetal position on my hotel bed longing for a gallon of ice cream.

As you read this section, please keep in mind that there is no One Way to publication. Especially as the industry changes, and more authors choose to go indie or hybrid. These are meant to be guidelines and suggestions, not rules.

Jill's Story

I had written half of a novel about a spy kid.

It was amazing.

In my mind, I was ready to be published yesterday. I mean, my story was *so brilliant*, I knew that when publishers got a look at it, they were going to fight over who got to buy it.

In my imagination, confidence was never a problem. In my imagination, all things work out perfectly. *grin*

Bolstered by my imagined success, I started looking into how I was going to make this dream come true. I mean, how hard could this be, really? My first task was to gather a pile of books that were similar to mine. I figured that the companies who put out these books might be willing to print mine as well. Once I had that list of potential publishers, I looked them up in the *Writer's Market* and went online to check each publisher's submission guidelines. Here's what I found on every site:

No unsolicited submissions.

Which meant, "Do not send us your manuscript unless we ask you to, which we won't because we have enough manuscripts to look at already. If you ignore this rule and send us your manuscript anyway, we will throw it in the trash or delete it. We will not notify you of this. You can plan on it happening. The only way we'll look at your manuscript is if your agent sends it to us."

Ouch.

Well, no big deal. I just needed to find an agent. How hard could *that* be? So I picked up my *Writer's Market* book again and started making a list of potential agents. But guess what I found when I sought out each agency's submission guidelines?

No unsolicited submissions.

That's right. It was a conspiracy. So totally unfair.

But in all my research, I *had* discovered a loophole.

The writers conference.

Writers conferences are events where writers come to learn from editors, agents, and published writers. These are opportunities to show editors and agents your manuscript despite the "No unsolicited submissions" rule.

I found a small, two-day conference in Anaheim, California and I went. I inhaled the information the speakers shared, and during one of the breaks, literary agent Steve Laube (pronounced: lobby) encouraged each of us to come up and give him our one-sentence logline or story pitch.

I had never heard of a one-sentence pitch until Steve Laube explained it, but I wasn't about to miss my chance to sell him my half-finished work of brilliance. I just knew that when he heard the genius of my idea, he'd sign me on the spot.

So I got in line and waited my turn. When I finally approached, and Mr. Laube gave me the go ahead, and I began to speak. I said something like this:

"My story is about a teenage boy named Spencer. He plays basketball and eats peanut butter out of the jar. Anyway, he gets recruited to join the Mission League organization. He thinks that's pretty dumb, but his grandma makes him go or whatever, so he goes to Moscow with a bunch of other kids he doesn't like. Oh, and Spencer has these visions and dreams and stuff and he is kind of a troublemaker . . ."

I went on and on.

You get the idea. Apparently I missed the part when Mr. Laube said to keep your pitch to *one sentence*. I also had no idea what my story problem was. I don't think I had one back then.

Mr. Laube's eyes had glazed over long before he finally cut me off. He said something about teens not liking books about missionaries, that the young adult genre was pretty much non-existent in the

Christian specialty market (which he worked in), and that he didn't represent YA authors anyway.

Oh. Okay.

I went up to my hotel room that night and bawled. It was the death of a dream and rejection hurt!

Once I had got *that* out of my system, my brain kicked back into high gear. Okay. Something had gone *way* wrong down there. I mean, I knew teens liked my story because I had teen readers giving me feedback. And my story wasn't about missionaries, it was about spies. You know, *Mission League/Mission Impossible*? Clearly I'd done a poor job explaining it.

I supposed it might be easier to explain if I finished the book and knew how it ended. Duh.

I realized in that moment that I hadn't respected my dream. When I was in high school, I'd wanted to be a fashion designer. I sewed daily, I subscribed to fashion magazines, I watched documentaries on famous designers, I went to a fashion design college, and I worked jobs in the industry. I knew my stuff where fashion design was concerned. I had respected that dream.

But writing? I'd spent six months writing half a book and expected to sell it for millions, and I didn't even know there were different markets for books.

Yeah . . . I'd been totally clueless.

So, I had a choice. Give up or keep at it.

I decided to keep at it.

As it turns out, my rejection wasn't the death of my dream at all, but the start of a realistic understanding of what it was going to take to achieve my dream. Over the next four years, I learned everything I could about writing, publishing, and the industry. I joined critique groups, I finished my book and rewrote it, I wrote more books, I read books on writing, and I had some articles published.

By the time I attended my next writers conference, I was ready.

And, by the way, one blunder with an agent doesn't seal your fate forever. Steve Laube and I are friendly acquaintances. I see him almost every year at writers conferences and we have fun catching up and talking about Alaska (turns out, we both grew up there).

The moral of my story? Respect your dream. Writing is hard

work. And the publishing industry is complex and overflowing with pre-published authors chasing their dreams. If you want to stand out from the crowd, you need to work hard to create the very best book you can, then do your best to seek out the right agents and editors who are looking for the kinds of stories you write.

> ### How to Find a Writers Conference
>
> There are all kinds of writers conferences. Searching the internet is the best way to find them. Be sure to look for conferences that are right for your book. Don't sign up for the Romance Writers of America conference if you're writing a middle grade historical novel.
>
> If you've never been to a writers conference, pick a small, local one for your first time, even if the right editors or agents won't be attending. You'll learn a lot.
>
> When you're ready to pitch your book, look for conferences that have the right editors and agents as part of their faculty and staff. The conference website should also list what each agent or editor is looking for and what they're *not* looking for. Pay attention to that. And if the conference website doesn't specify, do your own homework by looking up those agents and editors on their company websites to find out what kinds of stories they are interested in seeing.
>
> Another way to find conferences is to see whether or not the writing organizations you're part of are having a conference. Organizations like RWA (Romance Writers of America) and SCBWI (Society of Children's Book Writers and Illustrators) have their own conferences, as do many other organizations.

Step 3: Putting Yourself Out There

> For the artist who wishes to minimize the disconnect between creating and selling, what should marketing ultimately be if not a pursuit of, first, learning how to create something worth giving, and then learning how to give it in the best way?
> -K. M. Weiland

24 Pitching Your Novel

by Stephanie

While it's super tempting to start querying agents and editors as soon as you type The End, let me tell you it's no fun trying to throw your pitching materials together *after* an agent requests them. It leads to a night of scrambling around on the internet trying to figure out what the heck a synopsis is and how on earth you should write an author bio when the only credential to your name is being on the high school newspaper.

You might be tentatively raising your hand and asking, "But . . . what is a query?"

When we use that term, we mean short emails that you send to a literary agent (and rarely editors) telling them about you and your story, asking if they are interested in reading more. They're sales pitches, basically. We have some examples of queries for you in the next chapter, but first let's talk about what—besides the book—you need to have prepared before you start the querying process.

Before you send out a query, Jill and I suggest you know or have at least six things handy:

- Your genre
- Your target audience
- A hook for your book
- A paragraph description of your story, written in the style of back-cover copy
- The first three chapters of your book—formatted correctly
- A synopsis

With all that information ready, you'll be able to quickly put together pitching materials and a fiction book proposal when the opportunity arises.

Book proposals are typically for selling nonfiction, or selling fiction as an established author, but it doesn't hurt to have one. Former Blink/HarperCollins editor Jillian Manning has this to say about book proposals.

> "When it comes to fiction, few agents or editors expect or require book proposals. I certainly don't, though I have to admit that I am always happy to receive one. A book proposal helps me learn more about an author than a two-sentence bio. It gives me insight into marketing opportunities. And it provides a snapshot of the project that saves me hours of work when I'm preparing to evaluate a project."

Let's break down each of the six details on the above list.

Defining Your Genre
by Jill

Before you query or pitch your book in person, you need to define your genre. I struggled with genre when I first started out. I knew that I was writing for teens, but my first book had some supernatural elements, and I wasn't certain where the book fit. It was an adventure story . . . but it was about spies too, which maybe made it a mystery. Yeah. That was it. I was writing a teen mystery. But what about the supernatural part? Did that make it a supernatural book? Or was it paranormal or maybe urban fantasy?

I didn't know. I agonized over what to write on my query letter or what to say when an editor asked, "What genre do you write?"

The thing is, there are so many genres out there. If you can find your exact sub-genre, you'll have a better chance of selling your work and having your work stand out as unique in the market. Why? Because you're defining your target audience, and that helps an editor or agent know where your book might fit.

If you said, "This is a contemporary young adult novel." That can mean many things. It doesn't tell the editor or agent much about your book. Odds are, every teen reader won't like your story.

But if you said, "This is a contemporary novel about a teen swimmer." That's specific. And specific is the goal.

Here are some more examples:

"I've written a young adult medieval fantasy novel with a telepathy thread."

"I've written a contemporary science fiction/suspense novel for teens that deals with the subject of human cloning."

"I've written a young adult suspense novel about teen spies who fight supernatural beings."

"This young adult dystopian novel was inspired by the Babylonian exile from Jerusalem."

Make it Yours:

1. Think about what genres you would tag your book with. Historical? Contemporary? Sci-fi? Romance? Fantasy? Paranormal? If you're not sure, find books that are similar to yours and see how they've been classified, both in physical bookstores or libraries, and with online retailers.

2. Now try to come up with your unique twist to throw on the end. Is it a contemporary YA that confronts bullying? A fantasy novel with swords and technology?

Your Target Audience
by Jill

Another question an agent or editor might ask is, "Who is your target audience?"

If you're writing for teens, you might say, "Well, teens, of course."

But that's not the answer an agent or editor is looking for. They really don't want to hear that your book is for everyone, because that's impossible. Marketing people need a demographic to target. And, really, there's no book out there that everyone likes.

If you can give the editor or agent a very specific reader, the editor will perk up, knowing that such information will please the sales guys at the pub board meetings.

Here are some examples of specific target audiences:

Guys who love Fortnite will connect with this book because it has a similar storyworld.

Empty-nesters will relate to my protagonist's youngest child leaving home.

My book targets young mothers who have small children and are frazzled.

Guys who love to hunt will relate to my character when he's lost in the woods and needs to find his own food.

Female athletes will really connect with the journey of my main character to make the varsity basketball team despite her hardship of having lost her father.

The same book could have another audience.

Girls who've lost their father will relate to my heroine's loss.

The point is, know who your target reader is and what he's looking for in a novel. Then communicate that to the editor or agent.

Your Hook Sentences
by Stephanie

In your proposal—or if you're planning to pitch your novel to an agent or editor in person—you'll need to be able to describe your book in just a sentence or two. And since you chose to write your story using 80,000 words, not forty-two or twenty-seven or thirty-five, this can be incredibly difficult.

These go by multiple names—hooks, one-liners, one-line pitches, loglines (mostly for screenwriting), elevator pitches (refers to the oral version) and probably others that I don't know. We're going to call them hooks. Not only is it easier to type, it's descriptive of what you're trying to do with your one or two sentences.

It's helpful, I think, to start by thinking about the goal of a hook. The goal of your hook is to convey what your story is about in a way that stirs interest. Like if your friend says to you, "Do you want to join our book club? We're reading *Book You've Never Heard Of*." Your response will likely be, "What's it about?"

This is the moment you should keep in mind when you're writing your hook. The "What's it about?" moment. Your hook doesn't need to be strong *just* to convince an agent you've got what it takes to be a published author. Consider all the other ways your hook gets put to work:

Your newly-signed agent will be using it to sell your project. He or she will start calling up editors and saying, "I have this great project from a debut author. His book is about insert-the-hook-here."

The editor talks to other editors at the publishing house about it. "This book is great! It's about insert-the-hook-here."

The editor takes your book to the editorial and publishing committees to convince his coworkers that they want to buy this book, that it'll be profitable. "What's it about?" they'll ask. And your editor will say, "Insert-the-hook-here."

Then the sales team will go out to their clients—the bookstores— and convince them to dedicate shelf space to this debut author. "His book is great! It's about insert-the-hook-here."

And then the bookstore employees will be selling the books to their clients using your hook. "I think you'll like this book. It's about insert-the-hook-here."

Even *you* will have another use for it. Like when you're sitting at a book signing and a person walks up to you, picks up your book and says, "You're the author?"

You'll straighten your shoulders and beam a smile their way. "Yes, I am!" The next words out of their mouth will then be, "So, what's your book about?" (Or they might instead read your own bio out loud to you in a slightly mocking tone, before putting it back on the table and asking where the bathroom is. True story. But most people at least feign interest in your book.)

Do you see how much bigger the hook is than simply taking up space on the book proposal?

Your hook needs to contain these five elements in as few words as possible:

Character
Conflict
Setting
Uniqueness
Action

Let's take a look at how this plays out in books that many of us are familiar with:

> *Harry Potter and the Sorcerer's Stone* by J. K. Rowling: An abused orphaned boy discovers he's actually a celebrity wizard when he receives his invitation to attend wizarding school.
>
> *The Princess Diaries* by Meg Cabot: An uncool teenage girl learns in the same week that she's failing Algebra . . . and she's the princess of a European country.
>
> *The Sisterhood of the Travelling Pants* by Ann Brashares. Four friends discover a pair of jeans that magically fits them all, and it connects and empowers them when they are forced to spend the summer apart.

Another option for your hook is combining popular story ideas with settings or concepts. Such as:

Romeo and Juliet with vampires: *Twilight* by Stephenie Meyer

Gossip Girl set in the gilded age: The Luxe series by Anna Godbersen

Veronica Mars set in the 1920s: *The Lost Girl of Astor Street* by Stephanie Morrill

Teenage Superman: *Smallville*, which made a fortune pairing the perfect Superman with an imperfect teenager. (No offense, you teenagers, but I hope you can see how this makes it a great idea.)

Lawyers in trouble: John Grisham has made millions with this idea. Most lawyers lead a pretty dull life of paperwork, paperwork, and more paperwork, but not in Grisham's books.

Kid spies: This idea spawned Spy Kids, Agent Cody Banks, Alex Rider, Cherub: A division of MI6, and Jill Williamson's *Mission League* series.

(An aside: Sometimes this can be a wacky way to come up with book ideas—I'm convinced *Pride and Prejudice and Zombies* came from this tactic . . .)

These can be effective, particularly for an elevator pitch, but you'll still need to follow it up with your unique story details. So for *Twilight*, you could add, "A teenage girl falls in love with a vampire who doesn't kill people."

I love the way Blake Snyder (*Save the Cat*) describes effective loglines for movies. He says, "It must bloom in your mind when you hear it. A whole movie must be implied, often including a time frame."

And the same goes for the hooks in your pitching materials, they must imply a whole story, one that makes the hearer say, "Ooh, that sounds like something I'd like to read."

Your Back-Cover Copy
by Stephanie

Like a hook sentence, your back-cover copy is a tool for selling your book. First to agents and editors, but then to readers.

When people are perusing a bookstore, they'll flip the book over to read what your book is about. Or when you're being interviewed on blogs or in magazines, they'll often print the back-cover copy. Also, when you're on TV, they use your back-cover copy to explain your book to the audience.

The qualities of a good book blurb are similar to the qualities of a good hook. Your back-cover copy should include:

> **Character:** Who is the main character? Who is this story about?
> **Setting:** Where and when does it take place?
> **Conflict:** What are they trying to achieve? Why are they on this journey?
> **Action:** How do they go about doing this?
> **Uniqueness:** Why is this book different? Why should I invest the time in reading it?
> **Tone:** Is the book funny? Dark? Sarcastic? This should be hinted at in the blurb.
> **Mystery:** Often phrased in a question at the end, this is the part of the back-cover copy that triggers an itch in the reader's brain, that makes them scratch by starting to read.

And you need to do it as concisely as possible. But how do you boil your huge, beautiful masterpiece into just 150 to 200 words? Let's look at three examples from books that are very different from each other.

So Not Happening by Jenny B. Jones

> Isabella Kirkwood (CHARACTER) had it all: popularity at a prestigious private school in Manhattan, the latest fashions, and a life of privilege and luxury. Then her father, a plastic surgeon to the stars, decided to trade her mother in for a newer model. (CONFLICT)
> When her mother starts over with her new husband, Bella is forced to pack up (ACTION also CONFLICT) and leave all she knows to live with her new family in Oklahoma. (SETTING) Before her mother can even say "I do," Bella's life becomes a major "don't."
> Can Bella survive her crazy new family? Will the school survive Bella? How can a girl go on when her charmed life is gone and God gives her the total smackdown? (MYSTERY)

The "uniqueness" of a story isn't so easy to label, but for this book I would say there are lots of books about wealthy, snooty Manahattanite teens. This one just got dropped into small town Oklahoma, though. I also love that you can tell this is a humorous story by the tone throughout.

Let's look at the next example:

The Scorpio Races by Maggie Stiefvater

> It happens at the start of every November: the Scorpio Races. Riders attempt to keep hold of their water horses (UNIQUENESS) long enough to make it to the finish line. Some riders live. Others die. (ACTION, CONFLICT)
>
> At age nineteen, Sean Kendrick (CHARACTER) is the returning champion. He is a young man of few words, and if he has any fears, he keeps them buried deep, where no one else can see them. (MYSTERY)
>
> Puck Connolly is different. (CHARACTER) She never meant to ride in the Scorpio Races. But fate hasn't given her much of a chance. So she enters the competition — the first girl ever to do so. She is in no way prepared for what is going to happen. (MYSTERY)

Something interesting to note is that you can tell this is going to be a dual POV book by the way Sean and Puck's paragraphs are separated from each other.

Lastly, let's look at a fantasy example that sets up the storyworld as well as the characters:

King's Folly by Jill Williamson

> The gods are angry.
>
> Volcanic eruptions, sinkholes, ground shakers—everything points to their unhappiness. (CONFLICT, SETTING) At least that is what the king of Armania (SETTING) believes. His son, Prince Wilek, (CHARACTER) thinks his father's superstitions are nonsense, though he remains the ever dutiful heir apparent to the throne.
>
> When a messenger arrives and claims that the town of Farway has been swallowed by the earth, the king sends Wilek to investigate. But what Wilek discovers is more cataclysmic than one lost city. Even as the ground shifts beneath his feet, Wilek sets out on a desperate journey to save his people and his world. (ACTION) But can he do it before the entire land crumbles? (MYSTERY, UNIQUENESS)

Make it Yours:

Now it's your turn to try! Approach your back-cover copy the same way you might a novel. Don't worry about getting it perfect, zippy, and the correct length the first time, just get down something you can work with.

Your Author Bio
by Stephanie

When I first started writing bios for myself, I was convinced that I was doing it wrong. I guess I assumed that when you reached the level of professionalism that requires a bio, "your people" did it for you.

Nope.

Talking about myself in third person felt awkward and listing my accomplishments seemed wrong, but bios are necessary and a well-written one is an asset.

Let's start with a few pointers. Bios should be written in third person, especially if this is something you're putting in your book proposal. If it's on your website or blog, first person can work fine, but you still might want to have a traditional one somewhere online to help out those who are looking for something to copy and paste into an interview.

Your bio should reflect who you are and why you're qualified for whatever it is your bio is being applied to. By which I mean, why you're qualified to write your blog or write your manuscript or be speaking on such-and-such topic.

And this is where youth can be a drawback. Because—to put it frankly—you haven't really done much yet.

When I wrote my first bio, it was for my materials that I took to a conference to pitch *Me, Just Different*. I was 23, and my bio read:

> Stephanie Morrill lives in Orlando, Florida. She is a member of ACFW.

I had to beat those agents away with a stick!

Just kidding.

But what is there to say when you haven't done anything yet?

You write something that showcases your potential. Here are some thoughts on what you could include:

- What you write (your genre or brand of stories)
- Why you write it

- If you blog and where.
- Any special education you have that applies directly. (If you write books about World War II, then majoring in history at your university is applicable. If you write contemporaries, it's not.)
- Something that qualifies you to write this book. So if you're writing about missionaries in Africa and you were raised in Africa by missionaries, you should mention that.
- A few unique things you're passionate about.
- Any writing societies you're a part of, awards you've won, or articles you've had published.

So let's give that a try using my unpublished writer self:

> Stephanie Morrill is passionate about quality Young Adult fiction, perhaps because her teen years aren't too far behind her. She's a member of ACFW and won the award for the best new writer at the Florida Christian Writers conference in 2007. She lives in Orlando, Florida and enjoys rocking out to songs about heartbreak, despite being happily married.

It's not a dream bio or anything, but it has far more personality than my original.

Let's do another example. My main character in *The Revised Life of Ellie Sweet* is a teen who aspires to be a novelist, but she writes historicals. Here's a bio I wrote for her:

> Gabrielle Sweet lives in Visalia, California, though she often fantasizes about being born in a different time and place. This is probably why she writes medieval romances for teens. She is a member of American Fiction Writers and blogs obsessively about her journey as a young novelist. She's passionate about indie rock, novels with strong heroines, and lattes with the perfect amount of foam.

In that last sentence I could have said, "She likes music, reading, and coffee," but that doesn't tell you much about Gabrielle, because I bet in two minutes you can name 50 people who like music, reading, and coffee. This puts a unique twist on her tastes. Plus the "novels with strong heroines" part also communicates something you can expect from one of Gabrielle's manuscripts.

Hopefully this gives you an idea of what you can do with a bio when you don't have a ton of writing credentials to your name. Like all things writing related, if you want to get better at writing bios, it's a good idea to read lots of them. Surf the web for bios and see what connects with you and what doesn't.

Your Synopsis
by Stephanie

I know it's weird, but I adore writing synopses. I've taught classes on them, and I always feel like a bit of a kook standing up there saying, "You don't have to hate synopses! They can be fun!" (Though if somebody tried to convince me that writing hook sentences could be fun, I would totally give them the stink eye.)

One of the things I used to hate about synopses was having to condense my 75,000 word novel into two pages of summary. I used to do all this work going through my book, writing down what happened in each scene, and then trying to string it all together to make a synopsis. The result was always a stale, boring summary of my book.

Then—despite my stale synopses—I became a published author and the pitching process became different for me. Now I could sell projects *before* I wrote them . . . but they wanted some sample chapters and a synopsis.

I thought it was going to feel like torture. I thought there was no way I could churn out a decent synopsis for a book I hadn't even written yet.

Instead, it wasn't just the easiest synopsis I had ever written, it was the most fun I'd had writing one. It felt creative! I wasn't merely reciting details of my already-penned manuscript, I was creating. I was testing plot lines. I was envisioning the ending when I'd barely written two chapters. And not only was it more fun, the synopsis was super helpful when I wrote the book. When I got stuck, I could pull it out and get back on track.

So on your next project, if you're a seat-of-the-pants writer, consider writing a couple chapters, and then taking a break to write a synopsis. Even a rough one.

Jill is more of a plotter than I traditionally am, and she has a different way of putting together her synopses. When I asked about her method, she had this to say:

I write one sentence for each of the following things to create my one-paragraph blurb. I use this blurb in my query and cover letters.

1. The introduction, where the story starts
2. The hook at the end of Act One.
3. The big twist in the middle of the book.
4. The hook at the end of Act Two.
5. The climax and conclusion

Here's my five-sentence paragraph for *The New Recruit*:

(1) A teenage boy is forced to train in a Christian spy organization that he wants nothing to do with. **(2)** When he learns that his parents were also spies and that his dad betrayed his mom, he throws himself into being the best agent he can be. **(3)** He travels to Moscow on a training mission and discovers a connection between a Russian boy and a suspicious woman. **(4)** He witnesses the Russian boy sell information to the woman, betraying the local field office. **(5)** When our hero learns that the woman plans a final attempt to infiltrate the field office server, his only way to stop her forces him to draw near to the God who he feels abandoned him years ago.

Then, to write my synopsis, I take these five sentences and stretch each into a separate paragraph, adding more detail. This gives me a rough outline of my synopsis. I only need to add a bit more to make it flow nicely. I try to keep out most of the side characters and side plots so that I don't confuse the reader. I also learned at a writers conference that it's a nice touch to put the character's name in all caps the first time you type it in a synopsis.

You can read Jill's synopsis for *The New Recruit* at the end of this chapter. Let's talk about some additional techniques for writing a good one.

Format it right

Synopses are almost always written in third person present tense. ("When Stephanie is done with work for the day, she turns off her computer and goes upstairs to play with her kids.") You *can* get creative with this . . . but you do so at your own risk. Be mindful of the synopses' purpose—communicating your story. Don't make your creativity so bedazzling that the editor or agent can't fish the story out of all that glitz.

Also, for whatever reason, synopses are always single spaced. If the agent or editor doesn't request a specific length, one to three pages is a safe guess.

Include Backstory

While in story writing it's best to sprinkle in backstory, with the synopsis, you often get to lead with it. When I write mine, the first paragraph is typically backstory and setting up the story premise.

Tell, don't show

I know, right? It's like everything you learned about novel writing, you flip for writing a synopsis. In a synopsis you *should* tell rather than show. Sentences like, "Stephanie is happy with the way she finishes up her day," would mark you as an amateur in a novel, but telling is the technique for writing a strong synopsis.

Start with your main character

I often see synopses that start with something like, "What would you do if all your friends turned into rabbits, and it was up to you to make them people again? That's precisely what happens in THE RABBIT FETCHER, a story about John Smith who . . ."

That's fine for a query letter, but in your synopsis it's better to start with something catchy about the main character. Like, "Much to his embarrassment, twelve-year-old JOHN SMITH has always been scared of rabbits."

Show off your voice

I suppose it's because synopses feel more like the technical manual to your novel than anything else, but many writers scrub their voice out of it, which makes it way drier than it should be. You want the synopsis to reflect the feel of the story. So if your story is funny, there should be hints of humor in your synopsis.

One of the best examples I've seen recently was in the synopsis of an unpublished friend of mine, Susie. In her romance novel, a group of old church ladies is trying to fix up the hero and heroine. But Susie doesn't call them a group of old church ladies, she calls them "the cupid committee." Her using that phrase tells you something about her story, doesn't it? (It also tells *me* that Susie won't be an unpublished writer for long.)

You can do this with sarcasm as well. If you have a character who's a bit snarky or sarcastic, make sure that comes through in your synopsis. Or if your synopsis is for a historical novel, throw in the occasional historical word or phrase. A little goes along way with this, but by swapping out, "It's a shame," for "'Tis a shame" you'll steep historical flavor into your synopsis.

Don't clutter it up with names

Deciding who gets named and who doesn't in a synopsis can be tricky because if you name too many, it's tough to follow. If you don't name enough, your story can feel shallow. Here are some guidelines I use for using names when writing my synopsis:

> •Main and primary characters often get first and last names used at the first mention. I just like the feel of it. I think it subtly communicates, "This character is a big deal."
> •If a character is mentioned multiple times in the synopsis, or if he plays a big role in a twist in the story, first name only.
> •If he only gets mentioned once in the synopsis, then I just call him by his relationship. (Her good friend, his teacher, his sister, etc.)

Don't tell the story in perfect chronological order

This has the feel of a chapter-by-chapter outline but without all the, "In chapter two," stuff. Unless the agent or editor has specifically asked for a chapter-by-chapter synopsis, that's not what you want.

Instead you want to sit on the various plot lines for a bit. So say throughout the story your character is having problems with her mother, but she's also having problems at work. (Your character likely has a lot more than two problems, but I'm sticking with two for simplicity's sake.) Maybe in the book the breakdown looks like this:

> **Chapter 10**—Character learns Mom has boyfriend.
> **Chapter 11**—At work, the character drops a milkshake on a customer but fortunately her boss isn't there.
> **Chapter 12**—Character fights with Mom.
> **Chapter 13**—At work, character's boss learned about milkshake and threatens to fire her if it happens again.
> **Chapter 14**—Mom tells character that she's getting remarried.
> **Chapter 15**—Character drops milkshake on customer again.

But in your synopsis, you'll group the mom stuff together, build it up to a tense point, and then cut away to the work stuff. It might look like this:

> When Character learns her mom has been dating her biology teacher, she's furious. She's even more furious when she learns they're getting married. How could her mother do this to her? Meanwhile things are horrible at work. Character drops a milkshake on a customer, and even though her boss isn't there, he hears about it from a snitch coworker. He threatens Character that if there are any more shenanigans, she'll be hanging up her apron. And when a cute boy has Character flustered, and when she drops yet another milkshake on his lap, she fears the worst.

So even though those storylines alternate on-stage time in the book, in your synopsis you want to consolidate.

Tell Your Ending

This isn't the time to hold back plot twists or your fabulous ending. You want to divulge it all because the agent or editor is trying to gauge how well your story is crafted. I often end my synopses with the feeling the character is left with, and I noticed Jill did the same thing at the end of her one-page synopsis for *The New Recruit*, which you can read on the next page.

The New Recruit
Synopsis

When two strangers appear on his front porch, SPENCER GARMOND is certain that GRANDMA ALICE GARMOND is sending him to military school for getting into too many fights. The men are Christian spies, however, who have come to recruit Spencer into their organization. He wants nothing to do with them, but Grandma Alice insists he accept his call to be a spy or enjoy life at military school.

Spencer reluctantly begins training. He makes a friend and an enemy among the other recruits, and struggles to fit in. An uncle he never knew tells him that his family has been spies for generations, including his parents. His dad sold out, and his treachery led to the death of Spencer's mother. Spencer vows to avenge his mother and works toward being the best agent ever.

He arrives in Moscow on a training mission. On a tour of the local field office, Spencer recognizes the face of a foreign woman on an assignment dossier. She has haunted his dreams for years. He prints out the paper on the woman named ANYA VSEVELODA, desperate to know who she is and why he dreamed about her.

Spencer befriends PASHA IVANOVICH, a homeless Russian boy, and notices Pasha's labyrinth tattoo. When Spencer sees Anya in a subway station, he follows her and discovers she has the same tattoo as Pasha.

Spencer's investigation leads him to a local Internet cafe where he learns about a cult called Bratva that uses the tattoo symbol for their logo. He visits Bratva headquarters to find out more and is nearly captured.

Spencer is furious when he witnesses Pasha selling information to Anya. Pasha betrayed his family like Spencer's dad betrayed his. He struggles to forgive his new friend.

Spencer finds out through conversations in a chat room that Anya plans a final attempt to infiltrate the field office server. His only way to stop her forces him to return to Bratva Headquarters and trust God who he feels abandoned him years ago.

Although Anya gets away, and Spencer is reprimanded for breaking protocol, his efforts provide valuable information into Bratva, and his experience draws him closer to God.

Before the Americans head back, a smug Anya approaches Spencer, bragging that he failed to stop her. She warns him that she knows who he is and who he is meant to become. She promises to make sure he fails.

The New Recruit is the first in a series of four novels about Spencer's experiences in the Mission League.

Compiling it All into a Book Proposal
by Jill

Once you've figured out your genre, target audience, hook, back-cover copy, and synopsis, you're well on your way to having a book proposal put together. What you include in a book proposal depends on who you're submitting to and what that editor or agent wants to see, so it's good to stay flexible. Most houses and agencies have submission guidelines on their website or listed in a writer's market book. Follow their guidelines exactly. If there are no guidelines, here are some things you might include.

Overview

Give the title, word count, genre, target audience, hook sentence, and back-cover copy. You'll want them in a format that an editor can glance at quickly, bullet points (when appropriate), and lots of white space.

You might also include a blurb about how your target readers will connect with your book's main character or what inspired your story. Here's mine from my book proposal for *RoboTales*.

> My son and I were talking books one day, and I told him we should write one together. We came up with the idea of writing fairytales for boys. The ideas were endless, as there are so many fairytales out there, but it wasn't until we came up with the title *RoboTales*, that we really got excited. Something fun, designed for boys, that could have both science fiction and fantasy elements, where the readers could gather clues in each story, learn something about science, and enjoy the adventure. And, of course, what boy doesn't love a robot dog?

Market Analysis and Competitive Titles

This is where you talk about the market and why your idea is timely. Include a list of books that are like yours, mention similar movies that have been popular, and any world events that may coincide with the release of your novel. If you have any well-known authors who've agreed to read your book for possible endorsement, list them in this area.

Synopsis

Stephanie went over how to write a synopsis earlier in this chapter.

Author Information

In this section, put a short author bio, maybe a half-page long. Stephanie talked about writing author bios earlier in this chapter.

Make sure to list any published works. If you're a published novelist, you'll include sales information on each title here. If you've only published articles or short stories, you can list them. Here are a few of my entries:

> "The Perfect Gift." Shine Brightly, December, 2007, pp. 16-17. ($35)
> "Grieved." Devo'Zine, July/August, 2007, pp. 9. ($15)

You'll also include information about your platform here. List your websites, blogs, and their stats.

Marketing and Promotion

If you have marketing ideas for your book, you can put them in this section. They're not mandatory, but it won't hurt to add them. The more of a complete package you can hand the editor, the better chance you have of getting the publishing board to say yes.

You can also mention any connections you have, like friends who work for the news, radio, or the local newspapers. Don't worry if you don't have these things. Include what you can and leave the rest off. For most debut authors, the editor or agent will mostly focus on your writing.

I posted my book proposal for *Captives* on my website. Again, it's best to stay flexible because every agency and house seems to ask for different things, but it's helpful to at least see one proposal that did its job and landed a book deal. You'll find it at this link:

http://www.jillwilliamson.com/teenage-authors/examples/

Endorsements

An endorsement is a short, positive review from a published author. Once you have a book contract, you want one of these if you can get one, but only from a well-known author in your genre. If you're writing science fiction (unless it's a science fiction romance) an endorsement from Janet Evanovich isn't going to help.

Brainstorm a list of potential endorsement candidates based on authors who write books similar to yours.

Start asking for endorsements as soon as you sign the contract. Most authors expect to get several months or so to read books for endorsement. Don't rush endorsers. You'll annoy them. If they agree to read your book, wait patiently. If you don't get the endorsement by the date you asked for it, you can send one, polite reminder email. And if they send the endorsement to you late, you can still use it, even if it's too late to go in the book.

If the author never gets back to you, don't think of it as a personal attack. Authors are busy. The mere fact that they tried to fit you in is a compliment. Be thankful. They also might not love your story. This happens. Don't keep emailing them and put them on the spot to find out.

After I signed my contract for *By Darkness Hid*, I emailed twelve authors for an endorsement. Five said yes. Three of those five actually wrote an endorsement for me. I never heard from the other two. Of the seven others, some said they'd love to but were too busy. One said he didn't like stories with telepathy and felt that his prejudice wouldn't be fair to me. A few never responded.

If you didn't get the endorsement in time for the book, what can you do with it?

-Post it on your Amazon page.
-Post it on your website.
-Add it to your press release.
-Add it to your promotional postcard or bookmark.

Wherever you post it, it can give your book instant credibility. Here's the email I used to approach potential endorsers:

> Mr. Author,
>
> I recently contracted my medieval fantasy novel with Marcher Lord Press. It will release April 1, 2009. I am seeking a possible endorsement for the book. Since you also write fantasy novels, I decided to ask you. Here is the blurb for my novel, which is called *By Darkness Hid*, book one in the *Blood of Kings* series:
>
> Blurb: Given the chance to train as a squire, kitchen servant Achan Cham hopes to pull himself out of his pitiful life and become a Kingsguard Knight. When Achan's owner learns of his training, he forces Achan to spar with the Crown Prince, more of a death sentence than an honor. As Achan struggles to serve the prince without being maimed, strange voices in his head cause him to fear he's going mad. He travels with a procession escorting the prince to a council presentation. Along the way, their convoy is attacked. Achan is wounded, arrested, and escapes from prison only to be brought back before the rulers of the land. There he discovers a secret about himself he never believed possible.
>
> Would you consider reading the book for a possible endorsement? You can read a sample chapter to see if you like the writing style at this link: www.jillwilliamson.com/books/blood-of-kings-trilogy/by-darkness-hid-sample-chapter
>
> Endorsements that are received by February 28, 2009 will be listed in the front of the book. If you are willing, I can send you an advanced reader copy or a .pdf copy.
>
> Thanks for considering this.
>
> Jill Williamson

Notice that I gave as much information as I could. The publisher and release date, a blurb, the date the publisher needs it by, and a link to sample chapters. I also was very polite and in no way assumed that the author would say yes. If you approach endorsements in this manner, you'll increase your chances of success.

A book proposal is your opportunity to make a sales pitch for your book. It's your chance to say everything you want to say to editors about why your book will be successful. Take the time to get everything just right.

Step 4
Finding a Good Literary Agent

A note from Stephanie

My search for an agent was time consuming, heartbreaking, and full of frustration. And it was a search for *an* agent. Not *the* agent. I was up for anyone who would take me on, and I think that's a normal feeling for an unpublished writer. When we're told again and again how hard it is to find an agent, it doesn't feel like we have any right to be picky. It feels like we should be grateful to whoever is willing to take a chance on us.

And even though I knew in my pre-agented days that a bad agent, or even an iffy agent, wasn't a good idea, I didn't fully understand how damaging it could be. Something I urge you to be mindful of is that literary agents have a reputation tied to them. It's a reputation that causes editors to either pick up their phones when that agent is calling them . . . or to let it go into voicemail. And whatever their reputation is, it affects you. (You can see how that plays out in Chapter 22 when the merits of *The Crowl* were being tossed around.)

I'm now represented by my first-choice agent. The second time around, I was smart enough to know to ask questions like:

- What kind of career guidance do you offer your clients?
- How many YA authors do you represent?
- Do you prefer to be contacted through email or the phone? How long should I expect to wait for a response?

But something I wish I had asked her during that initial phone conversation was what *her* goals are as an agent. What does she hope to accomplish? And what does she need from me for that to happen?

Understanding an agent's business philosophies and ambitions can help you to determine if this is indeed the right business relationship for you. I urge you to be patient. And though it's tempting to be desperate—I certainly was—I urge you to believe you're deserving of good representation, all the while continuing to grow your writing craft.

A note from Jill

An agent should be an author's helper. Someone who can do things the author cannot. Once you've written a few books, an agent is crucial. There's just too much going on to handle it all on your own. New authors, however, don't necessarily need an agent.

I know. I know. I didn't believe that when I started out. Everyone also said, "Don't sign on with the first agent to come along." But I did. And my first agent was a good agent. He did a good job. But we were not the best match. And parting ways was difficult for me. Plus, I didn't do the parting the way I should have. And it was really hard. I wish I could go back and do things better and smarter, but I can't.

So, please don't be in a hurry to get an agent! Get to know lots of people in the industry. Make friends. And when the time is right, you will find the right agent.

I did. And when I met the agent I have now, it was the perfect match. We get along very well. She understands me, she knows my genre, and best of all, she likes the speculative books I write.

What could be better?

> When I finally find that one willing agent, I'll have found my prize in the Cracker Jack box.
> –Richelle E. Goodrich

25 Literary Agents

How to Find Literary Agents
by Jill

Because there are so many aspiring writers out there, there are lots of people who prey on a writer's desire to be published, from vanity presses who pretend to be otherwise, to people who claim to be agents but have no credentials to their name.

You don't have to pay a dime to an agent until the agent makes a sale. A good agent will ask for 15 percent of your sales, no more, no less. You also don't have to sign the rights to your book away or anything like that.

Agents don't represent every type of book, so you need to seek out one who represents the type of book you've written. Here are some ways you can find agents and learn what he or she represents.

1. Buy a copy of the *Writer's Market* (or find one at your public library), and look through the agent section, making notes or highlighting the agents who deal in your genre. If you're writing for kids, you'll need the *Children's Writers and Illustrator's Market* instead. There is also a *Christian Writer's Market Guide* for those targeting that specialty market. All these books are updated annually, so try and find the right book for your needs and the most recent copy

you can.

2. Google something like "writers conference, looking for, YA horror" (or whatever your genre is). Sometimes writers' conferences post which agents are attending and what they will be looking for. Google some variations of keywords until you get a nice list of names. Then you can Google those agents until you find their agency website and their submission guidelines.

3. Attend a writers' conference and talk to agents there.

4. Look at the acknowledgement section of books in your genre, and see if the author thanked their agent, then Google the agent's name.

5. Ask your writer friends who their agent is. This is another good reason to join some professional writers' organizations, so you can start networking with other writers.

But don't expect your author friend to get their agent to like your book. All your friend can do is tell you who her agent is and maybe ask if her agent will take a look at your query. The decision is in the agent's hands alone. Don't sever author friendships because an agent rejects you. It's not your friend's fault. It's not personal, either.

Try not to be in a hurry. I know it's frustrating. You've worked really hard to complete that manuscript, and now you're ready to get connected and sell it. But the wrong agent can tie up your manuscript for years—or sell it to the wrong house.

It's better to have no agent than to have a bad agent.

Make a list of the qualities you're looking for in an agent. Every author is different. We all want an agent who will sell our books, but even the best agents get rejections from publishers. So how do you know if the two of you might be a good fit?

Try and meet the agent first. It might be impossible, but there's a feeling you get when you meet someone face-to-face. It's an important thing to trust. Do you like the agent? Or does something about them bug you?

If an agent has offered to represent you, here are some things to consider:

1. Does the agent have the connections you need? Ask for a list of recent sales. Did those books come from publishers that your book might be right for? If not, it could be that this agent doesn't know the

market for your book.

2. Ask for the names of at least two of the agent's clients so that you can email them and ask for feedback on working with the agent. This is standard procedure and won't be seen as a rude request.

3. Ask about his process and what he does for his clients. Does he insist on helping edit your manuscript before he sends it out? Does he do career building? Do you want an agent who does these things or not? Every agent is different. Know what you're looking for.

5. What kind of contract is he offering? Many agents have a thirty-day contract, which enables both parties to sever the relationship within thirty-days if one is unhappy. This is a nice thing because you're not locked into working with an agent for years.

6. Ask if he plans to represent only this book or if he's interested in other books you have written or will write.

7. Does he communicate in a manner that works for you? Some agents are phone people. Some are email people. Many are way too busy to talk unless it's an emergency. If you're looking for a mentor in your agent, be sure and ask if he does that sort of thing.

I wanted a female agent because I tend to have a difficult time emotionally working that closely with men. That's just one of my quirks. More than anything, I wanted an agent who loved my writing. There are many agents who'll see that you can write and believe they can sell your book. And that's good. But you need an agent you can work with for a long time. Be patient. The right agent will come.

The Publishing Auction

One thing an agent can do for you that you can't do for yourself is put your novel on auction. This means that several publishers are interested in your book and willing to go to auction over the right to buy it. It's about the most exciting thing that can happen to an author. It is more common in the nonfiction market, so for a fiction book to go to auction is sort of rare.

Your agent would be the one who decides how to run the auction, and there are different methods of going about it. The author doesn't always choose the highest bidder. There's more than money to consider when signing a book contract, so the agent and author will look at the entire offer and choose the best.

This is every author's dream.

It's also every agent's dream.

How to Query
by Jill

When you get to the point of wanting to query an agent or editor, you'll need to write a query letter as a means of introducing yourself. Like Stephanie talked about in chapter twenty-four, when we say querying, we're talking about a short email you send to agents telling them about you, your book, and inviting them to read more.

These days almost everything is done through email rather than snail mail. But how do you know? You find out in a writer's market guide, by reading the submission guidelines the agency or publishing house provides on their website, or when an agent or editor extends an invitation.

Even though you're emailing, professionalism still matters. An email query or cover letter should be just as professional as a snail mail one. These are business communications to prospective employers and should be treated as such.

The Email Query Letter

A query letter is a one-page document introducing you and the story/article/book you have written. It's a sales pitch.

What agents and editors **don't** want to see in a query:

- More than one page! (If you think your email might be too long, type it in a word processing program first, then copy and paste into your email.)
- The wrong name or misspelling of the agent or editor's name.
- Your life story.
- That your mom loves your book.
- A list of books you like and why.
- Your opinion of how great of a writer you think you are.
- How this is your first try writing and it was so easy.
- That you are the next J. K. Rowling.
- That God gave you this story, that it's His will that it get published, and they'll be sorry if they turn you down!

What they **do** want to see:

- One page!
- The editor or agent's name, spelled correctly.
- A professional and spell-checked letter.
- A reminder if they met you and asked you to submit. (Agents and editors meet a lot of people. You can't expect them to remember every name, so a reminder is helpful.)
- Your one-sentence hook or tag line.
- A back-cover copy-type description of your project.
- Your word count and genre.
- That your book is complete. (If it's fiction, don't bother sending a query if your book is not finished. You're not ready to sell your story until it has been finished and polished.)
- A small paragraph about you and your credentials.

Try to stick to this format: A paragraph or two for the hook and book blurb, a paragraph for the information about yourself, and a closing paragraph. If you've met the agent or editor and have an inside joke, reference it. If not, stay professional. Let's take a look at some examples on the following pages.

> To: susan.love@romancebooksrus.com
> Subject: Query, romantic suspense, Mysterious Stranger
>
> Dear Ms. Love,
>
> What starts out as a bad day sends Katie Willis into the arms of the man of her dreams—or so she thinks. My novel, *Mysterious Stranger*, takes the reader on a wild ride of suspense, danger, and romance. It is complete at approximately 80,000 words.
>
> Always in the wrong place at the wrong time, Katie Willis becomes a hostage in a bank robbery. Another hostage, Brooks Gibson, rescues her and they flee. The bank robbers want their eye witnesses out of the picture, however, and Katie and Brooks are forced to go on the run. As they journey toward the state line, Katie starts to fall for Brooks until events unfold that cause her to doubt his intentions. Could he be involved with the bad guys? Katie struggles to discover the true identity of this mysterious stranger.
>
> I worked for six years as a vault supervisor for Bank of America, which gives me great insight about bank security. I am in two critique groups, one local and one online. Both groups have extensively critiqued my manuscript. I am a member of Romance Writers of America. *Mysterious Stranger* is my first novel.
>
> Thank you for considering, *Mysterious Stranger*. I look forward to hearing from you.
>
> Sincerely,
>
> Beth Author

    This email is short and sweet. The subject line includes only the pertinent information: that this is a query, the genre, and the title. The email itself starts out with a hook and informs the editor that the book is complete and how long it is.

    Next Beth gives a tight, one-paragraph summary that leaves the editor hanging. It's good to do this in a query letter.

    Then there's a short paragraph that includes mention of Beth's experience working at Bank of America. That's important. Since she's writing about a bank robbery, her work experience gives her first-hand knowledge of the inner-workings of a bank, which should make the story more believable. She also mentions a few of her writing activities, just enough to let the editor know that she's putting time into her writing career.

And she closes with a thank you.

When I was working as an editor, I would have been thrilled to receive such a concise query, and I would have emailed the author back and asked for three sample chapters.

Here's the query letter for what became *By Darkness Hid*. I submitted this letter with a sample chapter to an editor at a writers' conference, and he bought the book. Paper business letters should also include a header. If you need to write a paper letter to submit at a conference, Google "formatting a business letter" for help.

Dear Mr. Gerke:

Bloodvoicing is a gift, an endowment to communicate from one gifted mind to another. For a slave to have the gift is unheard of, yet one slave has more power than all the rest combined.

A young adult fantasy novel, *Prince Gidon* tells the story of two young people with a unique, ancestral ability to speak to, and hear, the minds of others: a slave forced to serve a prince who wants him dead and a young woman masquerading as a boy to avoid a forced marriage. The novel alternates between their points of view until their stories collide on the battlefield.

Judging from the steady stream of medieval fantasy novels on the bestseller lists, young adult readers remain fascinated by epic fantasy adventures. Projects similar to mine like *Eragon*, *Dragonspell*, *Chosen*, and *The Bark of the Bog Owl* bring a fun mixture of fantasy and faith to the Christian market.

I have two books contracted. *Jason Farms* will release in spring 2009 (a YA novel from The Wild Rose Press), and *A Mango and a Mud Church* will release in 2010 (an "all reader" book from Beacon Hill Press). My articles have appeared in *Brio*, *Brio & Beyond*, *Shine Brightly*, and *Devo'Zine*. My husband and I have worked with teens in the youth pastor role for nine years. I researched medieval life and swordsmanship for three months before writing this novel and can provide a works cited page.

If the premise appeals to you, I would be happy to meet with you to discuss the project. My agent, So and So at Such and Such Literary Agency, can provide a marketing proposal and the complete 96,000-word manuscript.

Sincerely,
Jill Williamson

When I met with the editor, he told me this was one of the best query letters he'd seen. What impressed him was my opening hook and how I smoothly went right into my case as to why my story would work in the current market. I'd written a compelling hook, and I had done my homework. If you do the same, you'll have an easier time getting an editor's interest.

The Email Cover Letter

An email cover letter accompanies a submission to an agent or editor. It's not so much a pitch as it is a reminder of who you are and why you are emailing them something. If an editor or agent responds to your query asking for sample chapters, you would send an email cover letter along with them. If an author friend recommended you to her agent and the agent told you to email your manuscript, you would send an email cover letter along too.

It's a good idea to put the hook from your query in the cover letter, in case the editor or agent doesn't remember or has never heard it.

The first example is a cover letter I wrote for an agent who requested my first three chapters. It's a bit long, but it worked for me. A month later, she requested the full.

To: agent.chappel@literaryagency.com
Subject: Query, young adult, The New Recruit

Dear Ms. Chappel:

I enjoyed meeting with you at Mount Hermon Christian Writers Conference. I appreciate your willingness to review my proposal for *The New Recruit*, a young adult novel of approximately 80,000 words.

The New Recruit pits the powers of darkness against undercover agents working for God. Teens love action and adventure and have eaten up similar spy projects such as; Anthony Horowitz's Alex Rider Series, Frank Peretti's Veritas Project series, MGM's *Agent Cody Banks*, and Miramax's *Spy Kids*.

When two strangers appear on his front porch, Spencer Garmond is certain that his Grandma Alice is sending him to military school for getting into too many fights. The men are Christian spies . . .

> . . . however, who have come to recruit Spencer into their organization. He wants nothing to do with them, but Grandma Alice insists he accept his call to be a spy or enjoy life at military school.
>
> Spencer travels to Moscow with other agents-in-training and stumbles onto a mysterious case. A local runaway betrayed the field office by selling information to a suspicious woman. When Spencer discovers the woman plans to infiltrate the field office database, he must stop her from exposing the secrets of his counter-cult organization.
>
> My husband and I have worked with teens in the youth pastor role for eight years. I also run a website and critique group for teen authors. I participate in two online critique groups, both of which have extensively critiqued my manuscript. My work for teens has appeared in *Brio*, *Brio & Beyond*, *Shine Brightly*, and *Devo'Zine*.
>
> Thank you for considering *The New Recruit*. I look forward to hearing from you.
>
> Sincerely,
> Jill Williamson

When that agent requested the full manuscript, I sent a much shorter cover letter along with the attachment. She didn't need such a long reminder of who I was this time. Also, I changed my subject line. I took out the word "query" and replaced it with "requested materials." This is good because the agent will see that and it will stand out as something she asked for. Never use the words "requested materials" if the agent did not request them from you.

> To: agent.chappel@literaryagency.com
> Subject: Requested materials, young adult, The New Recruit full manuscript
>
> Dear Ms. Chappel:
>
> Thanks for your interest in *The New Recruit*. I've enclosed the full manuscript for your review. Should you be interested, I can provide you with a marketing and series proposal.
>
> I look forward to hearing from you.
>
> Sincerely,
>
> Jill Williamson

Work hard on your query and cover letters before you send them out. Have your critique partners help you. As long as you are clear and professional, you'll get the job done.

Good luck! Let us know what happens.

> A rejection is nothing more than a necessary step in the pursuit of success.
> –Bo Bennett

26 Dealing with Rejection

by Stephanie

Rejection is part of the writing life. Really, it's just part of LIFE. But since writing is a choice we make, when the rejection (or the fear of rejection) grows intense and strong, it's easy to think, "Why am I even doing this?!"

This is normal. All writers go through it. Even those writers you love and admire.

I encourage you to accept that rejection is part of this path. Try to view the rejections you get from agents and editors as preparation for mean-spirited Amazon reviews or bloggers who bash books for sport. Or for the really tough ones—the reviewers who offer criticism that you maybe, sorta, if-you're-being-100-percent-honest, agree with.

When rejection comes—especially when you're just starting out—it's completely normal to feel like the victim of a drive-by shooting. The first time I queried literary agents, I was living in an apartment by myself. It's not too far from where I live now, and when I drive by there I always think about standing in the little mail room, ripping open the responses, and then racing back to my apartment before I burst into tears.

In the beginning, I put a lot of pressure on myself to take rejection like a pro. To not let it bother me. Don't do that. It's okay to cry and be upset. Thick skin takes time to build and even now I'm not so sure how thick mine is.

When you get a rejection do not, whatever you do, write a nasty blog post about who rejected you or vent about it on Facebook. It's a bad, bad, *bad* idea. Agents and editors often Google authors who they're interested in working with. You do *not* want to be caught writing something nasty like that.

Instead, have a friend you can call when you hear bad news. This doesn't have to be a writer friend, but he or she does need to "get it." I've never discussed this with the person I call, but we have a silent agreement that in that initial conversation, WE are not the problem, nor is our book. THEY have the problem. THEY are short sighted. THEY just passed up a huge opportunity.

After the sting of the rejection has worn off a bit, we might allow that maybe, just maybe, the editor was right about a particular thing she said. But only that! The rest is hogwash! Oh, well, she *did* make kind of a good point when she said such-and-such . . . and how could we incorporate this suggestion into the manuscript, because that's really not a bad idea. In fact, hadn't we already decided that this character was a bit flat . . . ?

Those conversations are the best. I encourage you to build that kind of relationship with someone.

So if you can't blast the editor or agent on the internet, how *should* you respond when you get a rejection letter? Write them a thank you note. On real paper, with a real stamp, and all that good stuff. You tell them thank you for taking the time to look at your submission, thank you for the feedback (if they provided any), and you stick it in the mail within a day of the initial rejection.

This won't change their mind, of course, but it takes away the power the rejection has over you. I don't know the science behind that statement, but when I write my "Thanks for that great rejection!" notes, it feels like closure. I can breathe better after I drop it in the box.

The same goes for when I receive emails from not-so-happy readers. I never respond right away, but within a week I put a smile on my face and type out a, "Thanks for taking the time to email me!" kind of email. I always feel freer after clicking SEND.

Of course your rejection might be coming from a contest rather than an agent/editor. Back in 2008, I entered the first chapter of *Me, Just Different* in ACFW's Genesis contest. My judges were kind, but they were also honest. The biggest complaint was they hated Skylar. After a month of grumbling, I realized they were right. And without their criticism, I wouldn't have done my rewrite and *Me, Just Different* never would have been published.

This isn't to say that everything you read in a rejection letter is going to be good advice, so if something feels off or wrong to you, even after you've calmed down, it's fine to ignore it. As we've said elsewhere in the book, if you continue to hear the same feedback from readers, it's something you'll want to pay attention to.

A Note From Jill on Rejection

One of the first books on craft I read was Stephen King's *On Writing*. The number of times teenaged Stephen had been rejected before he finally published something was probably over a hundred.

So I got it in my head that I might get rejected at least one hundred times too, and if I wanted this thing badly enough, I was going to have to deal with that. So, when I got my first rejection, I danced. Only ninety-nine to go, I told myself. Whoo hoo!

That philosophy kept me thinking positive about rejections. It gave me the chance to learn to write without putting all my hopes in every email I sent out. And, yeah. I was still disappointed when I got rejected, but it helped to remind myself that I was learning and these things take time.

The cool thing? I only received about sixteen rejections before I published my first article.

Something else to remember as you wrestle with rejection is that agents, editors, contest judges, etc. are not rejecting *you*, just your book. I know how personal your projects feel because mine feel the same way. It's important to regularly remind yourself that they aren't calling *you* a self-absorbed brat, just your character.

When you get a rejection, or a particularly harsh critique from your writing group, don't be afraid to step back and indulge in something that recharges you. Then get your brave on and put yourself out there again.

Step 5
Building a Career

Be a Writer Who Grows
by Stephanie

Something I both love and hate about writing is that it's an ongoing journey. I'm never going to be a perfect writer. There will always be ways I can grow and deepen my skills. There will always be more practicing to do.

Which is why it deeply saddens me on the occasion that I come across a know-it-all writer . . . who has only been writing for a couple years. If that.

They ask for advice, but they don't want advice—they want validation that they should totally be published by now. They want you to critique their work, but when you do, they argue with every issue you bring up. You recommend a craft book or an online class that you took and found helpful, and they tell you they don't need it; they're already exemplifying all that advice in their manuscripts.

Sometimes, in extreme situations, they offer paid critiques or have a blog that hands out writing advice . . . even though they've never even finished a story.

You don't want to be that person, do you? Neither do I. And anytime I notice myself slipping into unteachable behavior, I try hard to shift my perspective and think, "What can I learn from this?"

These are nine behaviors I've observed in writers who continue to grow both as a writer and as someone who contributes to the publishing industry:

They keep reading.

There's a sad amount of published writers who say writing makes them too busy to read, or that they just can't enjoy a book because of their inner editor. Not only is this just not a smart move professionally (you've got to keep tabs on what's going on in your genre) but it smacks of arrogance.

They keep learning about writing.

Even after being a published writer since 2009, when I take writing classes, listen to podcasts, or read craft books, I almost always walk away with *something* I can apply. I've certainly sat through some writing classes that were so boring, basic, or biased that I walked out without having learned a thing, but that's rare.

They spend more time writing than they do talking about writing.

Building onto that last item, it's easy to slip into the trap of spending most your time *learning* about writing and *talking* about writing and *thinking* about writing without actually, you know, *writing*. I've definitely been guilty of this. When Jill and I were putting together the first edition of this book on top of maintaining the Go Teen Writers blog, I felt the balance tip too far away from actually writing. Maybe a season of life will look like that for you too, but don't make it a lifestyle.

They don't compare.

I don't think we mean to do it, but us writers tend to group ourselves into different categories: Writers who haven't been writing long. Writers who have written a few books and seem close to getting an agent. Writers who are self-published. Writers who have an agent but no contract. Writers who have a contract. Writers who are multi-published.

The danger with this comes when our perception of being "ahead" leads to us being jealous or angry when another writer who is "behind" us achieves something.

When Roseanna White and I met, we were in similar places in our writing journey. Both of us had loved writing for a long time, had written as teens, and we were both at the place where our writing was close to publishable. At the conference where we met, Roseanna walked away with an agent who was excited about her and an editor who loved her. Meanwhile, I walked away with some mediocre leads and a very tired back. (I was quite pregnant.)

But in an odd turn of events, I wound up with a surprise agent and a three-book deal, all within six months, while Roseanna had to bide her time for a few *years* while she waited for her first contract.

Then several years later, I went through a seven-year drought between traditional contracts while Roseanna got several contract offers out of the blue.

If we'd insisted on comparing ourselves to each other all those years, we would have become two bitter writers. That wouldn't have been as much fun as being friends has been, nor would we have had the support we've both needed on our writing journeys.

Nobody wins with the comparison game. We're all on our own unique writing journey, and it's best to embrace yours and learn from others when you can, whether they seem to be ahead of you or behind.

They accept that all feedback is a gift.

My pastor once talked about a time that he was deeply hurt by a critique. He went to his mentor, wanting what we would all want in that moment—to be assured that the other person was a moron and that he should just ignore the feedback. Instead his mentor told him, "All feedback is a gift."

I don't like having my mistakes pointed out. (I'm much more fragile than I would like to be.) I want to have caught all my errors, and I want my manuscript to be perfect. I'm learning to embrace this idea, though, that all feedback is a gift. It all reveals something—even if it's just our heart or the character of the person who is critiquing for us—and we're wise to be thankful for it even when it hurts.

I love how Jack Deere puts it: "That which offends the mind reveals the heart."

They try something new with each book.

I used to think that as I wrote books, I would eventually land on My Perfect Book-Writing System. A system that made my first drafts structurally sound, my edits organized, and my hair from turning increasingly white.

But I think even if such a system exists—which I'm no longer convinced it does because book writing is just a messy, creative business—there would be a danger in it. When we think we have it all figured out, that's when we stop considering how we can improve. I learned from bestselling novelist Angela Hunt to intentionally look for something new that I can try with each book. There are countless new things you could try. A character who's darker than you normally write. Writing in first person instead of third. A different method of plotting. Present tense instead of past. More (or fewer) point of view characters. The list of new things to try is as limitless as your creativity.

They shut down thoughts like, "I should be published by now."

I have been an impatient, pre-published writer. I would read published books that didn't seem nearly as good as mine. Or writers who had written only one book were getting published when I was on my fourth and didn't seem any closer. *When is it ever going to be my turn? I should be published by now!*

Have you felt this way before? Let's say you're right. Your writing is excellent and that editor truly just didn't "get it." But what do you gain from the mindset of, "I should be published by now"? Nothing. This thought—or variations of it like, "My book should be selling better!" or "I should have another contract by now!"—has never produced a single healthy thought or action.

What does produce something useful is a question like, "Why am I not yet published?" This question can actually generate answers that help you. Is your genre a tougher sell than others? Is the opening of your story not interesting enough? Or have you just not been able to access the right editor or agent?

They don't tear down other writers.

As with the behavior above, it just doesn't do anything positive for you. Maybe the book really does have a sucky plot and bad characters and a predictable ending. But if it sold to a publisher, or if it's on bestseller charts, it's smart to ask why. What is it about this book that reaches people? What can you learn from it?

They don't burn bridges.

If someone in the industry—an agent, an editor, a published writer, or even an unpublished writer in your critique group—gives you a "gift of feedback" that you would've preferred not to unwrap, the wise writer says something like, "Thank you. I'll think about that," and doesn't (publicly) get more emotional than that.

Writers, agents, editors, and everyone else who make the book world go round talk to each other, so guard your reputation by being kind, honest, and considerate to all.

Even writers who are very careful with agents and editors often burn bridges with other writers. Sometimes they do it in the name of honesty, like, "It just wouldn't be fair for me to write you anything more than a 1-star shredding review on Amazon. My integrity is at stake here!"

While the literary community does value honesty, you'll get much further if your honesty is spoken with kindness and grace.

Remember Why You Write!
by Jill

I started out writing with a goal of making a difference with my stories. When I realized I had so much to learn, that distracted me from my original goal. Publication became the new goal. Getting published would be my way of measuring success—of proving I was good enough to go back to that original goal of making a difference with my stories.

My logic was a bit flawed. Anyone can make a difference in the world at any moment. One doesn't need to have a published book to do so. But publication became my obsession, and I didn't stop until I found success.

Looking back on my journey, I see myself hustling for my worth. I'm old enough now to know that drive was fueled by a lie I believed. You know how we come up with lies that our characters believe about themselves? It works because people do it in real life too. One of my lies is that if I work hard enough and have lots to show for myself, I will matter. The world cannot prove otherwise.

But that's just not true. It's not what I do in life that gives me worth. I matter already. I have worth because I exist. And so do you.

Now that I'm able to separate the lie from my motivation, yes, I still want to write stories that make a difference in the world. But now I can relax and not stress about how that's achieved or worry about measuring my numbers. My writing will impact who it is meant to impact. I don't get to control that. I don't have to. That's not my job. (Hooray!) My job is to be obedient to my calling as a writer, to write the very best books I can, and to communicate my "make a difference" message to those who read my stories.

Now, some people are called to write one book and that's all. One story that's on their heart. They write it and put it out into the world, and they're done. Others have more to say. If the latter sounds like you, then read on for my advice for career authors.

Write

The only way you will improve your writing craft is to write books. So write. Rewrite. Edit. Finish. Then repeat the process. Write another book. And another. You can also write blog posts, articles, or short stories. Just be sure to write, write, and write some more. No matter what, keep on writing.

Read

Stephanie talked about this already, but I agree so much that I must chime in. If you're not reading, you're not participating in your own industry. Read other writers' books. Buy new books. Request that your local library order books, then check them out and read them. Get books circulating. Join in the conversations about popular books. Share books you liked with your family, friends, and fellow readers. Talk about them on social media. Make reading and talking about books part of your life. Give books as gifts. Go all in.

Build Relationships

I prefer this subject to what the industry calls "platform." Forget the numbers of your social media followers or how many email subscribers you have. Just go out into the world and make friends. Build relationships. Be kind and supportive. Give more than you take. This also goes for your readers and for other authors, editors, agents, and people who can bring about marketing connections.

Author Mary Weber said that publishing is not all about who you know. But it is all about people. And that those people out in the world want to be seen (not used) just like you and me.

So don't just push your books or your email sign-up. Don't continually count your Instagram followers and stress when the numbers go down. Make it your goal to care about all people, whether or not they follow back or buy your book.

Live

You only get one life, so live it! True, the vast majority of writers are introverts, but that's no excuse to be a hermit. It's important to know yourself—what you can and can't handle. If you go out and have a busy, people-filled, extrovert kind of day, you might need to stay home the following day to unwind (recover). But get out there in the world and experience the beauty and wonder of people and this planet we all live on. Purposely avoiding what is difficult for you is an excuse that can keep you from experiencing life, so find ways to take baby steps. Do it scared! You'll be okay. It will be worth it.

It's also important to rest. Whether you traditionally publish, self-publish, or end up working as a hybrid author, you'll be an entrepreneur. When you work for yourself, it's easy to fall into work-a-holic patterns. Don't do that! Remember that writing is a job. You need to set work hours and off-the-clock hours. Sure, there will be days when you need to work some overtime, but don't make that the norm. Don't live life at your computer. Fight hard to rest. Make family and friends a priority. What does it matter if you spend your life putting stories out into the world to change lives when those closest to you feel abandoned? Set priorities and live by them.

Grow

Stephanie talked about growing as an author. I echo everything she said. It's so important to your career. But I also encourage you to grow as a person.

Take note of your bad habits and work at changing them. Discover the lies you believe and learn how to set yourself free from that bondage. Find things that interest you and learn. Grow stronger and healthier in your mindsets. Extend grace. All this will help you see people better and, as a result, write stronger characters. It will make you more authentic, and it will mature you as a human being.

Remember Why You Write

It's easy to get caught up in the numbers and what feels like success or failure. Remind yourself daily why you write, for what audience, and what you want to say. If you have to, write a mission statement, print it out, and keep it by your computer. Read it every morning before you start working. Here is mine.

Why I Write

> I write for readers who are struggling to either discover or remember who they are. I write to show people that we are all human, we are all fallible, and we need grace. I write to communicate these truths, knowing that the truth can set my readers free from the lies they believe. When my readers close one of my books, I want them to feel their value and know they are loved.

Along with the reason you write, I hope, is that you also enjoy it. Don't work so hard that you take all the joy out of writing. Having the ability to create is a gift, and while it is hard work, it should also be fun and rewarding.

Repeat

Do these things again and again. That's all there is to it except to stay humble and teachable, because those qualities are necessary for one who wields the power of the written word. It is a privilege to be able to speak into people's lives. Readers let us into their minds, the most private place anyone can go. Respect that gift and use it wisely.

In Closing . . .

We wish we could clean up the road for you.

We wish we could break down those obstacles like the hole in your story that you can't seem to figure out, or the nerves tightening your gut when you pitch to an agent at a conference, or the bite of a rejection from a dream publisher. We wish we could remove those horrible moments, like when you spend a year writing and perfecting a story . . . only to find out that an established author *just* released one that's eerily similar.

As much as we wish to, we can't prepare the road for you. But we can prepare *you* for the road.

That's what we strive to do at GoTeenWriters.com, and it's why we wrote this book. We know the tenacity it takes to stick with writing, and we know the heartache involved. We know sometimes you'll wish you *could* quit. You'll wish you didn't love writing so much, that writing stories didn't make you feel so complete and purposeful, because you're tired of reworking this story, and you just want to hang up your pen or close down your word processor forever.

We get that.

(Chocolate sometimes helps, by the way.)

But much like the characters that you send out on journeys, you have your own unique quest to go on. You have your own story to live, and writing is part of your story. And what's a good story without conflict, twists, and obstacles?

You want to be a writer. Don't take shortcuts.

Because when you:

- Squelch your pride while you listen to your critique group review your book,
- Go over your manuscript with a red pen *yet again*,
- Scrap that beginning that isn't working and start over,
- Pay for a quality freelance editor instead of a vanity press,
- Sit down and write, even when you don't feel like it,
- Save your allowance for a writers' conference,
- Set aside that first manuscript and start a new one,

- Send out another batch of queries to literary agents you've researched,
- Keep on writing despite all the rejections you've received,

That is when you're respecting the journey you're on rather than looking for shortcuts. That's when you're living a good story.

Dare to dream on.

With encouragement,

                                Stephanie and Jill

Extras:
Lists and Resources

The Go Teen Writers Self-Editing Checklist

This is meant to be a resource for your personal editing use, not a replacement for a professional editor.

Macro Edit

Plot

Story's Beginning
- Is my story problem established early? Why should the reader care?
- Have I shown my main character in his home world?
- Do I establish my main character's goal?
- Is my inciting incident strong?
- Did I present my main character with an invitation to go on a journey?
- Have I given my main character a compelling reason to choose the journey?
- Do the stakes increase throughout act one?

Story's Middle
- Does my main character have multiple people, places, activities, objects, etc. to pursue and fight for?
- Does my story build in a way that feels natural? ("Because this happened, now this happens.")
- Are my plot twists surprising yet logical?
- Have I imposed deadlines or ticking clocks on my characters to increase their urgency?
- How is my balance of good and bad things that happen to my characters?
- Do I have a big middle scene where my main character has a moment of introspection?
- Does the midpoint scene change the course of action for the main character?

- Do the obstacles following the midpoint push my main character toward the climax of the story?
- Have I created a clear disaster that leads to an "all hope is lost" moment for my character?
- Are the other characters (antagonists and support characters) active throughout the middle?

Story's End
- Does my main character experience a battle of some sort?
- Does my main character experience a convincing win or loss?
- Does my main character and antagonist drive the action in the concluding scenes?
- Does my conclusion feel surprising but logical?
- How does my *denoument* wrap up the story?
- What emotion am I leaving the reader with at the end?

Characters

Main Character(s)
- Does my MC have a goal?
- Do I know why this is his goal?
- Do others oppose his goal?
- What is his inner desire? (Love, respect, honor, etc.)
- What lie does he believe?
- What is the origin of this lie? How has it been reinforced to this character?
- What truth does he need?
- Does he have multiple people, places, or objects he cares about?

Antagonist(s)
- Does my antagonist have a goal?
- Do I know why this is his goal?
- Do others oppose his goal?
- What is his inner desire? (Love, respect, honor, etc.)

- What lie does he believe?
- What is the origin of this lie? How has it been reinforced to this character?
- What truth does he need?
- Does he have multiple people, places, or objects he cares about?
- Does he actively work to stop my main character?

Other major characters
- Do they have goals?
- Do I know why these are their goals?
- Do others oppose their goals?
- Do they believe in a lie?
- What is the origin of this lie? How has it been reinforced to this character?
- What truths do they need?
- Why are they necessary to the main character's story?
- Do they oppose or challenge my main character's worldview?

Setting

- Have I taken time to consider my main character's feelings about the setting?
- What needs to be researched still?
- What are the "laws" for my setting or magic and are they consistent with each other? (Applies mostly to fantasy/sci-fi.)

Theme

- Did any themes grow organically when I wrote the story? If so, what are they?
- Is there a way I can draw them out further?
- Is there a symbol I can use?
- Is this a theme my antagonist embraces as well or no?

Micro Edit

Scene Structure

- Does this scene impact the plot? If I cut it, would it matter?
- Does this scene build on the previous scene? Is the story progressing in a logical way?
- Do I open the scene in a compelling way that makes the reader curious about what will happen?
- Am I telling this story from the correct point of view?
- Do I provide context for my readers? (Who, what, when, where, why?)
- Do I end my scene in a way that makes my readers want to read the next scene?

Point of View

- Did I do a good job picking my POV character for each scene?
- Did I share anything that the POV character wouldn't know? Do they make too many assumptions about what other characters think?
- Do I jump into anyone else's thoughts *or* do I try too hard to broadcast the thoughts and feelings of another character in the scene?
- How is my balance of inner monologue? Am I letting the reader draw close to the character?

Backstory and Flashbacks

- Did I over-explain anything in this scene?
- Did I tell the backstory from the POV character's worldview?
- If a flashback is used, did I put it at a time that makes sense?

Dialogue

- Did I punctuate my dialogue in a way that makes my meanings clear?
- Did my characters use different words and phrases from each other?
- Have I considered this conversation from the views of all participants?
- Run a search for "said," "asked," and other dialogue tags I use often. Is there an action tag or thought beat that would work better?
- Why is my character saying this *now*? Why does she feel this is the right/best time?
- Are there places where I info dump in my dialogue? Pay close attention to spots where I refer to time. ("Since today is Thursday, your assignment is due in two days.")
- In group conversations, how is the pacing? Is everyone pulling their own weight in the conversation?

Telling and Showing

- Run a search for telling words: notice, found, spotted, experienced, looked, feeling, felt, watched, wondered, listened, tried, seemed, and thought. Did I use these words well? Or did I rely on them for telling the story instead of showing it?
- Search for telling adverbs. Am I saying "he walked quickly" when I could say "he rushed?"
- Run a search for the phrase "with a" and see if I tried to sneak in some telling that way too.

Description

- Did I give context for my scenes within the first paragraph (location, characters, time)?
- Did I describe using the filter of my POV character?
- Did I mention any items that may be important later? (If someone throws a vase at the end of the scene, make sure to mention it when describing the room.)
- Was I smart about my word choice? Did I pick specific nouns, verbs, and adjectives that help set the mood for my story?
- What senses (taste, touch, smell, feel, hear) have I used in each scene? Can I use more or different ones?
- Did I tone down the description in high action scenes?

Freshening and Tightening Your Writing

- Check the first and last line of each chapter and scene to make sure I start and end in the best place to keep readers turning the pages.
- Survey the length of sentences. Do I need to vary them?
- Can I break up any long paragraphs?
- Am I staying in the right tense?
- Read the scene for clichés and overused phrases.
- Apply the words of George Orwell to every sentence:
- What am I trying to say?
- What words will best express it?
- Is there an image or idiom that will make it clear?
- Is this image fresh enough to have an effect?
- Run a search for the word "it" and see if I can use a more specific word, especially if it's the start of a sentence.
- Are there places I used two words when I could use one instead?
- Have I chosen the best possible words? Active, concrete words?
- Search for the words: as, when, while, after, and continued to. Make sure those sentences are in a logical order—action, then

reaction.
- Hunt down passive phrases—search each scene for "was" or "is" depending on the tense of the book.
- Check any sentences that begin with —ing words.
- Check any sentences that use the phrases "began to" or "started to."

Have I formatted everything correctly?

- Is my title page single spaced and my manuscript double spaced?
- Am I using 12-point Times New Roman or Courier font?
- Does each chapter begin on a new page?
- Do I have one space after punctuation, not two?

Run Spell Check
Double-check for correct punctuation, grammar, homonym errors, and common typos:

- Run a search for those tricky words and any others I tend to misspell (i.e. its/it's, past/passed, though/through/thought)
- "Chance" when I meant "change"
- Have I consistently used the same spelling for character and place names?

Run a search for my placeholders.

What's a placeholder?

Many writers, when they come across something they need to research or write in more detail but don't want to take the time right then, they'll put in a placeholder word or symbol to mark that they need to come back.

Stephanie uses the word "GIRAFFE" for things she needs to fill in or an asterisk (*) if she's not happy with a phrase but doesn't have the brainpower at the moment to fix it. Jill tends to highlight the place that needs a little more love, or she'll add a comment to remind herself what she needs to come back and finish.

While typically you'll have fixed them all by the end of the micro edit, always run a check for your placeholders just to be sure!

Self-Editing Dialogue Checklist

A writer on the Go Teen Writers blog asked if we could make one of these. Hopefully you find it helpful as well!

___ Are you trusting your dialogue and using action beats, or are you trying to make up for weak dialogue with lots of, "she retorted" and "he exclaimed" and she "expostulated"?

___ Are your characters strategic about what they say, or are they just blurting things out? Did they enter the conversation with a plan?

___ When your characters receive tough news or bad breaks, are they processing the situation and experiencing grief in a realistic way?

___ Have you fallen into a "Q & A" pattern anywhere? Where one character is doing nothing but asking questions and the other character is doing nothing but answering them?

___ Do your characters use different words for the same thing, or are their phrasings too similar? (Grocery store can also be the market, purses can also be handbags.)

___ Are you letting character/story information come out naturally, or are you trying to explain too much with your dialogue? ("Gee, Bob, I'm so glad it's our anniversary today and that we've been married for seven years and have two beautiful children!")

___ Does every character behave and interact as though they believe *they* are the main character?

___ Are you using contractions?

___ Is your dialogue age-appropriate? Or are your toddlers elegant and your grannies saying words like "peeps" for anything other than marshmallow chicks. (*Shudder.* Don't know why, but I *hate* the word peeps.)

___ Do you have too many "group" conversations? (Conversations with four or more.)

___ Is "small talk" bogging down your story? (Hi, how are you? Good, how are you? Good. Nice day we're having. Sure is. And so on.)

___ Do you have a good balance of internal thoughts and dialogue? Does the reader get a sense of not only what the point-of-view character is saying, but *why* he's saying it and what he *feels* about the conversation in general?

___ Have you considered conversations from the perspective of all the characters involved, not just the point-of-view character?

Stephanie & Jill's Weasel Words & Phrases

These are words we overuse or that sneak into our first drafts despite our best efforts to keep them out.

Stephanie's

Quirked (my characters are always quirking eyebrows)
So-and-so rolled her eyes/ran her hands through her hair
Like
Just
Were
Was
Said
Asked
Very
Smile(d)
Sigh(ed)
Really

"Or something" (I like to throw that in to the end of a lot of my sentences for some reason. "We should go to the movies or something.")

Past/Passed—I have issues remembering which is correct.

It—Especially at the start of sentences. Often "it" should be replaced with something more specific.

Jill's

Vague words

Many, few, lots, a lot of, a little, some, most, almost, more, a few, rather, might, perhaps, much, often, for the most part, like, seem, etc.

Absolutes

Every, very, entire, everyone, everything, etc.

Verbs that facilitate telling

Feel/felt, see/saw, hear/heard, think/thought, look, watch, taste, smell, wonder, decide, notice, remember, recall, consider, ponder, is, am, are, was, were, has, had, have, etc.

Infinite Verb Phrases (Starting sentences with —ing words)

Continuous action words

As, when, while, after, continued to.

Pronouns

Overuse of "they" or "them" tends to create the feel of an omniscient POV.

Time transitions

Just, then, as, the next day, all at once, soon, etc.

Adverbs

Softly, angrily, sadly, really, basically, immediately, very, actually, surely, usually, truly, suddenly, etc.

Double verbs

Started to, began to.

Some other words on my list

There, it, be, being, been, became, that, well, poor, anyway, quite, however, about, thought/though/through, think/thing, loose/lose.

Story Brainstorming Questions

When you have a new story idea, these questions are meant to help you take it deeper.

Character Questions (for major characters)

Who is my character?
What is she named and why?
If I had to describe her in one word, it would be:
What's her family like?
What does she value?
What lie does she believe?
Why does she believe that lie? What happened in her past that caused her to believe it?
What is her main goal in the story?
Why is she ideal for the journey and why is she not?
Who are her allies and who are her enemies?
What will my main character sacrifice?
How does she need to change?
What happens if she doesn't meet her goals? Why are her goals important? How can I make that worse for her? Who else could it impact?
In what ways is she operating against society and in what ways is she operating within?
What part of her past can come back to haunt her?
What is her greatest fear?

Other Character Questions

What does the antagonist want?
Does my antagonist have a secret he's trying to keep?
Who will make sacrifices for my main character throughout the story?
What character could come out of the shadows and "shine?"

Story Questions

What's the best place for the story to start?

How do I think it will end? What is the climax?

Does my story have a theme? Why does this book matter?

What kind of hurdles will there be in the journey? How can I make these harder? How can I make them "cost" my main character more?

What is my storyworld like? Are there political, historical, or environmental situations that might affect my character's journey?

Is there magic in my story? If so, how does it work? What are the rules, costs, and limitations for it?

Extras: Lists & Resources

Story Plotting Charts

These can help in the early stages of planning your book or when editing to help you see what's missing. Download the full-sized documents at: www.jillwilliamson.com/helps/

Scene Plotting Chart

STORY TITLE:
Beginning:
Inciting Incident:
Second Thoughts:
Climax of act 1:
Obstacle:
Obstacle:
Midpoint twist:
Obstacle:
Disaster:
Crisis:
Climax of act 2:
Climax of act 3:
Obstacles:
Denouement:
End:

Scene Plotting Chart for Two Points of View

_____'s POINT OF VIEW	_____'s POINT OF VIEW
Beginning:	Beginning:
Inciting Incident:	Inciting Incident:
Second Thoughts:	Second Thoughts:
Climax of act 1:	Climax of act 1:
Obstacle:	Obstacle:
Obstacle:	Obstacle:
Midpoint twist:	Midpoint twist:
Obstacle:	Obstacle:
Disaster:	Disaster:
Crisis:	Crisis:
Climax of act 2:	Climax of act 2:
Climax of act 3:	Climax of act 3:
Obstacles:	Obstacles:
Denouement:	Denouement:
End:	End:

Copyediting Symbols

These days, most editors will edit your book with Microsoft Word's Track Changes, but in the event you receive any physical pages with copyediting notes, here is a list of what some of the most common symbols mean.

Character Archetypes

This is a fun list that can help you with brainstorming your characters.

Analyst: Can explain anything rationally. Ex: Mr. Spock
Anti-hero: The hero who didn't ask to get involved but does. Ex: Sarah Connor, Wolverine
Benefactor: Has a whole lot of something he wants to share. Ex: Miss Havisham
Bully: Has no tolerance for weakness, especially in himself. Ex: Scut Farkus (*Christmas Story*)
Bureaucrat: Follows the rules no matter what. Ex: Hermione Granger
Caretaker: Cares for others. Ex: Digory Kirke
Catalyst: Makes things happen.
Child: Could be a literal child or just living like one. Ex: Wally McDoogle, Peter Pan
Coward: Afraid of everything, controlled by fear. Ex: Adrian Monk, Cowardly Lion, Alexandra Rover
Curmudgeon: Irritable and cynical and proud of it. Ex: Ebenezer Scrooge
Dreamer: Longs to be something else. Ex: Annie, William Thatcher (*A Knight's Tale*)
Elder/mentor/teacher/parent: Been around long enough to know some vital information. Ex: Ben Kenobi, Mufassa
Explorer/wanderer: Wants to see the world—could be running from something.
Extraordinary man: The guy who can do anything. Ex: Indiana Jones, James Bond
Gossip: Must be the first to know everything and the one to pass it on. Ex: Rachel Lynde
Guardian: Protects the weak.
Hedonist/thrill-seeker: Lives for today in case tomorrow never comes.
Herald/messenger: The bringer of news, good, bad, or necessary.

Hermit/loner: Just wants to be left alone. Ex: Phil Hercules, Martin Riggs (*Lethal Weapon*)
Hunter/predator: Can catch or kill anything. Ex: Terminator
Innocent: An inexperienced individual exposed to the evils in the world. Ex: Dorothy Gale
Introvert: Lives inside his shell to prevent anyone from seeing the real him. Ex: Gabriella Montez (*High School Musical*)
Investigator: Thrives on puzzles and riddles. Ex: Nancy Drew, Sherlock Holmes
Judge/mediator: The arbitrator or peacemaker in a conflict.
Leader: Always knows the best thing to do—and the people follow him. Ex: William Wallace
Magician/wizard/superhero: Has special powers or abilities. Ex: Superman, Harry Potter
Manipulator: Plays with people and situations to get what he wants. Ex: Scarlett O'Hara
Martyr: Willing to suffer or die for others or a cause.
Masochist: Finds pleasure in torturing himself, denying himself—may take on too much.
Masquerader: Pretends to be something he's not.
Monster: A depraved beast. Ex: Gollum, Grendel (*Beowulf*)
Ordinary man: Your average Joe, just like you or me or the guy across the street. Ex: Dr. Richard Kimball, Frodo Baggins.
Penitent: Lives to atone for his sin.
Perfectionist: Every action and word must be flawless.
Pleaser/show-off: Craves approval from anyone and may do anything to get it.
Poet: Life is art, be that through story, song, painting, or sculpture.
Rebel/revolutionary: Stands opposed to the status quo and fights for his cause.
Rogue: Looks out for himself and no one else. Ex: Han Solo
Saboteur/betrayer: For whatever reason, he will make sure something fails. Ex: Edmund Pevensie
Samaritan: Does good deeds wherever he goes.
Scholar: Wants to learn.
Sensualist: Addicted to feeling good about himself.
Slave: Does not belong to himself. Ex: Dobby the house elf

Survivor: Pulls through no matter what happens, doesn't give up.

Sycophant: Self-seeking, flatterer, who works to please those in power. Ex: Smee (*Peter Pan*)

Temptress: Uses power (intellect, magic, beauty) to make others weak. Ex: Megara (*Hercules*)

Thief: Takes what he wants or needs. Ex: Philippe Gaston (*LadyHawke*), Jean Valjean

Trickster/jester: Always looking for the humor in a situation. Ex: Fred and George Weasley

Tyrant: Must be in control at all times. Ex: Captain Hook

Victim: Was hurt by someone or lives in fear that someone will hurt him. Ex: Claireece "Precious" Jones

Villain: Seeks to destroy/trap the hero. Ex: Evil Queen in *Snow White*, Lex Luthor

Waif: Appears innocent and weak and often relies on the pity of others. Ex: The Kid (*Dick Tracy*)

Hobbies & Skills Brainstorming List

Are all your characters writers or artists or soccer players? Here's a list that can help you shake things up.

Art and Crafts

Airbrushing	Fly tying (for fly fishing)	Photography
Beading	Glass blowing	Pottery
Blacksmithing	Graphic design	Quilting
Bridge building	Jewelry making	Scrapbooking
Calligraphy	Knitting	Sculpture
Candle making	Leather crafting	Sewing
Cartoons	Macramé	Soap making
Carving	Map making	Stained glass
Crochet	Model cars	Taxidermy
Cross-stich	Model rockets	Tie dying
Dollhouses	Model ships	Weaving
Drawing	Needlepoint	Woodworking
Embroidery	Origami	
Engraving	Painting	

Collecting

Action figures	Collector cards	Petals
Antiques	Comic books	Postcards
Artwork	Diecast	Posters
Barbies	Dolls	Rocks
Books	Guns	Seashells
Buttons	Insects	Sports cards
Cars	Leaves	Stamps
Clothing	Memorabilia	Toys
Coins	Music	

Exercise

Aerobics	Spinning	Yoga
Cardio kickboxing	Sports (see sports list)	Zumba
Pilates	Weight training	

Food

Baking	Canning
Cake decorating	Cooking

Games

Air hockey	Chess	Lawn darts
Backgammon	Crossword puzzles	Online gaming
Billiards	Darts	Paintball
Board games	Dominoes	Poker
Bridge	Dungeons and Dragons	Video games
Cards	Jigsaw puzzles	

Hobbies

Arcade games	Foreign languages	Reading
Astrology	Gambling	Reenactment:
Being a fan of . . .	Garage saleing	Medieval/Civil War
Body art	Genealogy	Remote control toys
Book reviewing	Geocaching	Robotics
Computers	Ham radios	Shopping
Construction	Journaling	Traveling
Domino set ups	Juggling	Trekkie (Star Trek Fan)
Educational courses	Knotting	Watching movies
Electronics	Legos	Watching sports
Fantasy Football	Magician	Watching TV
Fast cars	Modeling	Websites
Film making	Piloting an airplane	Yoyo
Fixing cars	Pinball machines	

Extras: Lists & Resources

Outdoors

Air sports	Fishing	Motorbikes
Archery	Flower competitions	Mountain climbing
Astronomy	Frisbee	Rafting
ATV riding	Gardening	Rock climbing
Beachcombing	Geology	Rodeo
Bicycling	Go-kart racing	Sailing
Bird watching	Gold panning	Scuba diving
Board sports	Hang gliding	Shooting guns
Boating	Hiking	Skateboarding
Bonsai trees	Horseback riding	Sky diving
Boomerangs	Hot air ballooning	Snorkeling
Building sandcastles	Hunting	Sunbathing
Butterfly watching	Kayaking	Surfing
Camping	Kite boarding	Treasure hunting
Canoeing	Kites	Water sports
Cave diving	Metal detecting	White water rafting
Dumpster diving	Motor sports	Windsurfing

Performance

A cappella singing	Cosplay	Radio
Acting	Dancing	Rock band
Baton twirling	Karaoke	Show choir
Beatboxing	Marching band	Singing
Bell choir	Orchestra/band	Theater sports
Choir	Playing an instrument	Worship team
Church choir	Podcasting	Youth band
Comedy	Puppetry	

Pets

Bee keeping	Fish	Pigs
Bird	Guinea pig	Snake
Cat	Hamster	Spider
Cows	Horses	Turtle
Dog	Lambs	
Falconry	Lizard	

Service

Big brother/sister	Reading to kids
Candy striper	Rescuing animals
Children's church	Retirement home volunteer
Food collection	Rocking sick babies
Habitat for Humanity	Tutoring
Lunch buddy	Volunteering
Reading to elderly	Youth group

Social

Bars	Dating
Chatting	Entertaining
Clubbing	Skype
Dancing	Texting
Dining out	

Writing

Blogging	Music- songs
Fan fiction	Newspaper
Fiction- novels	Playwright
Fiction- short stories	Poetry
Magazines	Scriptwriting
Music- composition	

Sports

Badminton	Field events	Running
Baseball	Figure skating	Snowboarding
Basketball	Football	Soccer
BMX tricks	Golf	Softball
Bowling	Gymnastics	Street racing
Car racing	Ice hockey	Swimming
Cheerleading	Martial arts	Tennis
Cricket	Parkour	Volleyball
Cross country skiing	Polo	Water polo
Diving	Racing bicycles	Wrestling
Downhill skiing	Racquetball	
Fencing	Rugby	

Character Traits Brainstorming List

For kicks, try closing your eyes and circling a few random ones!

active	cold-hearted	doesn't learn
adventurous	compassionate	domineering
affectionate	competitive	doubtful
afraid	complacent	dutiful
aggressive	compulsive	eager
ambitious	conceited	easygoing
amiable	confident	eloquent
angry	confused	encouraging
animated	considerate	energetic
annoyed	cooperative	enthusiastic
anti-social	courageous	fair
anxious	cowardly	faithful
argumentative	crafty	fearless
arrogant	critical	fidgety
attentive	cruel	fierce
babyish	cultured	finicky
blabbermouth	curious	foolish
bored	cynical	formal
bossy	dangerous	frank
brave	daring	friendly
brilliant	decisive	frustrated
busy	dependable	funny
calm	dependent	generous
careful	determined	gentle
cautious	diligent	giddy
charismatic	discreet	giving
charming	dishonest	glamorous
cheerful	disloyal	gloomy
childish	disobedient	grateful
clever	disparaging	greedy
clumsy	disrespectful	grouchy
coarse	dissatisfied	gullible

happy	insolent	noisy
harried	intelligent	obedient
hateful	jealous	obliging
haughty	judgmental	obnoxious
helpful	lackadaisical	observant
honest	languid	obsessive
hopeful	lazy	overindulgent
hopeless	liar	prejudice
hospitable	logical	procrastinator
humble	lonely	reckless
hyper	loving	rude
ignorant	loyal	sarcastic
ill-bred	lucky	selfish
imaginative	malicious	self-pitying
immature	mature	shy
impartial	mean	smart
impatient	meticulous	stubborn
impolite	mischievous	superficial
impudent	moody	tactless
impulsive	mundane	takes self too seriously
inappropriate	mysterious	too trusting
inconsiderate	naive	unable to commit
independent	negligent	uncommunicative
industrious	nervous	unconfident
innocent	never satisfied	unmannered
insensitive	no sense of humor	untrusting

Character Phobias Brainstorming List

abandoned
airplanes, birds overhead
beards (facial hair)
bees
being alone
being embarrassed
being looked at
being poor
being tortured
being touched
big crowds
birds
blood
bridges
bombs
cats
cell phones
cemeteries
changes
children
clocks
closets
clowns
colors (a certain one)
commitment
conspiracies
crossing roads
dark
death of a loved one
death of self
dirt
disappointing someone
dogs
dolls
dreams/nightmares
drowning/water
dust
elderly
elevators
enclosed spaces
endings
everything
failure
falling
fear
feet
fire
fish
flying
food someone else made
forests
frogs
frying pans
germs
getting arrested
getting fat
ghosts
going to sleep (never waking)
guns/weapons
heights
hospitals
household appliances
intimacy
ladders
leadership
losing things (therefore hoards)
making decisions
meat

medication	saying goodbye
men or women	scary movies
messes (or any untidiness)	seafood
mirrors	shadows
monsters	sharks
moths	sickness
needles or pointed objects	snakes
noises	speaking in public
nudity	spiders
numbers (a certain one)	stairs
oceans/lakes	staying single
old age (getting old)	strangers
open closets/doors	sunlight
outside	thunder and lightning
pain	traffic
police officers	trapped/small spaces/buried alive
raw food	turning out like parent
rejection	war
relationships	weather (storms)
riding in vehicles	worms
rollercoasters	x-rays

Historical Periods

Unsure about what historical genre your book falls in? This list can help. And this list only covers Europe and North America. You can also research historical periods for other parts of the world.

The Stone Age - The Beginning to 2000 BC
The Bronze Age - 3600 BC–600 BC
The Iron Age – 1200 BC–400 AD
Barbarian Invasions – 300 AD–700 AD
Medieval – 400 AD–1500 AD
Renaissance – 1500 AD–1700 AD
Elizabethan (UK) – 1558 AD–1603 AD
Jacobean (UK) – 1603 AD–1625 AD
Caroline (UK) - 1625–1649
Interregnum (UK) - 1649–1660
Restoration (UK) - 1660–1688
Georgian (UK) - 1714–1830
Napoleonic Era (FR) - 1799–1815
Regency (UK) - 1811–1837
Victorian (UK) - 1837–1901
Edwardian (UK) - 1901–1910
Colonial - 1492–1775
Native American - 1492–1900
Revolution - 1775–1800
Turn of the 19th Century - 1795–1810
West - 1800–1890
Regency era in Europe/Federal era in the US - 1811–1820
War of 1812 - 1812
Antebellum - 1820–1861
Victorian UK/US - 1837–1901
Frontier - 1845–1916
South - 1860–1920
Civil War - 1861–1865
Reconstruction - 1865–1887
Turn of the Century - 1890–1915

World War I - 1914–1918
Interwar period - 1918–1939
Roaring Twenties - 1920–1929
Great Depression - 1929–World War II
World War II - 1939–1945
Post WWII - 1945–1950
Atomic Age - after 1945
Post-war era - 1946–1962
Cold War (Soviet Union and US) -1945–1989 or 1991
Space Age - after 1957
The Sixties - 1960–1969
Turbulent 1960's/War in Vietnam
Post-Modern (Soviet Union and United States) -1973–present
Information Age - 1970–present
The Seventies - 1970–1979
The Eighties - 1980–1989
The Nineties - 1990–1999
The 2000s - 2000–2009
The Social Age - 2004–present
The Tens - 2010–2019
The Big Data age - 2001–present

Glossary of Terms

Abbreviations

ABA: American Booksellers Association
ARC: Advance reading copy
BCC: Back-cover copy
BEA: BookExpo America
CBA: Christian Booksellers Association
FMC: Female main character
GTW: Go Teen Writers
ISBN: International Standard Book Number
K: Thousand, as in an 80,000-word novel or 80K novel
MC: Main character
MMC: Male main character
MS: Manuscript *or* Microsoft (as in MS Word)
NaNoWriMo: National Novel Writing Month
OP: Out of print
POV: Point of view
SASE: Self-addressed stamped envelope
SCBWI: Society of Children's Book Writers and Illustrators
WC: Word count
WIP: Work in progress

Publishing Industry Terms

Acquisitions editor: A publishing house employee who reads incoming manuscripts to seek out publishable material.

Advance: A sum of money paid to the author in anticipation of royalty earnings, often paid in increments.

Agent: A person that represents an author's work and tries to sell it to editors.

Content editor (also known as a developmental or substantive editor): A person who edits a book for overall plot issues, character development, and continuity of the story.

Cover letter: An email or letter sent with requested materials to remind the editor or agent what is being sent and why.

Fiction: Works of the imagination, made-up stories.

Independent (Indie) author: An author who publishes on their own. This is also called being a self-published author.

Independent (Indie) publisher: A small publisher. Some pay an advance, some don't. Many are too small to get into bookstores, though some can.

Line editor: A person who goes over every sentence in a manuscript to make sure there are no errors.

Manuscript: A typed out story, article, or novel.

National Novel Writing Month: An organization that encourages participants to write at least 50,000 words in one month.

Nonfiction: Works that are not fictional.

Proofreader: A person who reads a final manuscript for errors.

Proposal: A thorough presentation of an author's book to an editor or agent for publication.

Query letter: An email or letter an author writes to propose his project to an editor or agent. Usually one page long.

Self-publishing (also called independent or indie publishing): When an author pays to publish his own ebook, audio book, or paperback.

Slush pile: The imaginary and sometimes literal "pile" of manuscripts that have been sent to an agent or editor without an invitation. (You don't want your manuscript here.)

Solicited (Requested Materials): Material that an agent or editor has asked to see.

Submission (Writing) Guidelines: Specifications from an agent, editor, or listed on a website for how to submit queries or completed manuscripts for consideration.

Synopsis: A one- to two-page summary of the plot of a novel.

Traditional publishing: This is the standard way an author gets a book published that should get his books into bookstores. In this type of publishing, the publisher pays the author for his book.

Unsolicited: When an author sends in her work to an editor or agent without permission to do so.

Word Count: The estimated number of words in a manuscript.

Writing Craft Terms

Action tag: Action used to identify the speaker of words spoken in quotes. Ex: "Fine!" <u>Sherry slammed the door.</u>

Back-cover copy: The text on the back of a book or on a book's online product page that introduces the story to a reader.

Backdrop: The setting of your story.

Backstory: What happened to your characters before your story began.

Beat: A pause in between speech or action. Also a moment of action or thought. This can also refer to plot points, especially in screenwriting. You might hear writers say they're putting together their "beat sheet" which is a list of critical scenes in their stories.

Cliché: An overused expression, character type, or plot.

Conflict: That which causes your character to struggle.

Flashback: Inserting an earlier event into the chronological structure of a story.

Narrative: When the story moves into narration, or telling, to explain what's happening outside a character point of view.

Point of view (POV): The position of the narrator who's telling the story at that moment.

Said tag: Used to identify the speaker of words spoken in quotes. Ex: "Do what you want," <u>Sherry said.</u>

Scene: A section of a story that represents a single episode or event.

Voice: The style, tone, and method of how an individual author writes. Also, the way a specific character sounds on the page.

Recommended Resources

These are books we've enjoyed, learned from, or written, listed in alphabetical order by the author's name. All of these books are targeted at adults, so we encourage you to read the back-cover copy and reviews to judge if it's age-appropriate for you or your young writer:

- *2k to 10k* by Rachel Aaron
- *Revisions and Self-Editing* by James Scott Bell
- *Write Your Book From The Middle* by James Scott Bell
- *The Art of War for Writers* by James Scott Bell
- *Self-Editing for Fiction Writers* by Renni Browne and Dave King
- *Story Genius* by Lisa Cron
- *Let's Get Digital: How to Self-Publish and Why You Should* by David Gaughran
- *Big Magic* by Elizabeth Gilbert
- *Writing Fiction for Dummies* by Randy Ingermanson and Peter Economy
- *On Writing* by Stephen King
- *Bird by Bird* by Anne Lamott
- *Writing the Breakout Novel* and *Writing the Breakout Novel Workbook* by Donald Maass
- *Successful Self-Publishing: How to Self-Publish and Market Your Book* by Joanna Penn
- *Save the Cat* by Blake Snyder (A book on screenwriting that will teach you a lot about how to tell a story.)
- *Stein on Writing* by Sol Stein
- *Creating Character Arcs* by K. M. Weiland
- *Structuring Your Novel* by K. M. Weiland
- *Storyworld First: Creating a Unique Fantasy World for Your Novel* by Jill Williamson

For grammar and punctuation, we recommend:

- *The Chicago Manual of Style*
- *The Elements of Style* by Strunk and White
- *Punctuation 101: A Fiction Writer's Guide to Getting it Right* by Jill Williamson

Other resources we love:

- HelpingWritersBecomeAuthors.com (also a great podcast!)
- Writing Excuses podcast
- TheCreativePenn.com and podcast, especially for self-publishing
- Traci Tyne Hilton's indie author column at The Write Conversation: https://bit.ly/2PrvFZr

Acknowledgements

From Stephanie

A big thank you to all the writers who hang out at Go Teen Writers and make it such a great community to be a part of. This book wouldn't exist without your great questions and your dedication to pursuing a literary life.

Jill Williamson, your heart, creativity, and hard work add so much to Go Teen Writers. It's such an honor to be your friend!

Shannon Dittemore, thank you for the wisdom and perspective you have brought to the site these last few years, as well as your support and encouragement as we prepared to re-release this book.

Roseanna White, thank you for encouraging the Go Teen Writers idea many moons ago and for commenting on those early posts so I didn't feel so lonely. Also, thank you for lending us your editing skills for the original version of this book, and your cover design skills for the new one. I'm lucky to count you as a friend!

Chris Kolmorgen, thanks for your sharp editing eye, encouraging comments, and all the great insights you provided in the first edition.

Thank you Lydia Howe, Keturah Lamb, and Hannah White for being generous with your time and helping us polish up this version of the book. And Ellyn Franklin, Rachelle Rea Cobb, and Gillian Bronte Adams for helping us out on the first edition.

And thank you to Sandra Bishop, my agent, for always being in my corner, and for making time for impromptu poolside conversations that I desperately needed, even if I kept saying, "I'm fine! I'm doing great!" with the fakest smile on my face.

Countless thanks to my husband, Ben. You vacuum, you fold laundry, and you lovingly encourage me even on my most dramatic, weepy, *why-am-I-doing-this?* writer girl days. Thank you for being an endless source of strength. And to McKenna, Connor, and Eli. You are more loving and encouraging than I ever imagined kids could be.

Also, thank you to my fantastic grandparents team! Thank you Mom, Dad, Ann, and Bruce for coming to the house weekly so I can pursue what I love while also being home with my kids.

From Jill

Thanks to Stephanie Morrill, who let me come and share in the great community she created at Go Teen Writers. I'm so glad that one guy *nudge, nudge* wanted us to meet. You're a fabulous writer and a fabulous friend.

Thanks to every teen writer out there. I love that you dream and create stories. Don't ever stop, even when you're not a teen anymore. A big hug to those of you who've found us online or at writers' conferences. I love hearing about your stories. Keep on writing!

Thanks to Roseanna and Chris for editing our book, and to Ellyn, Gillian, and Rachelle for your sharp proofreading eyes in the first edition. Thank you Lydia, Keturah, and Hannah for proofreading the second. We couldn't have published this book without you. You are all quite brilliant.

Thanks to Amanda Luedeke, my agent, who listens to all my random ideas and who graciously supported this project. You keep me sane. I'll get a bestseller for you one of these days, Amanda. I promise. ☺

Thanks to my family, who knows more than they ever wanted to about books and the publishing industry. Brad, who does laundry, cooks, and listens to my ramblings; Luke, who helps me brainstorm and builds Lego robots for my inspiration; and Kailtyn, who makes me smile and is always quick to find me a box of tissues when I'm not smiling. I love you all.

About the Authors

Stephanie Morrill writes books about girls who are on an adventure to discover their unique place in the world. She is the author of several contemporary young adult series, as well as the 1920s mystery, *The Lost Girl of Astor Street*, and the WWII era romance, *Within These Lines*. She lives in the Kansas City area, where she loves plotting big and small adventures to enjoy with her husband and three children. You can connect with Stephanie and learn more about her books at StephanieMorrill.com

Jill Williamson writes fantasy and science fiction for teens and adults. She's the author of over twenty books, including her debut novel, *By Darkness Hid*, which won several awards and was named a "Best Science Fiction, Fantasy, and Horror novel of 2009" by *VOYA* magazine. She also has written several books on the craft of writing fiction and teaches writing in person and online. She lives in the Pacific Northwest with her husband and two children. To learn more about her novels, visit her online at JillWilliamson.com.

Come hang out with us!
GoTeenWriters.com

Let's stay in touch!

Sign up to receive emails from Go Teen Writers. Not only will you get encouragement in your inbox every few weeks, you'll also get a free story workbook tutorial and template.
Go to:
GoTeenWriters.com/pri
or use the QR code:

HISTORICAL FICTION FROM STEPHANIE MORRILL

"Morrill has a keen eye for historical details and setting, making Jazz Age Chicago Piper's invisible yet omnipresent sidekick. Here's hoping this won't be the last case for this strong and admirable female sleuth to solve."
-Kirkus Reviews

"A fast-paced mystery that sparkles with the sights and sounds of 1920s Chicago. The strong characters and setting drew me in, and the twists and turns kept me hooked until the end." -Renee Collins, author of *Until We Meet Again*

"*Within These Lines* will both break your heart and awaken it. Evalina and Taichi's story not only navigates a precarious romance, but it challenges racism, injustice, and the temptation to stay silent. Their boldness and call to action will stick with you long after you turn the last page. I applaud Morrill's storytelling and cannot recommend this book enough—a must-read for all historical fiction fans!"
- Nadine Brandes, author of FAWKES

MORE WRITING RESOURCES FROM JILL WILLIAMSON

You don't need to be an expert in grammar and punctuation to write great novels, but you do need to learn the basics.

This handy reference book includes all the need-to-know punctuation rules for fiction writers, and it's presented in a clear, user-friendly format with many examples for the visual learner—including some from popular novels.

Punctuation 101 will save you time and energy, which you can spend writing your novel.

BUILDING A STORYWORLD? WONDERING WHERE TO START? THIS BOOK CAN HELP YOU.

Whether you're starting from scratch or looking to add depth to a world you've already created, *Storyworld First* will get you thinking.

Includes tips on the following worldbuilding subjects: astronomy, magic, government, map-making, history, religion, technology, languages, culture, and how it all works together.

TO LEARN MORE VISIT
WWW.JILLWILLIAMSON.COM

Don't just get even.
Write a novel.

When ousted by her lifelong friends, teen writer Ellie Sweet takes to story writing as self-therapy. She casts herself as Lady Gabrielle, a favorite in the medieval Italian court, her ex-friends as her catty rivals, and makes a pesky rake of the boy who thinks he's too good for her in real life. But when Ellie achieves the impossible and the details of her "coping mechanism" become public, she faces the consequences of using her pen for her sword.

Learn more at:
StephanieMorrill.com/ellie

AWARD-WINNING FANTASY FROM JILL WILLIAMSON

"Wonderfully written with a superb plot, this book is a sure-fire hit with almost any reader. An adventure tale with a touch of romance and enough intrigue to keep the pages turning practically by themselves."
—*VOYA* magazine

"This thoroughly entertaining and smart tale will appeal to fans of Donita K. Paul and J.R.R. Tolkien. Highly recommended for . . . fantasy collections."
—*Library Journal*

"Williamson crafts a complex and vividly portrayed epic fantasy reminiscent of George R.R. Martin's *A Song of Ice and Fire* series but less edgy."
—*Library Journal*

"[*King's Folly*] is an intense drama of biblical proportions... Wilek, Mielle, and Trevn in particular are intriguing, and the ending leaves readers wondering what adventures await this group of young people searching for truth."
—*RT Book Reviews*

TO LEARN MORE VISIT
WWW.JILLWILLIAMSON.COM

Made in the USA
Las Vegas, NV
12 October 2022